Praise for *Hear Us O Lord From Heaven Thy Dwelling Place*

"Lowry was not content to be an artist merely; he would not ignore reality, whether in the world without or within himself, in order to make a 'better' or more suitably ordered work. . . . I think he could serve as a model to every writer of any ambition." —*Commonweal*

"A maelstrom of a book. Reading it is like riding out a storm in a shaky vessel. . . . It is a tragic, brilliant, shattering book. Out of the mélange of emotion, experience, dream and disaster that was Lowry's private world, he has made a work of art—moving, noble."
—*The New York Times Book Review*

"Nothing is more satisfying than appreciating a neglected genius . . . demonstrating an exquisite, precise and highly articulate sensibility in an elegant, complex and careful style." —*San Francisco Chronicle*

"Lowry, Cambridge graduate and seaman, published in 1947 the brilliant, complex, critically acclaimed *Under the Volcano*. Now comes the posthumous collection of his stories, containing, quite probably, some of the finest writing of our times. There is an incredible shine and flexibility to all of it, as if an extraordinarily sensitive mind had been imprinted on the paper. Remarkable to read, and as a reverse record of the development of a mind and a writer, unique. One man's—everyman's—life is here." —*Kirkus*

"Lowry's prose has brilliance and vitality." —*The Atlantic*

HEAR US O LORD FROM HEAVEN THY DWELLING PLACE

Malcolm Lowry was born in 1909 at New Brighton and died in England in 1957. He was educated at the Leys School, Cambridge, and St Catherine's College. Between school and university he went to sea, working as a deck-hand and trimmer for about eighteen months. His first novel, *Ultramarine,* was accepted for publication in 1932, but the typescript was stolen and the whole thing had to be rewritten from the penultimate version. It was finally published in 1933. He went to Paris that autumn, married his first wife in 1934, and wrote several short stories in Paris and Chartres before going to New York. Here he started a new novel, *In Ballast to the White Sea,* which he completed in 1936. He then left for Mexico. His first marriage broke up in 1938, and in 1939 he remarried and settled in British Columbia. During 1941-4, when he was living in Dollarton, he worked on the final version of *Under the Volcano,* his masterpiece. In 1954 he finally returned to England. During half his writing life he lived in a squatter's shack, largely built by himself near Vancouver. His *Selected Letters,* edited by H. Breit and Margerie Bonner Lowry, was published in 1967, and *Lunar Caustic,* part of a larger, uncompleted work, appeared in 1968. Margerie Bonner Lowry and Douglas Day have completed, from Lowry's notes, the novel *Dark as the Grave Wherein My Friend is Laid* and *October Ferry to Gabriola.*

MALCOLM LOWRY

·

HEAR US O LORD FROM HEAVEN THY DWELLING PLACE

Carroll & Graf Publishers, inc.
New York

Published by arrangement with Literistic, Ltd.

First Carroll & Graf edition, 1986

Carroll & Graf Publishers, Inc.
260 Fifth Avenue
New York, NY 10001

Library of Congress Catalog Card Number 61-8688
ISBN: 0-88184-281-8

Manufactured in the United States of America

Foreword

Major novels are not written by minor novelists. That *Under the Volcano* ranks among the greatest achievements in 20th century fiction is generally not contested. Less secure in critical opinion are Malcolm Lowry's other works, many published posthumously. When Lowry died in the summer of 1957, a questionable suicide at the age of 48, he had been (typically) working on several books simultaneously. He left one novel nearing completion, notes and drafts for at least two more, a large number of poems, and the manuscript of *Hear Us O Lord From Heaven Thy Dwelling Place*.

Lowry had begun to think of these stories as a unit and to work on their interrelations of symbol, theme, image, and setting as early as 1951. He took the title from an old Manx fisherman's hymn (reproduced in this volume) whose words echo throughout the stories. He had prepared notes for "Through the Panama" on a voyage from Canada through the Canal to Europe in 1947, after *Under the Volcano* was published. Three of the stories, "Strange Comfort Afforded by the Profession," "Elephant and Colosseum" and "Present Estate of Pompeii" were planned in Italy in 1948 but not actually written until he and his wife returned the following year to the beach at Dollarton, near Vancouver, where they lived, for the most part, from 1940 to 1954. This is Eridanus, a place which takes on mythical proportions in the stories and is the setting of the short novel, "The Forest Path to the Spring."

Hear Us O Lord was nearly in final form when Lowry and his wife Margerie went abroad again in 1954, but Lowry was never truly satisfied and, as with all his works, continued to revise the stories. Only "The Bravest Boat" and "Strange Comfort" were published in periodicals during his lifetime and they are reprinted here in their original form. Margerie Lowry edited the remaining stories for posthumous publication, incorporating all of Lowry's revisions and working notes. Readers may be concerned that they are dealing with a "tampered–with" text, but one must consider that Lowry's wife participated in, worked on and edited all of her husband's mature works, including *Under the Volcano*.

The character Sigbjørn Wilderness, who appears in a number of these stories, was to have been a central figure in *The Voyage That Never Ends*, a sequence of six or possibly seven books that Lowry projected, of which *Under the Volcano* was to have formed the center. The final story, "The Forest Path to the Spring," with its affirmation of love and life, was to serve as the coda for the entire project.

The stories in *Hear Us O Lord* do not operate under conventional rules of plot and external action. They are meditations—more like descriptive lyrics than tales in traditional narrative or dramatic modes. They progress by hugging the contours of consciousness with all the tension and excitement of the motion of the mind. Lowry's characters are self–involved yet selfless, intoxicated but lucid, actually talking themselves into sobriety, for the proof of life lies in the action of mind.

Lowry begins the collection with "The Bravest Boat," one of the two stories to have seen publication previous to *Hear Us O Lord*, having been accepted in 1953 and published a year later in the *Partisan Review*. Here, we meet Astrid and Sigurd Storleson celebrating their seventh wedding anniversary by strolling through a park in Vancouver (near the fabled Eridanus). They reminisce about the occasion of their union, the "something miraculous in human destiny" that is threaded through all seven stories. That "something" in this case is a little toy boat whose cargo contained a secret message written by the once–ten–year–old Sigurd who had launched the boat five miles south of Cape Flattery. The drifting, little boat survived the twelve years of the sea's blustering ravages and was eventually discovered in the park by the seven–year–old Astrid. The gentle story is set 17 years later and the Storleson's happy marriage is revealed in their attitude of wise passiveness in the natural scene surrounding them. Lowry's prose, there, is like a telescope alternately distancing and focussing, demonstrating a narrative contraction and expansion that had been lacking in the brooding *Ultramarine*.

Other themes that cohere this volume are initially stated here. In fact, "The Bravest Boat" and the last story, "The Forest Path to the Spring," form a sort of mystical arc, a frame of hopeful affirmation in which the stories' fears and obsessions are realized and resolved: the encroachment of civilization on Eden, the ruthless yet unconscious power of destructive nature and how both work to "evict" man from his home "built or placed with some human need for beauty in mind."

"The Bravest Boat" is gentle and lyrical in tone, almost fragile in its attempt to reveal sentimentally the quality of "goodness" in love. Much more vigorous in argument and volatile in language is the novella, "Through the Panama: From the Journal of Sigbjørn Wilderness." Its premise is similar to that in *Ultramarine*: a young writer tries to compose a novel while at sea. The journal lunges forward with a hardy, heady stream–of–consciousness which at certain junctions resembles a system of free association designed to show a writer's mind at work. Sigbjørn recognizes the journal as a record of a record and stubbornly takes comfort in his own self–consciousness until he is no longer sure whether he is a writer writing or being written.

Sigbjørn's work is simultaneously inspired and interrupted by his lovely wife, Primrose, an always–deficient supply of liquor and the marginalia of Coleridge's "Ancient Mariner," whose albatross is seen as narcissim itself: "For alas, this is the way the majority of human beings see other human beings, as shadows, themselves the only reality." The journal spirals slowly downward as if in a dark well of self-pity whose deepening gloom is its only strange illumination.

Time after time, as if by nature, drink assumes a central position in Lowry's work. It becomes the agent with which the creative mind transcends the boundaries of reason. Conflict, to the creative mind, is all-important, and the real cause of alcoholism, Sigbjørn tells us, is the "ugliness and complete baffling sterility of existence as *sold* to you."

In the next story, "Strange Comfort Afforded by the Profession," Sigbjørn Wilderness visits the house in Rome where Keats died and reads behind a glass case the poet's words reported in his friend Severn's letter: "He says the continued stretch of his imagination has already killed him and were he to recover he would not write another line." These truly pathetic words affect Sigbjørn and he refuses to sign the visitor's book at the Keats House because the act would be proof of his morbid fascination with the poet's fate.

Sigbjørn's re–reading of his journal takes him back to a visit to Poe's house in Baltimore, to a desperate letter written by Poe, and then to his own unmailed letter similar in spirit which declares, however meekly, the poet's right, if not obligation, to self–indulge. He then retracts, pleading for aid: "For God's sake pity me and save me from destruction." Sigbjørn, here, makes a spiritual and psychological leap which tragically evades the Consul in *Under the Volcano*: he wants to be saved.

Aesthetically, "Strange Comfort" is deepened by a sense of emotional memory and by the legends of the Romantics (Keats, Shelley and Byron) whose image Lowry burnishes and polishes so that its coppery light is cast on to the figure of Sigbjørn himself.

"Elephant and Colosseum" spots another lonely writer, Kennish Cosnahan, lost and doubting his purpose in Rome. He sits, musing over his critical reputation. His ruminations are both gently cajoling and cautionary: "Rome, he thought, with mild paranoia . . . How right was that historian he must read: success invites self–neglect; by means of self–indulgence."

When Cosnahan becomes hopelessly lost in the labyrinthine streets of Rome, his first instinct is to take refuge in the Borghese zoo where he warmly invests mystical attributes to the elephants. He resolves to work and to try to be happy, for "all life must have a happy ending, it was our tragic sense that was the more frivolous, having been given us for aesthetic reasons alone."

In "Present Estate of Pompeii," Roderick Fairhaven and his wife tour the ancient city laid waste by Vesuvius. Again, travel awakens the consciousness by giving it a sense of its own isolation and aliention. Fairhaven's obsessions are parochial if not egocentric. He thinks only of his home in Eridanus and his fear of eviction—a threat which is more profoundly distressing to him than the threat of (something like) volcanic genocide.

The ruins of Pompeii become monuments because the originals were destroyed by natural forces, something greater than man. What troubles Fairhaven is the way modern man builds cities, where people huddle in "cowardly dependence on the presence of others," with an eye to their very destruction. Fairhaven fears that there is not enough time before the artifices and circumstances of his own life crumble.

"Gin and Goldenrod" is the most accessible and straightforward of the tales with its simple, effective narrative and passionate argument. It signals the return of Sigbjørn Wilderness who, with a raging hangover, is walking through the woods near Eridanus with his wife, Primrose. They are on their way to pay off a bootlegger. The lost paradise theme in a world in which "ruination and vulgarization had become a habit" is re–sounded here as the Wilderness' tempers are tried by the ruined meadows giving way to middle–class housing developments, the heat of concrete and tar, the shame of debt and the unclear paths of the mutilated forest. Lowry ends the story by reporting that a "kind of hope began to bloom again" with the promise of a cocktail when the couple reach home.

That hope is certainly counterfeit. Yet it is a temporary setback, for hope will bloom again along "The Forest Path to the Spring," which is probably the finest piece of writing Lowry completed other than *Under the Volcano*. The story clarifies themes posed throughout *Hear Us O Lord* and is something of a psychological and structural breakthrough for its author. In a letter to Harold Matson, his literary agent, Lowry wrote, "Some years back, I was not equipped to tackle a task of this nature: now it seems to me, I've gone through the necessary spiritual ordeals that have permitted me to see the truth of what I'm getting at." Though the narrative is in the first person, the complete self–absorption permeating the other stories lifts here like heat haze from a mountain. Now, the protagonist is a honeymooner who is protective of the privacy shared with his wife: "That's how selfish lovers are, without an idea in their heads for anyone save themselves."

Lowry's prose undergoes a remarkable chastening of form here, as if blessed by the hymn sung by the fishermen of Eridanus, "a poem of God's mercy." A religious impulse underlies the novella. The narrator walks the forest path like "a priest pacing in the aisles of a great cathedral at dusk." One could say that the best of Lowry reads like the slow panic of a deeply devoted soul whose very source of religious devotion is gradually removed from him.

The author and his wife struggle to make their Eridanus an emigrant Eden, a surrogate City Celestial. Lovely reveries, stopping short of sentimentality, are taken in the lush splendors of the natural world. But the intrusion of civilization, the "creator of deathscapes," encroaches in the form of excursion boats pointing out the narrator's home as "squatter shacks." Smog spills from the cities toward them. He is overcome by a sudden, violent hatred of man. Only his wife, who is "perhaps herself the eidolon of everything we loved in Eridanus, of all its shifting moods and tides and dark and suns and stars" with her "mysterious correspondence with all nature" can save him. She becomes his Beatrice, this daughter of Eve, who awakens his senses, becomes nature's language and leads him to the peaks of consciousness. She provides new contexts for him and quiets the doubts of his ephemeral identity: "And just for an instant I felt that had she not come down the path to meet me, I might indeed have disappeared, to spend the rest of my extraterrestrial existence searching for her in some limbo."

In *Under the Volcano*, the desperate isolation of consciousness is absolute. Geoffrey Firmin, the Consul, prays to be delivered "from the dreadful tyranny of self." Yet our narrator in "The Forest Path" settles down to "some horrendous extremity of self-observation . . . necessary to fulfill my project." With simplicity and composure, he and his wife have peacefully

> "progressed as if to a region where such words as spring, water, houses, trees, vines, laurels, mountains, wolves, bay, roses, beach, islands, forest, tides and deer and snow and fire, had realized their true being, or had their source: and as these words on a page once stood merely to what they symbolized, so did the reality we knew now stand to something else beyond that symbolized or reflected: it was as if we were clothed in the kind of reality which before we saw only at a distance."

This passage is emblematic of Lowry's genius for infusing abstraction with substance. If much of "The Forest Path" reads with an aeolian tone, we must realize that the characterization of the narrator is so successful and the poetic language so dramatically sustained, that reading it is like listening to and watching an expert actor in extended monologue. The story's plot dynamic tapers; the language of liquor is filtered like the spring in the final image of this book, "Laughing, we stooped down to the stream and drank."

It is this note of simplicity, acceptance and refreshment that might have signalled a new beginning for Malcolm Lowry. *Hear Us O Lord From Heaven Thy Dwelling Place* does not approach the magnificence of style or power of emotion found in *Under the Volcano*. Little does. The volume does, however, give us a glimpse of another Malcolm Lowry—one with a greater sense of irony and humor and one who begins to see a light that does not shudder with drunken trauma. Throughout Lowry's works, feelings persevere over logic. His reach was always for the universal. He constantly pushed at the limits of language, forming new ledges only to refer beyond them. If the depths of anguish in his works remain unfathomed, so do the peaks of hope for transcendence loom unscaled.

—John Donatich
Carroll & Graf Publishers

CONTENTS

HEAR US O LORD FROM HEAVEN
THY DWELLING PLACE

FISHERMEN'S HYMN
From the Isle of Man

THE BRAVEST BOAT

I⊤ was a day of spindrift and blowing sea-foam, with black clouds presaging rain driven over the mountains from the sea by a wild March wind.

But a clean silver sea light came from along the horizon where the sky itself was like glowing silver. And far away over in America the snowy volcanic peak of Mount Hood stood on high, disembodied, cut off from earth, yet much too close, which was an even surer presage of rain, as though the mountains had advanced, or were advancing.

In the park of the seaport the giant trees swayed, and taller than any were the tragic Seven Sisters, a constellation of seven noble red cedars that had grown there for hundreds of years, but were now dying, blasted, with bare peeled tops and stricken boughs. (They were dying rather than live longer near civilization. Yet though everyone had forgotten they were called after the Pleiades and thought they were named with civic pride after the seven daughters of a butcher, who seventy years before when the growing city was named Gaspool had all danced together in a shop window, nobody had the heart to cut them down.)

The angelic wings of the seagulls circling over the tree tops shone very white against the black sky. Fresh snow from the night before lay far down the slopes of the Canadian mountains, whose freezing summits, massed peak behind spire, jaggedly traversed the country northward as far as the eye could reach. And highest of all an eagle, with the poise of a skier, shot endlessly down the world.

In the mirror, reflecting this and much besides, of an old weighing machine with the legend *Your weight and your destiny* encircling its forehead and which stood on the embankment between the streetcar terminus and a hamburger stall, in this mirror along the reedy edge of the stretch of water below known as Lost Lagoon two figures in mackintoshes were approaching, a man and a beautiful passionate-looking girl, both bare-headed, and both extremely fair, and hand-in-hand, so that you would have taken them for young lovers, but that they were alike as brother and sister, and the man, although he walked with youthful nervous speed, now seemed older than the girl.

The man, fine-looking, tall, yet thick-set, very bronzed, and on approaching still closer obviously a good deal older than the girl, and wearing one of those blue belted trenchcoats favored by merchant marine officers of any country, though without any corresponding cap – moreover the trenchcoat was rather too short in the sleeve so that you could see some tattooing on his wrist, as he approached nearer still it seemed to be an anchor – whereas the girl's raincoat was of some sort of entrancing forest-green corduroy – the man paused every now and then to gaze into the lovely laughing face of his girl, and once or twice they both stopped, gulping in great draughts of salty clean sea and mountain air. A child smiled at them, and they smiled back. But the child belonged elsewhere, and the couple were unaccompanied.

In the lagoon swam wild swans, and many wild ducks: mallards and buffleheads and scaups, golden eyes, and cackling black coots with carved ivory bills. The little buffleheads often took flight from the water and some of them blew about like doves among the smaller trees. Under these trees lining the bank other ducks were sitting meekly on the sloping lawn, their beaks tucked into their plumage rumpled by the wind. The smaller trees were apples and hawthorns, some just opening into bloom even before they had foliage, and weeping willows, from whose branches small showers from the night's rain were scattered on the two figures as they passed.

A red-breasted merganser cruised in the lagoon, and at this swift and angry sea bird, with his proud disordered crest, the two were now gazing with a special sympathy, perhaps because he looked lonely without his mate. Ah, they were wrong. The red-breasted merganser was now joined by his wife and on a sudden duck's impulse and with immense fuss the two wild creatures flew off to settle on another part of the lagoon. And for some reason this simple fact appeared to make these two good people – for nearly all people are good who walk in parks – very happy again.

Now at a distance they saw a small boy, accompanied by his father who was kneeling on the bank, trying to sail a toy boat in the lagoon. But the blustery March wind soon slanted the tiny yacht into trouble and the father hauled it back, reaching out with his curved stick, and set it on an upright keel again for his son.

Your weight and your destiny.

Suddenly the girl's face, at close quarters in the weighing machine's mirror, seemed struggling with tears: she unbuttoned the top button of her coat to readjust her scarf, revealing, attached to a gold chain around her neck, a small gold cross. They were quite alone now, standing on top of the embankment by the machine, save for a few old men feeding the ducks below, and the father and his son with the toy yacht, all of whom had their backs turned, while an empty tram abruptly city-bound trundled around the minute terminus square; and the man, who had been trying to light his pipe, took her in his arms and tenderly kissed her, and then pressing his face against her cheek, held her a moment closely.

The couple, having gone down obliquely to the lagoon once more, had now passed the boy with his boat and his father. They were smiling again. Or as much as they could while eating hamburgers. And they were smiling still as they passed the slender reeds where a northwestern redwing was trying to pretend he had no notion of nesting, the northwestern redwing who like all birds in these parts may feel superior to man in that he is his own customs official, and can cross the wild border without let.

Along the far side of Lost Lagoon the green dragons grew thickly, their sheathed and cowled leaves giving off their peculiar animal-like odor. The two lovers were approaching the forest in which, ahead, several footpaths threaded the ancient trees. The park, seagirt, was very large, and like many parks throughout the Pacific Northwest, wisely left in places to the original wilderness. In fact, though its beauty was probably unique, it was quite like some American parks, you might have thought, save for the Union Jack that galloped evermore by a pavilion, and but for the apparition, at this moment, passing by on the carefully landscaped road slightly above, which led with its tunnels and detours to a suspension bridge, of a posse of Royal Canadian Mounted Policemen mounted royally upon the cushions of an American Chevrolet.

Nearer the forest were gardens with sheltered beds of snow-drops and here and there a few crocuses lifting their sweet chalices. The man and his girl now seemed lost in thought, breasting the buffeting wind that blew the girl's scarf out be-hind her like a pennant and blew the man's thick fair hair about his head.

A loudspeaker, enthroned on a wagon, barked from the city of Enochvilleport composed of dilapidated half-skyscrapers, at different levels, some with all kinds of scrap iron, even broken airplanes, on their roofs, others being moldy stock exchange buildings, new beer parlors crawling with verminous light even in mid-afternoon and resembling gigantic emerald-lit public lavatories for both sexes, masonries containing English tea-shoppes where your fortune could be told by a female relative of Maximilian of Mexico, totem pole factories, drapers' shops with the best Scotch tweed and opium dens in the basement (though no bars, as if, like some hideous old roué shuddering with every unmentionable secret vice, this city without gaiety had cackled 'No, I draw the line at that. — What would our wee laddies come to then?'), cerise conflagrations of cinemas, modern apart-ment buildings, and other soulless behemoths, housing, it might be, noble invisible struggles, of literature, the drama, art or music, the student's lamp and the rejected manuscript; or inde-scribable poverty and degradation, between which civic attrac-tions were squeezed occasional lovely dark ivy-clad old houses that seemed weeping, cut off from all light, on their knees, and elsewhere bankrupt hospitals, and one or two solid-stoned old banks, held up that afternoon; and among which appeared too, at infrequent intervals, beyond a melancholy never-striking black and white clock that said three, dwarfed spires belonging to frame façades with blackened rose windows, queer grimed

onion-shaped domes, and even Chinese pagodas, so that first
you thought you were in the Orient, then Turkey or Russia,
though finally, but for the fact that some of these were churches,
you would be sure you were in hell: despite that anyone who
had ever really been in hell must have given Enochvilleport a
nod of recognition, further affirmed by the spectacle, at first not
unpicturesque, of the numerous sawmills relentlessly smoking and champing away like demons, Molochs fed by whole
mountainsides of forests that never grew again, or by trees that
made way for grinning regiments of villas in the background
of 'our expanding and fair city,' mills that shook the very earth
with their tumult, filling the windy air with their sound as of a
wailing and gnashing of teeth: all these curious achievements
of man, together creating as we say 'the jewel of the Pacific,'
went as though down a great incline to a harbor more spectacular than Rio de Janeiro and San Francisco put together, with
deep-sea freighters moored at every angle for miles in the road-
stead, but to whose heroic prospect nearly the only human
dwellings visible on this side of the water that had any air of
belonging, or in which their inhabitants could be said any
longer to participate, were, paradoxically, a few lowly little self-
built shacks and floathouses, that might have been driven out of
the city altogether, down to the water's edge into the sea itself,
where they stood on piles, like fishermen's huts (which several
of them apparently were), or on rollers, some dark and tumble-
down, others freshly and prettily painted, these last quite evidently built or placed with some human need for beauty in mind,
even if under the permanent threat of eviction, and all standing,
even the most somber, with their fluted tin chimneys smoking
here and there like toy tramp steamers, as though in defiance
of the town, before eternity. In Enochvilleport itself some
ghastly-coloured neon signs had long since been going through
their unctuous twitchings and gesticulations that nostalgia and
love transform into a poetry of longing: more happily one began
to flicker: PALOMAR, LOUIS ARMSTRONG AND HIS OR-
CHESTRA. A huge new gray dead hotel that at sea might be a
landmark of romance, belched smoke out of its turreted haunted-
looking roof, as if it had caught fire, and beyond that all the

lamps were blazing within the grim courtyard of the law courts, equally at sea a trysting place of the heart, outside which one of the stone lions, having recently been blown up, was covered reverently with a white cloth, and inside which for a month a group of stainless citizens had been trying a sixteen-year-old boy for murder.

Nearer the park the apron lights appeared on a sort of pebble-dashed Y.M.C.A.-Hall-cum-variety-theater saying TAMMUZ *The Master Hypnotist, To-nite 8:30,* and running past this the tramlines, down which another parkwise streetcar was approaching, could be seen extending almost to the department store in whose show window Tammuz' subject, perhaps a somnolent descendant of the seven sisters whose fame had eclipsed even that of the Pleiades, but whose announced ambition was to become a female psychiatrist, had been sleeping happily and publicly in a double bed for the last three days as an advance publicity stunt for tonight's performance.

Above Lost Lagoon on the road now mounting toward the suspension bridge in the distance much as a piece of jazz music mounts towards a break, a newsboy cried: 'LASH ORDERED FOR SAINT PIERRE! SIXTEEN YEAR OLD BOY, CHILD-SLAYER, TO HANG! Read all about it!'

The weather too was foreboding. Yet, seeing the wandering lovers, the other passers-by on this side of the lagoon, a wounded soldier lying on a bench smoking a cigarette, and one or two of those destitute souls, the very old who haunt parks – since, faced with a choice, the very old will sometimes prefer, rather than to keep a room and starve, at least in such a city as this, somehow to eat and live outdoors – smiled too.

For as the girl walked along beside the man with her arm through his and as they smiled together and their eyes met with love, or they paused, watching the blowing seagulls, or the ever-changing scene of the snow-freaked Canadian mountains with their fleecy indigo chasms, or to listen to the deep-tongued majesty of a merchantman's echoing roar (these things that made Enochvilleport's ferocious aldermen imagine that it was the city itself that was beautiful, and maybe they were half right), the whistle of a ferryboat as it sidled across the inlet

northward, what memories might not be evoked in a poor soldier, in the breasts of the bereaved, the old, even, who knows,
in the mounted policemen, not merely of young love, but of
lovers, as they seemed to be, so much in love that they were
afraid to lose a moment of their time together?

Yet only a guardian angel of these two would have known –
and surely they must have possessed a guardian angel – the
strangest of all strange things of which they were thinking, save
that, since they had spoken of it so often before, and especially,
when they had opportunity, on this day of the year, each knew
of course that the other was thinking about it, to such an extent
indeed that it was no surprise, it only resembled the beginning
of a ritual when the man said, as they entered the main path of
the forest, through whose branches that shielded them from
the wind could be made out, from time to time, suggesting a
fragment of music manuscript, a bit of the suspension bridge
itself:

'It was a day just like this that I set the boat adrift. It was
twenty-nine years ago in June.'

'It was twenty-nine years ago in June, darling. And it was
June twenty-seventh.'

'It was five years before you were born, Astrid, and I was ten
years old and I came down to the bay with my father.'

'It was five years before I was born, you were ten years old,
and you came down to the wharf with your father. Your father
and grandfather had made you the boat between them and it
was a fine one, ten inches long, smoothly varnished and made
of wood from your model airplane box, with a new strong white
sail.'

'Yes, it was balsa wood from my model airplane box and my
father sat beside me, telling me what to write for a note to put
in it.'

'Your father sat beside you, telling you what to write,' Astrid
laughed, 'and you wrote:

'Hello.

'My name is Sigurd Storlesen. I am ten years old. Right now
I am sitting on the wharf at Fearnought Bay, Clallam County,
State of Washington, U.S.A., 5 miles south of Cape Flattery on

the Pacific side, and my Dad is beside me telling me what to write. Today is June 27, 1922. My Dad is a forest warden in the Olympic National Forest but my Granddad is the lighthouse keeper at Cape Flattery. Beside me is a small shiny canoe which you now hold in your hand. It is a windy day and my Dad said to put the canoe in the water when I have put this in and glued down the lid which is a piece of balsa wood from my model airplane box.

'Well must close this note now, but first I will ask you to tell the Seattle Star that you have found it, because I am going to start reading the paper from today and looking for a piece that says, who when and where it was found.

'Thanks. Sigurd Storlesen.'

'Yes, then my father and I put the note inside, and we glued down the lid and sealed it and put the boat on the water.'

'You put the boat on the water and the tide was going out and away it went. The current caught it right off and carried it out and you watched it till it was out of sight!'

The two had now reached a clearing in the forest where a few gray squirrels were scampering about on the grass. A dark-browed Indian in a windbreak, utterly absorbed by his friendly task, stood with a sleek black squirrel sitting on his shoulder nibbling popcorn he was giving it from a bag. This reminded them to get some peanuts to feed the bears, whose cages were over the way.

Ursus Horribilis: and now they tossed peanuts to the sad lumbering sleep-heavy creatures – though at least these two grizzlies were together, they even had a home – maybe still too sleepy to know where they were, still wrapped in a dream of their timberfalls and wild blueberries in the Cordilleras Sigurd and Astrid could see again, straight ahead of them, between the trees, beyond a bay.

But how should they stop thinking of the little boat?

Twelve years it had wandered. Through the tempests of winter, over sunny summer seas, what tide rips had caught it, what wild sea birds, shearwaters, storm petrels, jaegers, that follow the thrashing propellers, the dark albatross of these nor-thern waters, swooped upon it, or warm currents edged it lazily

toward land – and blue-water currents sailed it after the alba-
core, with fishing boats like white giraffes – or glacial drifts
tossed it about fuming Cape Flattery itself. Perhaps it had rested,
floating in a sheltered cove, where the killer whale smote,
lashed, the deep clear water; the eagle and the salmon had seen
it, a baby seal stared with her wondering eyes, only for the little
boat to be thrown aground, catching the rainy afternoon sun, on
cruel barnacled rocks by the waves, lying aground knocked from
side to side in an inch of water like a live thing, or a poor old
tin can, pushed, pounded ashore, and swung around, reversed
again, left high and dry, and then swept another yard up the
beach, or carried under a lonely salt-gray shack, to drive a seine
fisherman crazy all night with its faint plaintive knocking,
before it ebbed out in the dark autumn dawn, and found its
way afresh, over the deep, coming through thunder, to who
will ever know what fierce and desolate uninhabited shore,
known only to the dread Wendigo, where not even an Indian
could have found it, unfriended there, lost, until it was borne
out to sea once more by the great brimming black tides of
January, or the huge calm tides of the mid-summer moon, to
start its journey all over again –

Astrid and Sigurd came to a large enclosure, set back from a
walk, with two vine-leaved maple trees (their scarlet tassels,
delicate precursors of their leaves, already visible) growing
through the top, a sheltered cavernous part to one side for a lair,
and the whole, save for the barred front, covered with stout
large-meshed wire – considered sufficient protection for one of
the most Satanic beasts left living on earth.

Two animals inhabited the cage, spotted like deceitful pastel
leopards, and in appearance like decorated, maniacal-looking
cats: their ears were provided with huge tassels and, as if this
were in savage parody of the vine-leaved maples, from the
brute's chin tassels also depended. Their legs were as long as a
man's arm, and their paws, clothed in gray fur out of which shot
claws curved like scimitars, were as big as a man's clenched
fist.

And the two beautiful demonic creatures prowled and paced
endlessly, searching the base of their cage, between whose bars

19

there was just room to slip a murderous paw – always a hop out of reach an almost invisible sparrow went pecking away in the dust – searching with eternal voraciousness, yet seeking in desperation also some way out, passing and repassing each other rhythmically, as though truly damned and under some compelling enchantment.

And yet as they watched the terrifying Canadian lynx, in which seemed to be embodied in animal form all the pure ferocity of nature, as they watched, crunching peanuts themselves now and passing the bag between them, before the lovers' eyes still sailed that tiny boat, battling with the seas, at the mercy of a wilder ferocity yet, all those years before Astrid was born.

Ah, its absolute loneliness amid those wastes, those wildernesses, of rough rainy seas bereft even of sea birds, between contrary winds, or in the great dead windless swell that comes following a gale; and then with the wind springing up and blowing the spray across the sea like rain, like a vision of creation, blowing the little boat as it climbed the highlands into the skies, from which sizzled cobalt lightnings, and then sank down into the abyss, but already was climbing again, while the whole sea crested with foam like lambs' wool went furling off to leeward, the whole vast moon-driven expanse like the pastures and valleys and snow-capped ranges of a Sierra Madre in delirium, in ceaseless motion, rising and falling, and the little boat rising, and falling into a paralyzing sea of white drifting fire and smoking spume by which it seemed overwhelmed: and all this time a sound, like a high sound of singing, yet as sustained in harmony as telegraph wires, or like the unbelievably high perpetual sound of the wind where there is nobody to listen, which perhaps does not exist, or the ghost of the wind in the rigging of ships long lost, and perhaps it was the sound of the wind in its toy rigging, as again the boat slanted onward : but even then what further unfathomed deeps had it oversailed, until what birds of ill omen turned heavenly for it at last, what iron birds with saber wings skimming forever through the murk above the gray immeasurable swells, imparted mysteriously their own homing knowledge to it, the lonely buoyant little craft, nudging it with their beaks under golden sunsets in a blue sky, as it sailed close in to mountainous coasts of clouds with stars over them, or burning coasts at sunset once more, as it rounded not only the terrible spume-drenched rocks, like incinerators in sawmills, of Flattery, but other capes unknown, those twelve years, of giant pinnacles, images of barrenness and desolation, upon which the heart is thrown and impaled eternally! – And strangest of all how many ships themselves had threatened it, during that voyage of only some three score miles as the crow flies from its launching to its final port, looming out of the fog and passing by harmlessly all those years – those years too of the last sailing ships, rigged to the moonsail, sweeping by into their own oblivion – but ships cargoed with guns or iron for impending wars, what freighters now at the bottom of the sea he, Sigurd, had voyaged in for that matter, freighted with old marble and wine and cherries-in-brine, or whose engines even now were still somewhere murmuring: *Frère* Jacques! *Frère* Jacques!

What strange poem of God's mercy was this?

Suddenly across their vision a squirrel ran up a tree beside the cage and then, chattering shrilly, leaped from a branch and darted across the top of the wire mesh. Instantly, swift and deadly as lightning, one of the lynx sprang twenty feet into the air, hurtling straight to the top of the cage toward the squirrel, hitting the wire with a twang like a mammoth guitar, and simultaneously flashing through the wire its scimitar claws: Astrid cried out and covered her face.

But the squirrel, unhurt, untouched, was already running lightly along another branch, down to the tree, and away, while the infuriated lynx sprang straight up, sprang again, and again and again and again, as his mate crouched spitting and snarling below.

Sigurd and Astrid began to laugh. Then this seemed obscurely unfair to the lynx, now solemnly washing his mate's face. The innocent squirrel, for whom they felt such relief, might almost have been showing off, almost, unlike the oblivious sparrow, have been taunting the caged animal. The squirrel's hairbreadth escape – the thousand-to-one chance –

that on second thought must take place every day, seemed meaningless. But all at once it did not seem meaningless that they had been there to see it.

'You know how I watched the paper and waited,' Sigurd was saying, stooping to relight his pipe, as they walked on.

'The Seattle *Star*,' Astrid said.

'The Seattle *Star* . . . It was the first newspaper I ever read. Father always declared the boat had gone south – maybe to Mexico, and I seem to remember Granddad saying no, if it didn't break up on Tatoosh, the tide would take it right down Juan de Fuca Strait, maybe into Puget Sound itself. Well, I watched and waited for a long time and finally, as kids will, I stopped looking.'

'And the years went on –'

'And I grew up. Granddad was dead by then. And the old man, you know about him. Well, he's dead too now. But I never forgot. Twelve years! Think of it –! Why, it voyaged around longer than we've been married.'

'And we've been married seven years.'

'Seven years today –'

'It seems like a miracle!'

But their words fell like spent arrows before the target of this fact.

They were walking, as they left the forest, between two long rows of Japanese cherry trees, next month to be an airy avenue of celestial bloom. The cherry trees behind, the forest reappeared, to left and right of the wide clearing, and skirting two arms of the bay. As they approached the Pacific, down the gradual incline, on this side remote from the harbor the wind grew more boisterous: gulls, glaucous and raucous, wheeled and sailed overhead, yelling, and were suddenly far out to sea.

And it was the sea that lay before them, at the end of the slope that changed into the steep beach, the naked sea, running deeply below, without embankment or promenade, or any friendly shacks, though some prettily built homes showed to the left, with one light in a window, glowing warmly through the trees on the edge of the forest itself, as of some stalwart Columbian Adam, who had calmly stolen back with his

Eve into Paradise, under the flaming sword of the civic cheru-
bim.

The tide was low. Offshore, white horses were running
around a point. The headlong onrush of the tide of beaten silver
flashing over its crossflowing underset was so fast the very
surface of the sea seemed racing away.

Their path gave place to a cinder track in the familiar lee of
an old frame pavilion, a deserted tea house boarded up since
last summer. Dead leaves were slithering across the porch, past
which on the slope to the right picnic benches, tables, a derelict
swing, lay overturned, under a tempestuous grove of birches.
It seemed cold, sad, inhuman there, and beyond, with the roar of
that deep low tide. Yet there was that between the lovers which
moved like a warmth, and might have thrown open the shutters,
set the benches and tables aright, and filled the whole grove with
the voices and children's laughter of summer. Astrid paused for
a moment with a hand on Sigurd's arm while they were sheltered by the pavilion, and said, what she too had often said before, so that they always repeated these things almost like an
incantation:

'I'll never forget it. That day when I was seven years old,
coming to the park here on a picnic with my father and mother
and brother. After lunch my brother and I came down to the
beach to play. It was a fine summer day, and the tide was out,
but there'd been this very high tide in the night, and you could
see the lines of driftwood and seaweed where it had ebbed. . . . I
was playing on the beach, and I found your boat!'

'You were playing on the beach and you found my boat. And
the mast was broken.'

'The mast was broken and shreds of sail hung dirty and
limp. But your boat was still whole and unhurt, though it was
scratched and weatherbeaten and the varnish was gone. I ran to
my mother, and she saw the sealing wax over the cockpit, and,
darling, I found your note!'

'You found our note, my darling.'

Astrid drew from her pocket a scrap of paper and holding it
between them they bent over (though it was hardly legible by
now and they knew it off by heart) and read:

The Bravest Boat

Hello.

My name is Sigurd Storlesen. I am ten years old. Right now I am sitting on the wharf at Fearnought Bay, Clallam County, State of Washington, U.S.A., 5 miles south of Cape Flattery on the Pacific side, and my Dad is beside me telling me what to write. Today is June 27, 1922. My Dad is a forest warden in the Olympic National Forest but my Granddad is the lighthouse keeper at Cape Flattery. Beside me is a small shiny canoe which you now hold in your hand. It is a windy day and my Dad said to put the canoe in the water when I have put this in and glued down the lid which is a piece of balsa wood from my model airplane box.

Well must close this note now, but first I will ask you to tell the Seattle Star that you have found it, because I am going to start reading the paper from today and looking for a piece that says, who when and where it was found.

Thanks.

SIGURD STORLESEN.

They came to the desolate beach strewn with driftwood, sculptured, whorled, silvered, piled everywhere by tides so immense there was a tideline of seaweed and detritus on the grass behind them, and great logs and shingle-bolts and writhing snags, crucificial, or frozen in a fiery rage – or better, a few bits of lumber almost ready to burn, for someone to take home, and automatically they threw them up beyond the sea's reach for some passing soul, remembering their own winters of need – and more snags there at the foot of the grove and visible high on the sea-scythed forest banks on either side, in which riven trees were growing, yearning over the shore. And everywhere they looked was wreckage, the toll of winter's wrath: wrecked hencoops, wrecked floats, the wrecked side of a fisherman's hut, its boards once hammered together, with its wrenched shiplap and extruding nails. The fury had extended even to the beach itself, formed in hummocks and waves and barriers of shingle and shells they had to climb up in places. And everywhere too was the grotesque macabre fruit of the sea, with its exhilarating iodine smell, nightmarish bulbs of kelp like antiquated motor horns, trailing brown satin streamers twenty feet long, sea wrack like demons, or the discarded casements of evil spirits that had been cleansed. Then more wreckage: boots, a clock, torn fishing nets, demolished wheelhouse, a smashed wheel lying in the sand.

Nor was it possible to grasp for more than a moment that all this with its feeling of death and destruction and barrenness was only an appearance, that beneath the flotsam, under the very shells they crunched, within the trickling overflows of winterbournes they jumped over, down at the tide margin, existed, just as in the forest, a stirring and stretching of life, a seething of spring.

When Astrid and Sigurd were almost sheltered by an uprooted tree on one of these lower billows of beach they noticed that the clouds had lifted over the sea, though the sky was not blue but still that intense silver, so that they could see right across the Gulf and make out, or thought they could, the line of some Gulf Islands. A lone freighter with upraised derricks shipped seas on the horizon. A hint of the summit of Mount Hood remained, or it might have been clouds. They remarked too, in the southeast, on the sloping base of a hill, a triangle of storm-washed green, as if cut out of the overhanging murk there, in which were four pines, five telegraph posts, and a clearing resembling a cemetery. Behind them the icy mountains of Canada hid their savage peaks and snowfalls under still more savage clouds. And they saw that the sea was gray with whitecaps and currents charging offshore and spray blowing backwards from the rocks.

But when the full force of the wind caught them, looking from the shore, it was like gazing into chaos. The wind blew away their thoughts, their voices, almost their very senses, as they walked, crunching the shells, laughing and stumbling. Nor could they tell whether it was spume or rain that smote and stung their faces, whether spindrift from the sea or rain from which the sea was born, as now finally they were forced to a halt, standing there arm in arm. . . . And it was to this shore, through that chaos, by those currents, that their little boat with its innocent message had been brought out of the past finally to safety and a home.

But ah, the storms they had come through!

THROUGH THE PANAMA

From the Journal of Sigbjørn Wilderness

> Frère Jacques
> Frère Jacques
> Dormez-vous?
> Dormez-vous?
> Sonnez les matines!
> Sonnez les matines!
> Ding dang dong
> Ding dang dong ...

THIS is the ship's endless song.

This is the engine of the *Diderot*: the canon repeated endlessly ...

Leaving Vancouver, British Columbia, Canada, midnight, November 7, 1947, S.S. *Diderot*, for Rotterdam.

Rain, rain and dark skies all day.

We arrive at dusk, in a drizzle. Everything wet, dark, slippery. Dock building huge, dimly lit by tiny yellow bulbs at far intervals. Black geometry angled against dark sky. Cluster lamps glowing – they are loading cardboard cartons labeled *Product of Canada*.

(This morning, walking through the forest, a moment of intense emotion: the path, sodden, a morass of mud, the sad dripping trees and ocherous fallen leaves; here it all is. I cannot believe I won't be walking down the path tomorrow.)

Primrose and myself are the sole passengers aboard the freighter. The crew are all Bretons, the ship, French, its build, American. A Liberty ship about 5,000 tons, 10 knots, electric welded hull.

Longshoremen leave, skipper comes aboard. Sense of departure increases. Nothing happens for hours. We drink rum in cabin: Chief Gunner's cabin, between skipper and wireless operator. Primrose wearing all her Mexican silver bracelets, calmly tense, electrically beautiful and excited.

Then: the Immigration officers, very courteous and cheery. All had cognac together in the skipper's cabin.

Then: bells rang, hawsers were cast off, shouts from bridge, slowly, suddenly, we were moving. The little strip of black, oily water widened . . . The black cloudy sky was breaking and stars were brilliant overhead.

The Northern Cross.

Nov. 8. High salt wind, clear blue sky, hellishly rough sea (zig-zagged with a lashing tide rip) through the Juan de Fuca Strait.

– Whale geometry of Cape Flattery: finny phallic furious face of Flattery.

Cape Flattery, with spume drenched rocks, like incinerators in sawmills.

– Significance of sailing on the 7th. The point is that my character Martin, in the novel I'm furiously trying to get a first draft of (knowing damned well I'd never do any work on this voyage, which is to last precisely 7 weeks), had dreaded starting a journey on the 7th of any month. To begin with we were not going to leave for Europe until January. Then the message comes that our sailing has been canceled and we'll have to take advantage of the *Diderot*'s sailing on the 6th if we want to go at all. But she doesn't – she sails on the 7th. Martin Trumbaugh's really fatal date is November 15. So long as we don't leave Los Angeles on Nov. 15 for the long haul, all will be well. Why do I say that? The further point is that the novel is about a character who becomes enmeshed in the plot of the novel he has written, as I did in Mexico. But now I am becoming enmeshed in the plot of a novel I have scarcely begun. Idea is not new, at least so far as enmeshment with characters is concerned. Goethe, Wilhelm von Scholz, 'The Race with a Shadow.' Pirandello, etc. But did these people ever have it happen to *them*?

Turn this into triumph: the furies into mercies.

– The inenarrable inconceivably desolate sense of having no

27

right to be where you are; the billows of inexhaustible anguish haunted by the insatiable albatross of self.

There is an albatross, really.

Martin thought of the misty winter sunrise, through the windows of their little cabin; the sun, a tiny little sun, framed in one of the window panes, like a miniature, unreal, white, with three trees in it, though no other trees were to be seen, and reflected in the inlet, in a high calm icy tide. Fear something will happen to house in our absence. Novel is to be called *Dark as the Grave Wherein My Friend Is Laid*. Keep quiet about house or will spoil voyage for Primrose. Intolerable behavior : remember Fielding with dropsy, being hauled on board in a basket on voyage to Portugal. Gentleman and sense of humor. Had himself tapped for water every now and then. H'm.

This desolate sense of alienation possibly universal sense of dispossession.

The cramped cabin one's obvious place on earth.

Chief Gunner's cabin.

Curious agony of not having tipped steward. Whom to tip ? Not wishing to insult anybody.

Strindberg's horror at using people. Using one's wife as a rabbit for vivisection. Seems more honorable to use yourself. This idea unfortunately not new either.

Fitzgerald would have been saved by life in our shack, Martin thought (who had been reading *The Crack-Up*). The Last Laocöon. Impossible to find anybody less like Fitzgerald than Martin. Sad that F. hated the English. To my mind his latter work represents essentially best qualities of chivalry and decency now too often lacking in the English themselves. This quality true essentially of soul of America. Can this be expressed without obsequiousness ? Or good manners, with fidelity to the ghastly façade of Deathpic and Spaceclack, pulpy enemies of the earth and mankind. Read *Alc*, the weekly boozemagazine, etc.

– Would like to express cultural debt of England to America. It is enormous, even bigger than our national one, if possible. But what use have we made of it ? Public school boys fishing vicariously for Hemingway's trout. Or Deathpic and Spaceclack talk. The English are now so loathed in Canada we are rapidly becoming a tragic minority. Starve to death in Stanley Park rather than ask for help. It happens every day. Canada, whose heart is England but whose soul is Labrador. Of course I am a Scotsman. As a matter of fact I am Norwegian.

Frère Jacques
Frère Jacques

– Played by Louis Armstrong and his orchestra. Art Tatum on piano. Joe Venuti violin. *Battement de Tambours.*

And I think of O'Neill. *Iceman* is wonderful play. Wonder if similarity to the theme of *The Wild Duck* was conscious, in which drink is justified as 'life illusion.' I wish O'Neill had written more plays about the sea. The Norwegian barque? My grandfather, captain of the windjammer *The Scottish Isles*, went down with his ship in the Indian Ocean. He was bringing my mother a cockatoo. Remember the story told about him by Old Hands in Liverpool. The owners loaded his ship badly : he complained : was forced to take it out. So he sailed it right bang down to the Cape, and right bang back again to Liverpool and made them load it correctly.

– 'The man who went to sea because he read *The Hairy Ape* and *The Moon of the Caribbees*.' (That was me twenty years ago. Accounts partly for my depression on board, *Diderot* is totally different freighter to any in my experience though. Liberty ship – but really beautiful in my opinion, if of romantic slowness. Food is superb; and great gulps of pinard at every meal. A wonderful trip, really.)

– A long black albatross, like a flying machete – strictly 2 machetes . . . Albatross like a distant lone left wing three quarter at rugby, practicing . . .

An iron bird, with saber wings. Actually *is* black albatross, though captain says no.

But the captain, for once, is wrong. It is not a shearwater, though there is a sooty shearwater behind, Primrose says. Melville's hatred of shearwaters : birds of bad omen. Nonsense. Hope we do not sail on the 15th of November from Los Angeles.

We have crossed the border and are off the state of Washington.

ALBATROSS SLAIN, BRINGS GRIEF, PAIN

(Excerpt from a fragment of newspaper, left by steward in cabin):

Shaft Snapped, Leg Broken, Net Fouled
When Sea Tradition Defied.

Port Angeles, Wash. (A.P.) – A University of Washington faculty member who defied the tradition of the sea knows better now. His sad story came to light when the U.S. Fish and Wildlife Service's exploratory vessel put in here. The university research assistant, John Firmin, started it when he sighted a white albatross flying near the vessel, engaged in exploratory deep sea trawling off Cape Flattery. Firmin asked permission to shoot it and bring it to the university museum as the first known specimen of a white albatross seen in Washington coast waters.

Crew Horrified.

The seven crew men immediately shouted 'No!' reminding Firmin of the fate of Coleridge's 'Ancient Mariner' and the old tradition of bad luck which follows shooting an albatross. But because of the specimen's rarity – etc.

See, conversely, newspaper clipping I've been saving:

ALBATROSS SAVES SAILOR

Sydney, Friday. An English seaman who fell overboard from a liner owes his life to an albatross. It landed on his chest and guided a life-boat to him.

Seaman John Oakley, 53, of Southampton, fell from the stern of the 20,204 ton *Southern Cross* 10 miles off the New South Wales coast yesterday.

A little boy, a passenger, saw him fall and told the deck officer. The ship turned about and a lifeboat was lowered.

Oakley was obscured by waves until the albatross landed on his chest and served as a beacon to the rescuers. – *Reuters*.

– The albatross is one of the largest flying birds in the world with a wing span of 10 ft–12 ft and weighs about 17 lb.

Now there are three shearwaters.
Golden sunset in a blue sky.
Several large green meteors from Gemini.

Nov. 9. Primrose and Sigbjørn Wilderness are happy in their cramped Chief Gunner's cabin.

Martin Trumbaugh however is not very happy.

Trumbaugh : named after Trumbauer – Frankie. Beiderbecke, et al.

A dead storm petrel on the bows, with blue feet like a bat.

Off the coast of Oregon.

Thousands of white gulls. The crew are feeding them. Will our gulls starve without us ? Incredible jewel-like clearness of some days in November in the shack, a bell ringing in the mist. Mill-wheel reflections of sun on water, sliding down the shack. Such radiance for November! And turn the pine boughs into green chenille.

Nov. 11. The dramatic diatonic booming of fog horns, bells, whistles, on Golden Gate Bridge, in the fog, warping early in the morning into cold San Francisco. Past Alcatraz. Bird watcher who lives there.

Fog lifts; to the left, Oakland is dark, cloudy, bridge disappears into low gray clouds. To the right San Francisco, the sky is tender blue, the bridge arching away, incredible, with its cables and towers.

Skipper wearing fur-lined jacket, collar turned up, blue cap, formidable, with beaky profile against the sky. He is angry with longshoremen and shouting curses and orders in French and English. Pilot amused, bored, respectful. Various mates stand around tensely.

Brilliant comment of a person to whom I once lent *Ulysses* on returning it the next day. 'Thanks awfully. Very good.' (Lawrence also said: 'The whole is a strange assembly of apparently incongruous parts, slipping past one another.')

Leaving at night the jeweled city. Baguette diamonds on black velvet, says Primrose: ruby and emerald harbor lights. Topaz and gold lights on two bridges.

Primrose is very happy. We embrace in the dark, on deck.

Nov. 14. Los Angeles. A notice in a shed: *Watch the Hook It Can't Watch You.*

Warm blue satin sea and mild sun.

Nov. 15. Sure enough, off we go. Of course.

We have another passenger : his name? Charon. Naturally.

– Outward bound, from Los Angeles to Rotterdam, S.S. *Diderot* sailed November 15, in the evening.

(Mem. *Outward Bound*, seen at the Theatre Royal in Exeter with my mother and father in 1923. Eight bells ring up each curtain. Wonderful performance by Gladys Ffolliot.)

S. S. *Tidewater*, a black glistening oil tanker, very close, empty : red rails : *Marie Celeste* ?

Description of sunset : sailing into boiling Quink. Magenta scarves to starboard, from the galley, a smell of loaves, to the right, vermilion spare ribs, aft, a sort of violet porridge.

Frère *Jacques*
Frère *Jacques*

Gulls blowing, silhouettes. And more shearwaters.

Sailing close into a black mountainous coast of clouds, with stars over them.

And Mr Charon, he's there too.

Nov. 16. We have crossed the border in the night.

– At sunset, leaden clouds, black sky, with a long line of burning vermilion like a forest fire 3,000 miles long, far away between black sea and sky.

Strange islands, barren as icebergs, and nearly as white.

Rocks ! – The Lower California coast, giant pinnacles, images of barrenness and desolation, on which the heart is thrown and impaled eternally . . .

Frère Jacques, Frère Jacques Laruelle.

Baja California. In fact, Mexico to port. Thousands and thousands of miles of it.

– But nothing equaled now the inconceivable loneliness and desolate beauty of the interminable Mexican coast (down which the freighter now slowly made its way), with the furnace of the ship saying *Frère* Jacques : *Frère* Jacques : *dor*mez-vous : *dor*mez-vous, and a single lone digarilla floating, turning, against the purple frightful coast, and the sunset of misery –

32

> dormez-vous
> dormez-vous
> sonnez *lament*ina
> sonnez *lament*ina
> dong dong dong
> doom doom doom

The digarilla is the bosun bird, or frigate bird, or man-o'-war bird, with a tail like a swallow; it is a bird of ill omen in *Dark as the Grave Wherein My Friend Is Laid*. It was a bird of ill omen to Primrose and me in Acapulco three years ago. Yet one week after that *The Valley of the Shadow of Death* was accepted. The book will be divided into three parts, three novels. *Dark as the Grave Wherein My Friend Is Laid, Eridanus, La Mordida*. *Eridanus* is a sort of typical intermezzo and is about a shack in Canada. *Dark as the Grave* is about the death of Fernando, who is Dr Vigil in *The Valley of the Shadow*. *Real* death that is, we discovered. *La Mordida*, The Bite, is set in Acapulco. *The Valley of the Shadow* worked like an infernal machine. Dr Vigil is dead like the Consul – in reality that is. No wonder my letters were returned.

Someone has written an opera about another Consul. It hurts my feelings. This sort of thing is the theme of the book too.

Nov. 17. Mr Charon looking at Mexico.
Daemon on the job: 24 hours a day.
All noises of the engine set themselves to the tune of 'Frère Jacques' (Martin thought), sometimes the words were 'Cuernavaca, Cuernavaca' instead of 'Frère Jacques'; the engine had another trick too, of singing

> Please go *on*!
> Why not *die*!
> Sonnez les matines . . .

and what's more taken up by the ventilators, it would sing in harmony; I swear it, I heard aerial infernal choirs chanting in harmony, sometimes rising to a frightful pitch . . . And then it would begin again, saying something quite ridiculous, instead of ding dang dong:

33

Sans maison
Sans maison

and when it got literally into that groove it would never stop.

– The inability to breathe almost, as the heat grows worse – your mouth too becomes a sort of perpetual pulped vise, your face swollen so that you can scarcely open it save to mutter something inane, and always unfinished, like 'I thought it would be – or – ah, please dear it –'

Battement de Tambours

Dark as the Grave Wherein My Friend Is Laid. Fernando is buried in Villahermosa. Murdered. He ah drink too much mescal. Mehican whiky. Alfred Gordon Pym.

Title too long: why not just 'My Friend Is Laid' (Primrose suggested).

The distant inane motorcycle of the electric fan, whose breeze does not reach you, sitting below, watching the sweat pricking your hands, and seep out of your chest.

The crew are chipping rust: hammers on the brain.

White leathery pelicans in the afternoon.

Peaks like machetes, pointing down. Inverted swordfish. Barren mountains, sharp-finned, or peaked like cones. (Yeats's *Vision*?)

Waking in the night with eyes aching and twitching vision to wonder (for Martin Trumbaugh, for the Consul, likewise named Firmin, to wonder) where did I put my shoe, did I have a shoe? I did, and the lost one seemed in the right place, but then where are the cigarettes, and where am I? etc. Surely standing now in the corridor of a train vacantly; but then again the engine with its *Frère* Jacques, *Frère* Jacques, *dor*mez-vous, *dor*mez-vous: of course, you bloody well can't dormez.

I fear that was the consequence of a case of none too good American whisky bought in Los Angeles because I liked its name. Green River. Even so, there is not half enough for this voyage. But perhaps the captain would ask Sigbjørn Wilderness and his wife on to the bridge for an apéritif.

Nov. 18. – the long long dead cruel sorrowful uninhabited coast of Mexico.

Frère Jacques.

Wake at 3 a.m., stumble around dark cabin. Where am I?

5 a.m. Primrose goes out to watch dawn. Indigo sea, black tortured shapes of mountains and sharp-pointed islands, a beautiful nightmare against a gold sky. For two hours we pace and weave, in and out, out and in, from cabin to deck. Try to sleep and cannot. Too close to Mexico?

Day becomes stinking hot and still. Coast faded out of sight. We are crossing the mouth of the Gulf of California. The crew are painting ventilators, wearing wooden shoes.

The skipper says they are 'beautying up the ship.'

– at sunset, the Tres Marias Islands, two ships, three frigate birds, jet against amber sky, clouds like boiling cauliflower by Michelangelo : and later, the stars : but now Martin saw the fixity of the closed order of their system: death in short. The thought comes from Keyserling. (They are only *not dead* when I look at them with Primrose.) Wonderful truth in Lawrence about this. Somehow my life draws (he writes) strength from the depths of the universe, from the depths among the stars, from the great world! Think Primrose feels something like this. And how true was that of them in Eridanus! But he can only get the feeling vicariously on board this ship, as it takes him away inexorably from the only place on earth he has loved, and perhaps forever.

In his loneliness and fixedness the ancient Mariner yearneth towards the journeying Moon, and the stars that still sojourn, yet still move onward ; and everywhere the blue sky belongs to them, and is their appointed rest and their native country and their own natural homes, which they enter unannounced, as lords that are certainly expected, and yet there is a silent joy at their arrival.

Our Mr Charon, Mr Pierre Charon, is a Frenchman, but acting Norwegian Consul in Papeete, Tahiti. An excellent fellow. He will take boat from Cristobal. Bon vivant. Wears shorts and high white stockings and calls Henry Miller an atom bomb. Also was in foreign legion and goose-steps on the foredeck every now and then. Also he says: Vous n'avez pas de nation. La France est votre mère. Soldat de la Légion Étrangère. Now who in the world said that before? Why no one but a character in *The*

Valley of the Shadow of Death. And you know what happened to the Consul at that point, don't you, observed Sigbjørn Wilderness, helping himself to his fourth sarsaparilla.

Man not enmeshed by, but *killed* by his own book and the malign forces it arouses. Wonderful theme. Buy planchette to provide for necessary dictation.

– Death takes a holiday. On a Liberty ship.

– Or does he? All day I can hear him 'cackling like a pirate.' Robert Penn Warren's phrase. Charon is really a good fellow too, offers us cognac, says I look like Don José in my bandanna handkerchief tied round my head. But the Captain does not invite him on the bridge for an apéritif however *like he did us*. Case of two masters looking at each other face to face. And by the way, who is Don José? The chap who murders Carmen?

Everyone talks so fast I can't hear a word: admirable crew.

The book should not be 3 books but 6 books, to be called *The Voyage That Never Ends,* with the *Valley* in the middle. The *Valley* acts like a diabolic battery in the middle. Resolution should be triumphant, however. That is to say it is certainly in my power to make it so.

Nov. 19 – or 21? The French Government falls: our little princess is married. Gallantly, the French crew drink the health of Princess Elizabeth. The radio reporter, Carpentier, reads long radio report at dinner for our benefit: his English is peculiar:

'And at that moment Lord Mousebatten . . .'

'At *Book*ing'am Palace . . .'

They don't intend any offense.

These Bretons are wonderful sailors; chivalrous and kind-hearted people to a man.

Englishmen who pride themselves on speaking French, snazzily being great judges of wines, referring to 'my friend, the best cook in Normandy, of course,' with the object of discrediting American salads. Did you ever meet a Frenchman who prettied up his English or was a good judge of a tankard of bitter and a steak and kidney pudding?

– But I dream of death, a horrible dream, Grand Guignol, without merit: but so vivid, so palpable, it seemed to contain some actual and frightful tactile threat, or prophesy, or warning: first there is dissociation, I am not I. I am Martin Trumbaugh. But I am not Martin Trumbaugh or perhaps Firmin either, I am a voice, yet with physical feelings, I enter what can only be described – I won't describe it, with teeth, that snap tight behind me: at the same time, in an inexplicable way, this is like going through the Panama Canal, and what closes behind me is, as it were, a lock: in a sense I am now a ship, but I am also a voice and also Martin Trumbaugh, and now I am, or he is, in the realm of death: this realm is, rather unimaginatively, entirely full of noseless white whores and ronyons with pulpy faces, in fact their faces come to pieces when they touch them, like newspapers picked out of the sea; Death himself is a hideous looking redfaced keeper of a prison, with half his face shot away, and one shattered leg whose shreds are still left 'untied' (because he apologized for this); he is the keeper of

But the curse liveth for him in the eye of the dead men.

The Polar Spirit's fellow-demons, the invisible inhabitants of the element, take part in his wrong; and two of them relate, one to the other, that penance long and heavy for the ancient Mariner hath been accorded to the Polar Spirit, who returneth southward.

the prison, and leads him or me or it through the gates, beyond which is St Catherine's College, Cambridge, *and the very room* (I'm not sure what he means) but Death, although hideous, has a kindly voice, and even sweet in his gruesome fashion: he says it is a pity I have seen 'all the show' whereupon I remember the vaudeville show when I entered, that is to say I remember moving chairs (in the sense of moving staircases) on which one sat as at a cafeteria, and some of the ghouls were sitting on these chairs and some seemed to be performing in some way: he said this meant I was doomed, and gave me 40 days to live, which on the whole I considered very generous of him. How can the soul take this kind of battering and survive? It's a bit like the toy boat. It is hard to believe that a disgusting and wicked dream of this nature has only been produced by the soul itself, in its passionate supplication to its unscrupulous owner to be cleansed. But it has.

Must be something I ate despite eulogy to French cooking.

The Mariner
awakes, and his
penance begins anew.

Martin woke up weeping, however, never before having realized that he had such a passion for the wind and the sunrise.

Sir, hombre, that is tequila.

(This now seems ridiculous to me, having risen early and washed a shirt.)

– I am the chief steward of my fate, I am the fireman of my soul.

Nothing can exceed the boundless misery and desolation and

He despiseth the
creatures of the calm

wretchedness of a voyage like this. (Even though everyone is so decent and it is the nicest crew one could have encountered, the best food, etc. And the Trumbaughs were of course having a hell of a good time, etc., etc.)

A shearwater, reconnoitering doubtless.

Leviathan, by Julian Green. The short story.

Acapulco on the beam, and I recognize it immediately – before the skipper indeed. There is Larqueta, with the lighthouse going past so slowly, and it even seems we can make out the Quinta Eulalia.

Since passing Manzanillo Acapulco is the first sign of any life we have seen down the entire Mexican coast. Almost from the ship, I can hear them shouting, attracting people to the camiones: Culete! Culete!

– This, Acapulco, is the place that is the main scene of my novel that I have been writing about these past months: and this is where Martin Trumbaugh meets his nemesis. This is also where Primrose and Martin, in 1946, saw the digarilla. One week before the acceptance of *The Valley of the Shadow of Death*. Which is when 'it' all began to happen. Story of a man (Man himself no less) Joyced in his own petard. A sense of exile oppresses me. A sense of something else, beyond injustice and misery, extramundane, oppresses, more than desolates, more than confounds me. To pass this place like this. Would I, one day, pass England, home, like this, on this voyage perhaps by some quirk of fortune not to be able to set foot on it, what is worse, not want to set foot on it? Acapulco is also the first place where Martin ever set foot in Mexico. November 1936. Yes,

and on the Day of the Dead. I remember, going ashore, in a
boat, the madman foaming at the mouth, correcting his watch;
the mile-high bodiless vultures in the thunder. And all this somber horror is lying calmly to port, slowly going astern, innocent
as Southend-on-Sea. That is also when the Consul began. Scene
of first mescal is now abaft the beam. Intervening years spent
writing it – happiest of his life so far, with Primrose in shack –
and other things, mostly burned. I know what the feeling must
resemble; exactly that of a ghost who revisits some place on earth
to which it is irresistibly drawn. He longs to make himself seen
but, poor hovering gas bag, cannot even land. (And last, at sun-
down, the skipper said innocently: 'Look at the little Mexican
boat going down the coast with all its lights on. A coastwise
human soul. Isn't it pretty?') His feelings are equally compounded of a desire for revenge and an illimitable desire that
can never be fulfilled. Feeling is also like excommunication. In-
fringement of spiritual rights of man. Where else may he pray
to the Virgin of Guadeloupe? The Saint of Desperate and Dangerous Causes? Here. Filthy, mean little place. Acapulco is that.
Certainly not worth throwing a tragedy at. But Martin Trumbaugh was passing the theater of his whole life's struggle, his
whole future life's struggle, if any, in this endless passage down
the Mexican coast. Christ how those ferociously ignorant and
mean and wicked little men made the Trumbaughs suffer,
though, here – would like to get them, every one. The Minister
of the Interior of Death especially. Country of the Absolute
Devil. Protest to the United Nations. How many Americans,
Canadians, murdered there every year. Hushed up, without investigation, to save face – whose? Some Mexicans just as good
as others are evil. Don José – Ah, Don José, so that was the meaning of Mr Charon's remark? – for example, at the Quinta
Eulalia. Think of the risk he took for us. His charity. Mexicans
are the most beautiful people on earth, most lovely country.
Mexican government seems still controlled by Satan, that's the
only trouble. All Mexicans know it, fear it, do nothing about it,
finally, despite revolutions; at bottom it is more corrupt than in
the days of Diaz. Mem: *Juarez in exile landing secretly in
Acapulco* ...

Culete! Culete! in memory. The little buses, and the shaking man and the blaze of beach at Pied de la Cuesta and the sharks and the manta ray as big as a drawing room. And the tiny brilliant tropical fishes at Culete ... And Primrose's broken holiday, her first holiday in ten years. I'll get them for that, if it is the last thing I do, on paper anyhow.

Another digarilla. The bosun bird. Rapacious giant swallow of the Zapotecan Sea.

And envieth that they should live, and so many lie dead. The mournful song of the crawling ship, that rose and fell; the heartbreaking endless purple barren coast against which the great lone frigate bird, with bat's wings and a swallow tail, ceaselessly falls, silently turns, and turns, and soars again.

Nov. 20 – or 21.

> FRÈRE Jacques
> FRÈRE Jacques
> DORMEZ-vous?
> DORMEZ-vous?
> SONNEZ les matines!
> SONNEZ les matines!
> Doom doom doom!
> Doom doom doom!

If these things should be survived, Martin decided, he must never forget, and write down, to the accompaniment of Frère Jacques, etc.: for they represented to his mind the bottom of all sorrow and abjectness.

God help me

Frère Jacques Frère Jacques dormez-vous?
Was it, Sigbjørn thought, that he did not wish to survive?
At the moment, it seems, I have no ambition ...
Sigbjørn Wilderness (pity my name is such a good one because I can't use it) could only pray for a miracle, that miraculously some love of life would come back.
It has: apparently this retracing of a course was part of the main ordeal; and even at this moment Martin knew it to be no dream, but some strange symbolism of the future.

– The French Government falls again.

In spite of having spent the night wrestling with the torments of the d.t.'s Martin Trumbaugh put in a remarkably good appearance at breakfast, looking bronzed and hearty.

'You are in good form.'

'Bon appétit.'

'Il fait beau temps' . . . and so on.

(This gentleman with the d.t.'s is not myself. Everything written about drink is incidentally absurd. Have to do it all over again, what about conflict, appalling sadness that can lead equally to participation in the tragic human condition, self-knowledge, discipline. Conflict is all-important. Gin and orange juice best cure for alcoholism, real cause of which is ugliness and complete baffling sterility of existence as *sold* to you. Otherwise it would be greed. And, by God, it *is* greed. A good remark: Guess I'll turn in and catch a little delirium.)

A white dove comes on board.

And a jaeger flies by.

And the French Government falls once more.

The little church bells that chime the hours; for the curious thing about the ship's bells on the *Diderot* – they are slow, melancholy, like the infinitely sad bell-chimes from the cathedral in Oaxaca – Oaxaca, now to port, home of Fernando the Oaxaqueñian, and Dr Vigil, dead, murdered in Villahermosa.

'For she is the Virgin for those who have nobody them with.'

'Nobody goes there, only those who have nobody with.'

'For she is the virgin for those who have *nobody* them with.'

Dark as the Grave Wherein My Friend Is Laid. Where is his girl now, to whom he used to write his notes on old monastic walls? We should have looked her up.

Song for a Marimba
or
In the Wooden Brothel the Band Plays out of Tune

Oa-xa-ca! Oa-xa-ca!
Oa-xa-ca! Oa-xa-ca!
It is a name like
A bro-ken
A broken heart at night.

Wooden wooden wooden are those faces at night.
Wooden wooden wooden are those faces at night.
Broken hearts are wooden at night.
Wooden, are wooden, at night.

Limerick

There was a young man from Oaxaca
Who dreamed that he went to Mintaka
And dwelt in Orion
And not in the Lion
The pub where he drank, which was darker.

A Prayer

God give those drunkards drink who wake at dawn
Gibb ring on Beelzebub's bosom, all outworn
As once more through the windows they espy
Looming, the frightful Pontefract of day.

– From this you might get the impression that Martin was a gloomy and morbid fellow. Quite the contrary. One of Martin's happiest private memories: a bit of conversation accidentally overheard about himself – 'The very sight of that old bastard makes me happy for five days. No bloody fooling.'

It is my impression, from maritime law, that the ship can now go anywhere the Captain – or rather Commandant – pleases. He could play Ahab and get away with it. For France has no government. The crew, happy thought, might even mutiny if they wish, and it would be difficult for anyone – say in Oaxaca – to do anything about it. But the crew don't wish to mutiny for the simple reasons (a) this is a happy ship, (b) they want to be home for Christmas. And as for the Commandant, who unlike most captains has the respect and liking of everyone, it is a matter of sublime indifference how many governments fall. She is indeed, as the chief steward (a fellow rugby enthusiast) says, a ship bien chargé. Would that the world were such. All shades of political opinion on board this ship, but I have yet to hear an unkind word. Now if we had a world governed by Bretons !

Turkish bath of the toilet, and *forgetting* where the flush handle is . . .

Terror, too, in the toilet, scarcely daring to stir, will the Captain object? Martin Trumbaugh wondered. Between two stools. And between two stools the breech falls to the floor.

For Captain read Commandant : the Capitaine is the first mate of a French vessel. The second mate, the first lieutenant, etc. This has a naval, rather than mercantile flavor. The Commandant uses ancient regal privilege of dining alone. Wonder if my grandfather did that. From this you'd think the ship was undemocratic, nothing could be further from the truth, though. Everyone is equally courteous – first requisite of any democracy. Primrose's presence may have something to do with obvious manifestations of this, but the thing seems innate with the French. Nor do there seem any of the heartbreaking persecutions, petty snobberies, that used to pertain in an English freighter. As an old hand I can smell these things. I remember the eternal argument between the bosun and the carpenter as to who was the senior; in fact, the carpenter, though he is technically a tradesman. Also the poor fellow on his first voyage, so persecuted by the crew, he stood on the windward side in a storm praying to be washed overboard. To say nothing of the apprentice they kept in the chicken coop. By the time we got to Dairen (then Dalny and now part of Russia) half the crowd had the pox. There hasn't been a single case of V.D. on board this ship since it set off four months ago, says the 3rd mate, who acts as doctor and who should know. Something worth remembering since the British have the idea the French invented it. Still, grandmother invented penicillin. Wisdom and sanity of having wine with meals for all hands. And same food for everybody. And wonderful it is, ten times better than on dear old American bauxite ship we went to Haiti on, though stores on return voyages, be it remembered, all come from America. On English ship, though food used to be better than its reputation, they went to endless trouble to see that we, as the crew, had especially 'worse' food than the officers. I didn't eat a hot meal for two months on the outward voyage to China – 1927. Things are probably better now. Only advantage I can think of we had, being a coal burner, with the aid of a tarpaulin, we rigged up a bunker hatch as a swimming pool. There seems no way they can do that here, and it is a pity for the crew. Stokers and trimmers – I have been latter – no longer

43

suffer, to be sure : there are none : but engineers and greasers –
the machinists – do, as ever, as a consequence of which – superb
and sane compensation! – they are allowed twice as much wine
with meals. (One of the consequences of which, we sit at the
engineers' table, not without having been expressly and courteously invited, of course.)

– Who am I? –

– A great black bird sitting crucified on the cross-trees, its
wings so vast it obscures the foremast light; the Captain calls
us to see it, says: 'I will not shoot the eagle, or anything, I never
kill anything, but –' 'Shoot it! I should damned well think
not!' says Primrose. It is a condor (Gymnogyps Californianus)
with a $10\frac{1}{2}$-foot wingspread, and the sight one of the rarest in
the world, for the bird, a sort of super-xopilote or vulture by
Thomas Wolfe, is almost extinct; after a while it has vanished,
as mysteriously as it arrived.

The Captain (the Commandant) likes cats, is a first-rate chess
player, but likes to madden himself with some kind of contraption like a yo yo, drinks rum before dinner, sleeps in a hammock
on bridge because his room is too hot, refuses to discuss politics,
yet is in great tradition of captain who not only loves but *is* his
ship; at the same time cannot escape pathetic subterfuges of men
longing for their homes and wives. Gets a ton of sand for his
cats, Grisette and Piyu, each voyage. Admirable fellow, has
been in sail, like my grandfather. Humorous, kindly, charitable,
absolutely the best kind of person.

Nov. 22. The Gulf of Tehuantepec: sapphire calm, long, almost imperceptible swells, the surface like crepe (Primrose
says). Flying fish of electric blue with dragon-fly wings, skitting
and flying everywhere. Their sudden swift tracery on the water,
Prospero skimming winged souls, much as a boy skims stones;
and indeed their brief heavenly passage through the air is like
our moments of happiness on earth; old turtle breast-stroking
past solemnly, turns a quizzical eye on us. Astral body of Wal-
lace Stevens writing his wonderful poem about Tehuantepec

... A flying fish skidding over the sapphire sea toward an albatross floating to meet it: ecstasy. Primrose in seventh heaven ... The Zapotecan Sea ... Just under the bow a shark – a dark, shining shape with wicked fins, turning beautifully, swimming swiftly, then he dives, is green, blue – gone.

My faithful general Phenobarbus, treacherous to the last? (Note for Martin.)

Nov. 23. Going down the coast of Guatemala, we crossed the border from Mexico in late afternoon. Coast is tame here, the mountains rounded, green and pretty, now and then a river flows. I wish I could see it with volcanoes spitting fire into the night.

The skipper tells us a good story about his last voyage here: sweltering in the heat below; the volcanoes above cooling their heads with snow. The skipper, with magnificent hospitality, invites us almost every other day to have an apéritif with him, so that we have begun to look forward to this enjoyable interlude, nearly to look on it as a right.

The skipper tells another story: he found a beautiful Mediterranean island where he took his wife for a holiday; everything was perfect, a fine cheap hotel, good food, beach, swimming, and no one else there at all! What luck! But when they went to bed that night, they found out why: the rats. Thousands of rats, swarming through the windows and doors all night.

Primrose tells me: 'I was sitting in the sun on deck when the skipper invited me to the lower bridge for a drink. (You were asleep in the upper berth like the lion in the basket.) He is a friendly man, lonely and gay, stern, eager and boyish. I have mentioned the French crisis and he laughs and says:

' "I never hear the news. If they make another trouble I will run to Mexico."

'We discuss cats. I say Piyu speaks French and he is delighted. The cats go to their box and we have a long conversation re cats' cleanliness: he points to Piyu and Grisette digging holes, doing, and covering them up; he is like a proud parent watching his child playing a piece on the piano, noting everything and calling for my attention and applause.'

45

However:

Over the freedom of all people hangs the shadow of the Immigration Inspector, with his little card (not always the little card) sent you in advance (and his 5 children, his anxiety about his wife, his inadequate income, his fear of being fired, his allergy, and analogy, to the sprue, and his unfinished novel), asking you questions you never can answer viz.:

Information required from Passengers in Transit through or destined to the Canal Zone of the Republic of Panama. Informacion requerida de los *Pasajeros en transito o con destino* a la Zone del Canal or la Republica de Panama . . .

(1) Name

Nombre	Family (Apellido)	Given (Primero)
Sex		Race
Sexo		Raza

(2) Birth date   Place of birth
    Fecha de nacimiento   Lugar del nacimiento

    Citizen of
    Cindadeno da

(3) Occupation   Embarkation
    Ocupacion   Puerto de Embarque

(4) Passport no.   Issued at   Visas for
    Pasaporte no.   Expedido en   Visado para

(5) Arrival port   Name of vessel
    Puerto de llegada   Nombre del barco

    Arrival date
    Fecha de llegada

(6) Destination   Ticket   Date of departure
    Destino   Boleto   Fecha de salida

(7) Address on Isthmus   Purpose of visit
    Direccion en el Istimo   Objeto de la visita

(8) Date of last smallpox vaccination
    Fecha de la ultima vacuna contra la vizuela

(And now come the insults, to be completed by the Quarantine and Immigration Officer.)

Reasons ....
Medical and Immunization ....
Disposition of passport ....
Remarks ....-..................
                                        (Initials) ....
                        History after Arrival
Departed for ....
Vessel .... Date .... (Initials) ....

In this subtle way, the true freedom of every traveler is lost forever in his own world.

A sapphire sea. Would that one were a flying fish!

A turtle, swimming sleepily, is smacked by the boat but – he dives . . . Hope he is not hurt.

Whales spouting astern, just before sunset.

Strange to be sitting in the very seat of one's agony the day after, restored and in one's right mind, the miracle happened.

> Miraculous such nights as these
> Should be survived, how no one knows,
> Far less, how one reached finer air
> That never breathed on such despair.

I know you think Tennyson wrote that, but I did.

Nov. 24. Going down the coast of El Salvador – the latter out of sight however – usual angry-looking slate elephants and jagged coasts of sunset, and the changing light on the sea, every bit like in the newest supercinema at home; fine old dirty freighter on horizon keeping up with us; at evening, suddenly, Venus . . .

The agony of Martin Trumbaugh is related to the agony of repeating experiences.

Unripe bananas and porterhouse steak colored sunsets of Nicaragua.

Charon, lonely, peers with binoculars into the west. H'm . . .

And ever and anon throughout his future life an agony constraineth him to travel from land to land.

Ahead are four storms. Thunderheads, snow white on top, becoming more dark and deep as one's eyes travel down until at a distance above the horizon the cloud bank is black, cut off sharply in a straight horizontal line, with the

47

black sea below. Between are vertical lines, like pencil lines, of rain. The wind is blowing from that quarter and freshening.

Did I mention the new patented black oiled windlass, like a gigantic set of false teeth squatting on the foredeck?

A little albatross sitting on the mast, preening his feathers.

An elephant sitting on the horizon.

Venus swimming in a mauve cloud.

Engine that sings the 'Marseillaise.'

Venus, with a circle around it, like the moon . . .

Engine that sings 'The Kerry Dancers.'

Primrose . . . Primrose . . .

Nov. 25. Going down the coast of Costa Rica. Rain all day.

A plague on all Central American republics with their corruption, their cuteness, their dictators, their mordidas, their tourists, their fatuous revolutions, their volcanoes, their history and their heat!

The abomination of desolation, standing in the holy place.

Alarme

Le signal d'alarme consiste en 5 coups longs donnés par sonnerie et sifflet.

A ce signal :

— allez dans votre cabine

— couvrez-vous chaudement

— mettez votre gilet de sauvetage

— laissez-vous guider par le personnel et rendez-vous au Pont des Embarcations.

  Côté à l'Abri du vent

Abandon

Le signal d'abandon est donné par 6 coups brefs suivis d'un coup long.

A ce signal vous embarquerez dans le canot No. 1. Tribord
                                          ou 2. Babord

Selon la direction du vent.

Cie. Générale Transatlantique

Avis.   S.S. *Diderot*

                    (Sinister notice in saloon)

Through the Panama

Chacun est prié d'économiser l'eau attendu que nous ne pourrons
pas nous en approvisionner avant Rotterdam.

Au cas où le gaspillage serait trop grand, nous serions obligés de
rationner l'eau.

Bord le 22 November 1947
le/2ème Capitaine

(Samuel Taylor Coleridge)

Safety

Your lifebelt is in this stateroom.
Put it on as you would an ordinary jacket
Your arms through the shoulder straps
Never wear the lifebelt without the shoulder straps
Pull the two ends of the belt together across
Your chest and tie the tapes very securely

(Wilderness Carlos Wilderness)

(Mem:) – Passing San Francisco, below Mount Diablo, going
down past Monterrey and Cape Saint Martin, passing San Pedro,
forgetting Point Firmin (sic) down, down, at 404 fathoms at
Carlsbad on November 16 at 1,045 fathoms off Cape Colnet, at
midday on the 17th at 965 fathoms, still going down Lower
California, on the 18th at midday, having gone past Cape St
Lazaro (?) opposite Le Paz but still in the opposite peninsular
Cape Falso (Cape Falso is good) – *False Cape Horn* good name
for a novel – but disheartening – there *are* no False Cape Horns?
– and Cape S. Lucas, going down to 1,800 fathoms opposite the
Tres Marias, on the 19th, at midday on the 20th at 2,712 fathoms,
below Manzanillo, by Black Head, on the 21st, just passing
Acapulco, by Porta Malconda 2, 921 fathoms – Acapulco! – and
going out into the Gulf of Tehuantepec on the 22nd at midday
1,883 fathoms, on the 23rd – after the Gulf of Tehuantepec –
opposite San José, at 2,166 fathoms, on the 24th near the Guardian Bank, having passed El Salvador, at 1,850 fathoms.

After Acapulco: B. Dulce, Pta. Malconado, Morro Ayuca
(?), Salina Cruz, Tehuantepec, La Puerta, Sacapulco – getting
into Guatemala – S. Benito, Champerico, San José, and in El
Salvador, Acajutla, La Libertad, La Union indeed – passing

altogether the Golfo de Fonseca – Corinto, getting toward Costa Rica . . .

Death in Life . . .

Their beauty and their happiness.

He blesseth them in his heart.

– the albatross, at midnight, huddled upon the foremast, her great beak, from the captain's bridge, gold in the moving light: when her beak was there it made a third light. Finally her beak moved away and you could only see, from the port side, her tail feathers. This was the mother albatross. She stayed there all night, while on the mainmast, aft, there were 3 other young albatross, huddled together, black . . . The mother albatross had brought her little brood on board to rest.

Nov. 26. In the morning one of these was captured for Primrose by the crew. The baby albatross sitting on the after deck, with its red feet and blue enamel beak and soft fawn-colored feathers, hissing at us. Then, to my joy, they released it . . .

Frère Jacques. Frère Jacques. Dormez-vous? Dormez-vous?

The coast of Panama is like Wales. Old Charon would not come to see the albatross. After the capture of the albatross, there is further excitement, a ship on the horizon, that seems to be on fire; it is a Russian tramp, a coal burner?

Life in Death

But Life-in-Death begins her work on the ancient Mariner.

The burning ship turns out to be just some old haystack of a tramp, that passes very slow, billowing smoke from her funnel, like some sea-going Manchester, or the funereal pyre of the ship in Conrad's *Youth*, nothing wrong with her at all; I am vaguely disappointed, having visualized some rescue at sea, in which one took a heroic part.

Bad news: due to the unexpected arrival of more passengers in Cristobal, perhaps Primrose and I are to be separated, into different cabins . . .

Through the Panama

Death in life.

Facts and Figures on the Canal

Atlantic to Pacific length – 40 miles.
Minimum channel depth – 45 feet.
Maximum elevation above sea level – 85 feet.
Average time of ship transit – 8 hours.
Railroad time across Zone – 1 hour 25 minutes.
Canal opened to traffic – August 1914.
Total cost – $543,000,000.

(Fear of anyone seeing me write these valuable war secrets down. Giving aid and comfort to the enemy. Which enemy?)

Idea for part of a novel: Make the Trumbaughs somehow have this happen to them, in manner of the sad experience of two other people on the last trip, as recounted by skipper. Devoted married couple who fear they are going to be separated, at Balboa, into different cabins. Decide to write some of this, to take mind off possibility of its happening to us. Can't even think of being separated from Primrose.

Sailing into Balboa under a full moon against a strong ebb tide, cloud like picked mackerel bones and loomy Hercules – the disastrous alien sunsets for the alienated, of travel.

We are now approaching the Panama Canal

Francisco Pizarro, a native of Portugal who began life as a swineherd . . .

I beg your pardon.

(Martin was so distressed at the idea of their separation that for a while, as is sometimes the case in the face of actual disaster, he lost all sense of proportion, and for a moment indeed it was as if he forgot which was the more important, the threatened catastrophe of the separation itself, or the fact that having been unable to buy a bottle of Martell from the steward he was thus incumbent upon an invitation from the skipper for a drink which

William Paterson, founder of the great Bank of England, who was on the contrary a native of Scotland, who began life by walking backwards through England, with a pedlar's pack on his back, having been impressed by the memories of a British surgeon, Lionel Wafer, who had crossed the Isthmus on the way to Peru with one William Dampier, an author and freebooter, and who had subsequently remained – like,

51

later, William Blackstone – for some years living among the Indians, who had nursed him back to health from almost certain death, conceived, that is to say, William Paterson conceived the ennobling idea – no doubt feeling that in a vicarious sense this would be repaying the Indians' hospitality to the writer he so much admired – of capturing Havana and gaining possession of the Isthmus, and thus securing to Great Britain the keys of the universe, as they called it in those days, by which they meant that it enabled the possessor of those keys to give laws to both oceans and become arbiter of the commercial world.

Now this Paterson was a self-made man as who shall not say – however much we may pity him – that he was soon to become a self-unmade man also.

(I am constrained to mention that the majority of the information in this commentary I have obtained from the diverting book I hold in my hands, lent us by the 3rd mate of this vessel and called *The Bridge of Water* by Helen Nicolay, published by, etc. etc. And I

had never seemed more necessary and to which, since the skipper was the nearest representative of the company who had betrayed him, he had never felt more entitled. Primrose returned from the bridge without further news, and the prospect of the drink seemed even more remote, for the Commandant was now taking his vessel, against a strong ebb tide, under more clouds to the west like picked mackerel bones, into Balboa Harbor: in spite of this responsibility of the skipper who could not obviously be drinking himself in these circumstances – an assumption in which he was proved to be mistaken – Martin strongly resented the fact that they had not been invited: after a while Martin had an angry drink of cold water and there was something very strange now in the transformation of his emotion about the drink back to the sadness in hand: after a while too, as if this drink had miraculously been hard liquor, Martin Trumbaugh's glass of cold water began to take effect ... Nonetheless long after the ship had been anchored and was lying off the lights of Balboa, and the skipper had finished fishing off the stern, and had doubtless turned in, since his was the ordeal of taking the ship through the canal early on the morrow, Martin still found himself waiting futilely for their invitation, waiting, even though he had drunk at least two quarts of pinard at dinner in the meantime, and so his passions in that respect would have been thought partly at least to have been assuaged. But no: he was still on tenterhooks for the skipper's knock on the door, more anxious for that even than for the purser's knock, which would lead to the definite news of the disposal of their plight. My God, did poor stewards wait like this for a tip? Was this how, too, with this gnawing anxiety, Mexicans waited for La Mordida? A desire to go down and tip the steward immediately even if it meant getting him out of bed, assailed him and –)

Going out on deck Mr Charon was peering through his binoculars into the darkness, in the direction of the canal . . .

Nov. 27. Waked before dawn — sky still gray, with a moon — by second mate: immigration officers are in salle-à-manger and must see our papers before boat enters Panama. Dress stupidly, half asleep, myself angrily apprehensive, but really hate all immigration officers too much to fear them, and stagger down. Captain muy correcto in elaborate white dress uniform with

mention this because strange though it may seem I have never read a book about the Panama Canal before.)

Probably neither have you. It may be more intricate works on the subject are to be found in Tokyo, in Moscow – certainly in Acapulco – and even Glasgow, perhaps even at the Unesco, but the homely touch, such as evinced by Miss Nicolay, may well be rare. So my kind acknowledgements.

So at Bristol, we are told, William Paterson embarked for the Bahamas and the West Indies, where he made friends with the natives and buccaneers alike, teaching theology to the former and learning from the latter everything he could about the strange region in which he found himself.

(such as that there were no high mountains down toward the Gulf of Darien and that it would therefore be easy to make a canal at that point.)

Having developed this plan, says Helen Nicolay, he returned to England, hoping to interest the King, but disappointed, organized the Bank of England instead, though he soon withdrew from the Bank's management – perhaps, explains our good Miss Nicolay, because he had too many novel ideas to please the more conservative directors – and raising 900,000 pounds, founded now the Company of Scotland with a sudden upsurge of patriotism perhaps, because Scotland and England were not – as now – at that time united.

So in the year 1698 William Paterson sailed with 1,000 colonists on what came to be known as the Darien Expedition, landing in this region made famous by Balboa and Pedrarias – as in a different way by Keats – where he no doubt made friends once more with the natives and buccaneers alike, teaching theology to the former and learning from the latter everything that he could about the strange region in which he found himself – another traveler in the realms of gold – and in which, to make it seem more familiar, they called their colony Caledonia (much as later they called the region that is now British Columbia, New Caledonia), and the town they founded New Edinburgh. But the Spaniards, perhaps not approving of the theology, were unfriendly, and the Indians, perhaps not liking the name New Edinburgh, in

black and gold epaulettes, etc., drinking brandy with officers. Formalities – save that we don't get a drink – over in 5 minutes and we go on deck. Make amusing scene out of this with Martin. Ha ha. Digarillas floating around Balboa motionless. Dawn behind the *Henry B. Tucker* of Luckenbach Line.

Going down, at 7 a.m., between buoys, passing, at buoy 7, going the other way, the S.S. *Parthenia*, out of Glasgow; emerald palm trees, a road house on piles blinking its light, to the right; very green to right and left; to the left an island like a cupcake, completely flat, marshy land and a stretch of emerald jungle like chicory salad, and palms, with white houses showing through and what looks like a nice beach, buoys like little Eiffel Towers – ahead, the green light marks the first écloue (lock) – really beautiful beach to the left now beneath the chicory salad round the corner; Balboa to the right as we approach first buoy, palm trees and objects that look like country clubs, golf courses; left it gets more jungly – 20 or 30 frigate birds sailing motionless, circling – docks to the right, then a launch comes alongside and 20 Negroes carrying canvas bags climb up a pilot ladder.

Orion: old type American battle-ship and submarine.

Quite cool going through the canal – then to the right mud flats, a beached houseboat, striped stakes of an indeterminate purpose, then something innocent like a grove of alders at home: 1,000,000 country clubs or brothels beyond these; lighthouse like a chessman, ashore snowy egrets standing on mud flats by gigantic drain-pipe with this same background of chicory salad. The Canal now looks like a narrow, casual creek with muddy banks.

Swallows twittering on our masts and round our aerials, playing on the maintop, swallows skylarking – and a long-tailed grackle.

Gigantic frigate birds – digarillas – common as vultures in Mexico here, curious sense of land, birds singing.

Locks.

The first lock: Miraflores: 1913. Gigantic iron-studded gates very high but looking too narrow for a ship to steer into – but we do. Amuse Primrose by telling her silly Punch story of two country folk in London underground for first time. 'Coo, Martha, look at that, bang in the 'ole every time!'

We ascend 54 feet through double lock.

1,000 birds of bad omen.

addition to not approving of the theology, became downright disgusted.

But at this point the story becomes tragic – Fever; hundreds died, including poor Paterson's wife and child. While Panama and Cartagena gathered land and sea forces to expel the unwanted New Caledonians, and the English King, partly to placate Spain and partly the British merchants, forbade any kind of assistance whatever to the Darien colony from the Governors of Virginia, New England, Jamaica, the Barbadoes and New York.

Finally Paterson was driven almost insane – and the colony forced to abandon itself – and so, says Miss Nicolay, *in mid-ocean the disbanded and half dead colonists passed a vessel westward bound going to their own relief*, who when they arrived also gave up the struggle after ten months. Today all that remains of the grandiose dream, she says, are two names on the map: Caledonia Bay, and Port Escosses. And for more than a century little was heard about an Isthmian Canal.

For a great new era of enlightenment was dawning in the world. Rousseau, Voltaire, Adam Smith, electricity, Sir Isaac Newton, Halley, Linnaeus, Herschel, Whitefield, Swedenborg, Priestley, oxygen, inoculation, the penny post, tramways and the South Sea Bubble, England with her plans to develop her American colonies and then with her efforts to subdue them. Peter the Great and Catherine the II in Russia. Frederick the Great in Prussia, the three Louis', the French Revolution and the dictatorship of Napoleon. England fighting against France. France fighting against Spain. France and Germany and Alsace. Spain fighting against Portugal. Sweden attacking Denmark. Russia attacking the Ottoman Empire. France fighting Russia. England, France, Holland, Germany fighting Spain – and then crushing Napoleon – and then England fighting Spain nearly all this time and in 1780 sending two separate fleets to the Isthmus, one against the Spanish colonies on its eastern side, the other to gain possession of Lake Nicaragua and the San Juan River on the west, and the officer commanding this second expedition was Horatio Nelson. But despite Horatio Nelson, who reported that Lake Nicaragua was the key to the whole situation, an

Second lock: Pedro Miguel: 1913.

We ascend 31 feet in second, single lock (symbolic) in 10 minutes.

More salad with stuff like scarlet acacia and flamboyants. Hombres shouting, doubtless for La Mordida.

Culebra Cut.

Blackest history of canal's horror, failure, collapse, murder, suicide, fever, at Culebra Cut. Now one glides through a narrow canal, gorgeous jungle like a wall on both sides, 2 minutes lost here would mean death, or a very peculiar new life – monkeys, birds, orchids, sinister orchestrations from the jungle. Hot here as a Turkish bath in hell. Jungle has to be chopped back every day.

Memorial tablet on a rock.

Apparatus as for foghorns, remote waterfalls. Besetting fear, as a writer taking notes, of being taken for a spy. Diving floats. Gold flags, dredgers, targets, and the lonely stations with in each one a man peering through binoculars: high wiry towers: 'Many bananas trees,' says Charon, with his guttural Turkish laugh. 'Once there were many alligators, but not now.'

ROBERT CHARON
Consul of Norway
Tahiti Island   Society Islands

U.S. *Tuscada*, a dredger, visualize life on a dredger in the Panama,
muddy water. Down the Panama
Canal, all sorts of jungle, iguanas
rattling on a rock, parrots gibber-
ing, a train, quite like home in
England, lumbers along the side of
the canal, blossoms like honey-
suckle, a kind of cactus.

A ship: *The Manatee* – London.
Another ship from London, all
going the other way steaming very
swiftly as with current. (Bergson.)
These rude London bastards of
my countrymen give the Frenchmen the raspberry! I am thoroughly
ashamed. I dislike Londoners anyway, coming from Liverpool, or do
at this moment.

'Courtesy is no empty form, but
the assent to man's true being.' The
Mexicans for example ... It was
enough to make you weep, Martin
thought. With shame, when you
might have wept with joy. (Though
perhaps they were only giving *him*
the raspberry.)

Significance of *locks*: in each
one you are locked, Primrose says,
as it were, in an experience.

A buoy like a white swam and
behind thick jungle, little green
hills. The lighthouses like chessmen

Island of Gibraltar, which if
held by England would cut
Spanish America in two, you
would scarcely credit that so
many people for so many years
during this long era of
enlightenment could be so
goddamned stupid, could be
so ferociously ignorant, could
have learnt so little, that they
went on doing precisely this
same sort of bloody thing. But
that is what they apparently
did, for this is what it says
they did in this interesting
book by Miss Helen Nicolay
lent me by the 3rd mate. So
that I personally, although an
Englishman, or rather a
Scotsman, and so with a
sneaking sympathy for poor
old Paterson, who founded
the Bank of England, am
quite relieved to read what it
says here, that in 1846 the
United States concluded a
treaty with New Granada
whereby it obtained exclusively
right of transit across the
Isthmus from the borders of
Costa Rica and down to the
Gulf of Darien and promised
in return for this to insure the

neutrality of any canal it might establish and defend it from foreign attack which is exceptionally sporting of me since I mention nothing of an ancestor of mine who also had a plan for the Panama Canal that was very favorably received at a dinner given for De Lesseps in New York in 1884.
cunningly contrived to guide, the whole like a fantastic child's dream, or a sort of Rube Goldberg invention.

– Dead trees sticking right out of the water presumably on shore of old lake...

In Gatun Lake have lunch amid sense of unreality, as if on an engineless ship sailing through the jungle in a dream.

While as for poor old De Lesseps himself (Martin said – who felt himself without knowing why rather to resemble that gentleman – helping himself to pinard), seeing what nationality of vessel we are on, perhaps the less said the better.

For myself, while hereditarily disposed in favor of canals in general, while in short loving them – any child could figure one out, indeed it is the first piece of engineering a child does figure out – and in any case a canal here would have been arrived at eventually by some sort of Platonic sense of oversights – which is not to decry it as an achievement (in that sense maybe I'm a bit envious), my feeling is bugger them all if they cause that much trouble, my sympathy being 150% with the troublesome San Blas Indians, whose territory occupied by their descendants to this day remains practically unknown. But I'm not out of sympathy altogether with the two American gentlemen of wealth, George Law and William H. Aspinwall, who at length assumed responsibility for carrying the mails, if only because the latter gentleman gave his name to a town which in turn gave its name to a lighthouse which prompted a certain writer to write a story called *The Lighthouse Keeper of Aspinwall* I shall have occasion to mention later.

Other people who in the history of the Panama Canal as reported here by Miss Nicolay I find myself particularly in sympathy with in their sufferings are some 800 Chinese – who were imported here to build a railroad – in sympathy not because they were Chinese, but because they nearly all committed suicide when deprived of their customary opium, an old law being invoked '*Which forbade this on moral grounds*,' as a consequence of which 'they strangled or hanged themselves with their long queues (this has now become a universal habit of the English) or sat down on the beach and waited for the tide to come up and drown them.'

(How long I wonder is it to Colon? Or Cristobal? Or Aspinwall? And will we be able to go ashore there and get some liquor? Have the immigration inspectors gone? Or are they starting on the second bottle?)

Which reminds me that it says here too somewhere that when the actual work of digging began on the De Lesseps Canal, 'this marked a season of festivity, to which Sarah Bernhardt added brilliance by journeying all the way from Paris to perform in Panama's playhouse': while meantime some Englishman, who had evidently not lived in Liverpool, had the gall to write on arrival in Panama at this period 'that it would be difficult to find elsewhere on the earth's surface a place in which so much villainy and disease and moral and physical abomination were concentrated.'

And that is about all — save for the persistence and foresight and skill and enterprise and heroism of its final builders, of course, which we take for granted, and La Mordida, which is always with us — save that this book tells us some things about the operations of the canal we perhaps wouldn't have known even though we're going through it at this moment. That our engines are locked and sealed. That our sailors — which is maybe why the chief engineer is on deck looking so hot and upset — are obeying the orders of the pilot. That perhaps we couldn't go through at all — for the water hyacinths would render navigation impossible — but for some dredging outfit poetically known as the 'Hyacinth Fleet.' That our good captain is only a decoration, temporarily, despite his epaulettes and his bottle of Martell —

After lunch the jungle looks like a gigantic conglomeration of spinach against the horizon with occasional lonely wild familiar-look- — and that man over there sitting on the control tower on the central wall, has a model of the canal locks before him, carefully built, which registers electrically the exact depth of the water and every movement of every lever and thus is able – ghastly image of the modern world – to see what is happening at every moment – and has possibly even seen me taking notes – That great chain that is rising suddenly from the water, is doing so to prevent us from going too far forward, and that water swirling upwards from the opening near the bottom of the lock, is making us rise at the rate of about 3 feet a minute, soundlessly, and without orders.

That those small squat electric engines that are following us and which seem such a far cry from the camels of the Suez Canal are called 'mules' and are attached by hawsers to the ship –

All in all though, gentlemen, what I would like to say about the Panama Canal is that finally it is a work of genius – I would say, like a work of child's genius – something like a novel – in fact just such a novel as I, Sigbjørn Wilderness, if I may say so, might have written myself – indeed without knowing it am perhaps in the course of writing, with both ends different in character, governed under different laws, yet part of the same

ing trees, such as one might see in Westmorland, under a windy cloudy summer sky . . .

The Last Lock

Gatun Lock

We descend 85 feet through triple lock.

The Hawaiian Banker: Wilmington, Delaware: rising from a grave of lock, as from Atlantis: Americans having wonderful time on bridge.

And ourselves, watching, happy, happy at the news we won't be separated after all.

Gigantic concrete street lamps as on a great boulevard, with grass walks, a lighthouse apparently on a bowling green, the sun beating down ferociously in the foreground and beyond a little lake, entirely surrounded by jungle over which floated vultures as a black storm was gathering: little isolated palm trees blew on the bowling green, and in the immediate foreground the vast ship from Wilmington, Delaware, slowly rising, blocking the view, elsewhere other ships were rising, or sinking, Negroes were pulling ropes, and from the rising and sinking ships people were taking photos. Little electric cars were trundling along the wharf.

Where Kilroy had also been and a little American family stood, with black glasses, waving their hands (I wave too) the children eating all day suckers. A great hook dangling against the sky – three great ships on three different levels – the lighthouse now alone, the American flag flying, and the Tricolor – and again now emerging, sun, dark clouds, concrete, the jungle and the lake disclosing itself once again : driving blackness now over the once innocent Westmorland horizon, little streetcar stations on the bowling green, and cable cars with cabins on either end (and a drum in the middle) like roller coasters – chute-the-chutes – and the xopilotes slowly slowly ascending into the tempest over the jungle – there were seagulls blowing in every direction : for we have reached the Caribbean Sea.

Danger – Capacity 4 Persons. (Martin takes this to heart.)

An old Negro with mackintosh, solar topee and rolled umbrella and gaiters limping along the lock wharf – why are there always these poor old men limping along wharves? ME.

And a lone loon diving in the last lock.

Looking back on it – The Panama – from the Caribbean is like looking back on a fairground with chute-the-chutes and great dippers: even the lighthouses contribute to community, the one end full of boiler and repair shops, and the other full of clubhouses – with the jungle on every side, with the one end copying the other's worst features, which was a town anyhow of the Middle Ages, and where at any moment one expects to see ambulances carrying yellow fever patients, or piles of coffins lying on the dock but where actually all you see are these small squat electric engines called mules attached by hawsers to the ship – for it works, God how the whole thing beautifully and silently works, this celestial meccano – with its chains that rise sullenly from the water, and the great steel gates moving in perfect silence, and with perfect ease at the touch of that man sitting up in the control tower high above the topmost lock who, by the way, is myself, and who would feel perfectly comfortable if only he did not know that there was yet another man sitting yet higher above him in *his* invisible control tower, who also has a model of the canal locks before him, carefully built, which registers electrically the exact depth of everything *I* do, and who thus is able to see everything that is happening to me at every moment – and worse everything that is *going* to happen –

And lastly, to the right, gentlemen – Cristobal, with houses described by Miss Nicolay here as perched on concrete pillars to outwit termites – making an interesting contrast with the legs of the beds in De Lesseps' hospital, which legs were placed in little cups of water to protect the patient from the crawling insects that instead of crawling liked to breed in these little cups of water prior to flitting from bed to bed, and from person to person, thus to provide more patients for De Lesseps' hospitals. For this is the way civilization advances, so that now we have the concrete pillars of Cristobal and rows and rows of electric-lighted dry closets screened in black gauze, with their woodwork painted white, instead of the legs of the beds in little cups of water which in itself was an advance in the days when Cristobal was once criticized for having too low a death rate. And talking of little cups of water I can see without being told that one is not even going to get a little cup of water here whether this is Cristobal or Colon (or even Aspinwall). Though here is a thing that is worthy of mention where Miss Nicolay says that the completion of the canal passed almost unnoticed.

the illusion, being something like the English helter-skelter.

De Lesseps' old canal goes off to the right into a swamp, a sad monument to unfinished projects, though actually *it is worse than that*.

Hot rain, coconut palms, pelicans.

Saying good-by to Charon : dropping the pilot, after the passage through the canal.

– Whatever Cristobal may be like ashore – not a town but a dormitory as a friend of mine (J.L.D.) said – from the sea, in the rain, at 3 o'clock in the afternoon, it is one of the dreariest places, imaginable on God's earth ; on one side of the harbor, a row of houses, all exactly the same type of architecture, and precisely the same in every detail, resembling square electric generators, with tin roofs, the masonry of some tanned substance, rimmed at the window lines with yellow, stand under the jungle, seemingly alone : surprised by that I turned my binoculars on Cristobal itself, where, although at first one saw what might have been an old Spanish building, with arches, suggesting arcades, I was astonished to discover that here too, lining the waterfront, were likewise these houses, row after row of them, resembling electric generators; turning my glasses now upon what, perhaps wrongly, I surmised to be Colon, I saw that this was also entirely composed of these electric generators half hidden by the murk: the only other objects of interest being a gas-works and what seemed to be a Methodist church, I now turned my glasses back to that section which, as if it were Fairhaven to New Bedford, I had first looked at the same generators, and leading from that, a long breakwater of broken stones with a skeletal lighthouse on it – Point Manzanillo – that now shone green (or red), later there were more passengers and farewell to Mr Charon, 'We will see each other, not in Jerusalem, but in Tahiti,' he said (what does he mean by that, and what is Martin in for?) – coming on board in the rain.

I had forgotten to mention that the tragedy of the Trumbaughs' separation had now been replaced by another; they were still to have their cabin as before, but they were not, on the other hand, to be allowed to go ashore in Cristobal; instead, as has been seen, they dropped anchor well outside, the passengers were to come aboard by launch, it was rough and murky, and the skipper was planning to get away as soon as possible, as a consequence it was impossible to go

That plans of the United States for a naval parade were abandoned. For Nature does not celebrate her victories in noisy ways, she observes, but works silently, and when the task is done lets the consequences proclaim it. Which is something for all novelists to remember!

But I almost forgot The Lighthouse Keeper of Aspinwall. And there he is. Or rather there he once lived. In the imagination of another novelist, over there, through the hot rain, somewhere in that direction, from which direction nothing shall be provided for our own illumination, though that was the whole point about the poor lighthouse keeper of Aspinwall. That in having another kind of illumination himself, he failed to provide illumination for his lighthouse, in fact went to sleep, which no lighthouse keeper should do even if spiritually advanced enough to have an illumination in Aspinwall. And so in imagination I ask you to behold, through that hot rain, the lighthouse made famous by the famous Polish author, Henryk Sienkiewicz, whose works are probably at the moment no longer on sale in

Poland, though they will be but whose great novel is even now I hear being filmed in Rome with an enormous cast of thousands and which some years from now will doubtless be seen by many in America – and appropriately I address you in America too, since it's your canal – seen not for the first time – though for the first time at such popular prices ranging I dare say from $1.25 to $2.40 or nearly an English pound, to sit in a cinema. A project that while it might in fact have benefited Henryk Sienkiewicz would certainly have astonished Mr Paterson, a Scotsman, and the founder of the Bank of England, even though he began life walking backwards through England, and who first conceived the Panama Canal – All prices include taxes of course – And of course you know the book to which I refer:

QUO VADIS?

ashore and get any rum or other supplies. For a moment the thought had flashed through one's mind that the American *Amberjack* (why not apple jack?), the boat manned by Negroes running alongside the most closely and dangerously, with a bunch of bananas on the bow, could possibly be countermanded to go ashore and get some liquor, but the bananas – for one dollar – having been refused by the chief steward, the *Amberjack* turned off at a tangent and dashed into the murk again; the other launches that had been following dropped behind, and likewise turned away toward Cristobal, soon our new passengers were on board, we were waving good-by to Mr Charon, disappearing into the rain on the American *Owl*, and we were underway ourselves. Underway themselves, were the Trumbaughs, with their cabin, but no liquor.

Can it be imagined? Martin had little gratitude for this, and no sympathy either for the skipper, who had spent eight hours on the bridge: he scarcely dared let himself out of his room on to the deck lest he be asked for an apéritif, and miss the invitation. Finally he shaved, and as a final act of desperation, even, in the washbasin, washed his feet, a feat he had not attempted for many months, afterward making an attempt to cut his toenails, an even greater feat, doubtless not attempted for many years: and yet even these latter paradoxical preparations were being made, in a sense, for the apéritif to which they were not going to be invited. It was Primrose who finally broke down and suggested, as Martin gazed mournfully at a ship, on the

gloomy horizon, the shape of the Empire State Building, that
he should buy some wine from the steward. (Try and find
reasons for Martin's inability to do this – and also for his finally
sending Primrose to ask the skipper.) Sure they could buy
wine. (But Martin, stingy bastard, wanted to buy pinard.) But
the skipper was in the same boat as they were. Well naturally.
Nor was he sure they would even be able to get supplies in
Curaçao. But perhaps he would cable forward, radio forward,
getting the Company to get in some stores ... The long day
dragged onward until dinner, at which Martin sat silent, drinking too much pinard – half hating it because he could *only* drink
it at dinner – unable, almost, to speak to the poor Salvadoreans,
and another gloomy personage, whom he had glimpsed through
a door, putting on a pair of new wooden shoes. Was it imaginable, but even after dinner, even after the skipper must have
long been asleep, that Martin should even think, still hesitating,
upon his still relatively clean, if swollen, feet, upon the thres-
hold, and still as it were waiting – God knows for what – that
he distinguished, among the hoarse cossack choir of the wind,
the electric fan, the engine and the sea, the word 'apéritif,
apéritif,' endlessly, as if to the tune of 'Frère Jacques,' repeated ...

Silent on a peak in Bragman's Bluff.
Silent on a peak in Monkey Point.
– Keats could scarcely have written.

To the territory of La Mordida – good-by, and may Christ
send you sorrow! (Well, I take this back : Christ has already
sent you enough. May you live, rather, bloody Mexico, to afford
to man an example of the Christian charity you profess, else
the abomination destroy you!)

Nov. 27. But that was nothing to the torments (while they
were almost out of the Gulf of Darien, opposite Barranquilla –
the little barranca?) Martin suffered on the next day, although
he rose early, did his hardest Indian exercises, and cleaned his
teeth – gingerly – for in the strain of creation – and also the

urge toward cleanliness – of the previous almost liquorless day
he had cleaned them no less than 8 times. It was a healthy day
on the whole, spent mostly in the sun. On the other hand, it
appearing likely that now they would stop in Curaçao in the
morning, and not at night (as had been feared), but on a
Sunday, Martin remembered that then all the shops would be
shut, everything indeed save the church, the 4th mate inadver-
tently and tactlessly said 'No whisky no interesting.' (In actual
fact this remark pertained to a bleakly uninhabited island they
were passing to starboard.) Later that afternoon, trying to study
French with Primrose and the 3rd mate, in the windy salle-à-
manger with books of matches and cigarettes blowing about,
the red-faced engineer came in, angrily helped himself, out of
the frig., to 3 glasses of wine. 'Hullo, Mr Wilderness.' (Earlier
it had been Sigbjørn.) Later it seemed Martin heard his name
being vilified: 'Il fait beau temps' – 'But if there is this *wind*,'
shouted the engineer, 'then Mr Wilderness won't be able to
go ashore in Curaçao and get his whisky!' What the hell. This
suggested to me however to have Martin think that the story had
now gone round. Later, the agony of inarticulate neuroses, the
fear – perfectly imaginary – of rebuffs: they get some St. Julien
(Martin still vainly tried to buy pinard off the steward, who is now
going to bake a cake on their wedding anniversary. But what is
that cake going to demand of the Trumbaughs? The cake itself
seems a nightmare. In spite of stars, wind, and sun, Martin had
almost foundered in some complicated and absurd abyss of self,
could only pray for another miracle to get out of it . . .).

In fact, Primrose tells me, the Chief Engineer is furious
with the wind because it may put us into Curaçao at night
– where we only stop to refuel – and then *no one* will be
able to buy liquor and everyone, including the skipper, is dry.

Seaweed like an amber necklace, Primrose says.

Nov. 30. Three days, plodding across the South Caribbean,
off the coast of Colombia, past the Gulf of Maracaibo, the coast
of Venezuela.

Situation in France is now serious, I read in Panamanian paper Primrose borrowed from our new passengers; 2 million on strike – no transportation – riots, etc.

CURAÇAO

Sailing into Curaçao in the early morning. Low, barren, tree-less, grassless hills with sideways peaks and the bright neat town. A sea wall – the Dutch just can't resist their dykes, says Primrose – like an ancient fort. But where is the harbor ? The ships ? Then suddenly we sail into a narrow channel, and bang ! right through the main street of Willemstadt. Pontoon bridge sweeps open for us and the channel then opens out abruptly into a huge inland harbor with hundreds of ships.

In Curaçao, *Havendienst II*, a black motorboat, and the beau-tiful swinging pontoon bridge across the canal – which is the main street – a delightful town, very clean and neat and Dutch, pointed red roofs, like a Dutch fairy tale sitting in the tropics. Olive-green water with a film of oil. Sea breeze stinks.

Having laid in a case of rum from the ship's chandlers we went ashore : Streets : Amstelstraat : 10c store, Pinto and Vinck.

Koninklyke Nederlandsche.

Stoomboot-Maatschappy N.V.

– and

> Hoogspanning
> Levensgevaar
> Peligro de Muerte
> Electricidad
> Danger

We had a happy time !

– Seamen, visit your home : Cinelandia : Klipstraat (well named ?) : Step into Ice Cold Beer : Restaurant La Maria :

Emma Straat: Cornelis Dirksweg: Leonard B. Smith–Plein: Borrairestraat : *Jupiter* – Amsterdam . . .

Angel trees like flat umbrellas.

In a street of strange solid Sunday-shut banks that remind me of *Buddenbrooks*, we took refuge from a shower in the Wonder Bar – a characterless place, with an open front, 3 tables (like an ice cream parlor, Primrose says) and a 6 foot bar: 2 Negro bartenders speak English with a Dutch accent: this will be a happy memory, drinking Bols and feeling like Hansel and Gretel with the Sunday shower, the Sunday crowds outside, held up at the scything, sweeping pontoon bridge, and the great ships hurtling down the main street.

Back at the ship in the oil dock, all colors (and all smells) are on the water: surrounding the ship are something like sand dunes at Hoylake, only infinitely more desolate, more like slag-heaps in a Welsh mining town, or the worst of the desert in Sonora, Mexico, with the masts of 3 little frigates, as if wrecked, sticking up above small cliffs: the abomination of desolation. Oil tanks, the twin cupolas of a church, like Port-au-Prince, just rising over the roofs of the blue-gray-dun-colored character-less mud houses with windows like small black rectangles.

The entrance to Curaçao is the most dramatic in the world. Hans Andersen would have loved the town. There is a more enormous sense of sea and ships in Curaçao than in any other part of the world I know of, except Liverpool.

From where we are moored ten ships: Argentine, British, Costa Rican, Norwegian, Greek, etc., can be seen, with a wild background of oil refineries (factory chimneys) giving an effect of Detroit rather than of a remote West Indian island, beneath a rainy water-color sky, showing patches of green. *Taverns* – Torrens? English ship. *Rio Atuel* Argentine *Matilde* unspeci-fied probably Venezuela. CPIM – on pillbox-like tank.

Dalfoun – Stavanger (Norsk): *Jagner* – Goteborg (Swed-ish): *Clio* – Curaçao: *Plato* – Curaçao: pink-tiled roofs on the wharf. Verboden te Ankeren: S.E.L. Maduro and Sons: *Jupiter* – Amsterdam. Highland Prince: Seaman's Home: Casa Cohen: Club de Gezelligheid: El Crystal Photo Studio: Troost Ship: Chandler: G. Troost: Kelogovia: Joyeria.

Ridiculous mass exercises, people running up and down the long bridges of ship in shorts – probably very sensible – on board the Norwegian oil tanker.

It brought back to me the horror of 'crocodiles,' discipline at school; I try to visualize life on an oil tanker: the pure aseptic horror of it: almost better (it seemed for a moment) the clap-stricken death of the ships of Martin's own day . . .

– A letter came on board causing me much anxiety: my brother reports my mother is seriously ill in England. This is the first time I shall have seen her, as I still hope to, in 20 years. Last time I saw her was at Rock Ferry Station, Birkenhead (where Nathaniel Hawthorne was Consul), when she saw me off on the London train. Where, alas, did she think I was going? Where did I go? But I never came back. Nevertheless I wrote, regularly, which was more than I did for myself very often.

Leaving Curaçao . . .

> Frère Jacques
> Frère Jacques
> Dormez-vous?
> Dormez-vous?
> Sonnez les matines!
> Sonnez les matines!

The entrance – now exit – of Curaçao harbor – on the Venezuela side: final impression of its sweeping pontoon bridge, its immediate sense of the character and originality of an individual people.

Now the desolate coast; a little lagoon, with a tiny church standing at the right of the entrance, a dun-colored hill behind that, wine-colored hill behind that, violet hill behind that.

A house.

On the extreme right (looking to port) are sinister lead-colored, gun-metal-colored tanks, each with a tiny polka dot in the middle (shadow like a man on one), like barrels of sawed-off guns, with oil tankers lying below, 'where the goats wear green spectacles to eat the morning newspaper . . .' And a castle, with to the right a gigantic Montana-like bluff: more medieval castles rising up between oil tanks, a little lagoon with sailboats, going into a sort of wild Yorkshire moor . . .

Little shadowed islands at sunset; formations like Stonehenge.

Last sight : 3 lone angel trees on long long flat sandbar.

Reaction to magniloquent sunset.

– resolution –

Dec. 1. . . . Situation now reversed : Martin wanting to invite *skipper* for apéritif, after getting liquor at Curaçao. Martin got a case of rum, only $20, thanks to the skipper. 'But why not two cases, Monsieur? I myself shall buy two, perhaps three at this price.' Why not? Because Martin wanted to appear as if he did not need two cases. How wrong he was! How right the skipper. Already he can scarcely broach the case because he is thinking of wanting the second one they don't have – the skipper knows this too, that's why he charitably dodged having an apéritif with them. Nonetheless, Martin, who has acquired a mother too, doesn't want to use her as an excuse to get drunk. This sort of absolutely bona fide excuse supplied at such a moment is the dirtiest trick of the gods.

– Resolution ! –

Other passengers.

The Hungarian from Nueva Mordida boarded at Colon. As I entered the saloon he was saying in answer to the El Salvadoreans, who have just said in Spanish they think I won't understand :

'And who drove you out then?'

'The police.'

'And what had you done?'

The Hungarian, spreading his hands and lowering his voice as I approached : 'Nothing.'

The Hungarian drinks out of a private silver tankard, looks sadly at the sea, wants to sail a small boat on it.

'I go to Soviet territory . . .' He shrugs his shoulders. 'Under Russian rule. Of course I risk my life. But,' he adds, 'my family . . . And of course I am a sportsman.'

That's right, brother.

The Salvadoreans, tiny little people, a couple and their son, about 14 years old, seem Jewish, are wholly delightful: going to Paris. New Life. But I feel they have suffered some sort of persecution too – perhaps anti-Semitic – quien sabe? Somerset Maugham would find out. But it's just curiosity that makes me loathe all writers, and incidentally prevents them from being human. Primrose and Señora Mai sitting in the sun on deck, twittering like birds and painting each other's finger nails and toe nails. Primrose chattering atrocious French and worse Spanish to the Señora, who speaks no English, and both laughing and giggling at Primrose's mistakes. (I myself speak terrible French and a sinister Spanish.) Later we play parchesi with them and like them very much. (Snobbery of novelists whose characters always speak atrocious French and drink 'something that passed for coffee.')

In addition: three Dutch engineers returning. to Holland from Curaçao: Mynheer von Peeperhorn, Mynheer von Peeperhorn, and Mynheer von Peeperhorn. They too are delightful and kindly, but the only way Martin can think of opening conversation is by saying: Now as we were saying about Hieronymus Bosch – so he says nothing. Alcoholics Hieronymus.

Would do for description of novels about alcoholics. Alcoholics Hieronymus. Bosh!

We are cutting due northeast across the Caribbean and tomorrow will be in the Atlantic . . .

Dec. 2. Our anniversary. At noon, in the distance, on the horizon, a lighthouse to starboard: Sombrero Island. (Mem: story, very pertinent, about Sombrero: in Baring Gould.) Am exceedingly grieved about my mother but it is no use thinking about it.

The Cake, survived, somehow even eaten, at lunch. Extra wine, too. Many toasts and congratulations.

We make the Anegada Passage and are in the Atlantic.

Seaweed like gold tinsel, says Primrose. Sargasso Sea directly north. Isle of Lost Ships, featuring Stuart Rome, Moreton Cinema, Cheshire, England, Matinee at 3 p.m. My brother and I missed 26 years ago. Now we enter the Western Ocean and the 4,000 miles before we sight land at Bishop's Point, at Land's End. But to what end?

The Atlantic Highlands – long deep swell. Atlanterhavet.

Montserrat not far away to starboard where I altered geography books by climbing Chance's Mountain in 1929, in company with two Roman Catholics: Lindsey, a Negro, and Gomez, a Portuguese.

One albatross.

Six bottles of beer on top of mountain.

Primrose says, I'm afraid of this boat, thrown together in wartime by makers of washing machines . . . But for myself, I like her, though she rolls worse than the ship Conrad loaded with one third of the weight 'above the beams' in Amsterdam. It is wrong to suppose the poor old Liberty ship hasn't got a soul by this time, just because she was thrown together in 48 hours by washing machine makers. What about me? – thrown together by a cotton broker in less than 5 minutes. 5 seconds perhaps?

Another ship to starboard: Flying Enterprise. Pretty name.

Dec. 3. Great storm to leeward near sunset, sweeping diagonally past.

Commandant, meaning well, hunts out old American magazines for me. Old *Harper's*. Terrifying ancient brilliant and even profound article by De Voto on later work of Mark Twain. (Mem: Discuss this a little: problem of the double, the triple, the quadruple 'I'.) Almost pathological (I feel) cruelty to Thomas Wolfe. Would De Voto like to know what I think of him, in his Easy Chair, lambasting a great soul – and why? because he is a man – who, as N. might say, cannot answer? Mem: quote Satan in *The Mysterious Stranger*. And then on top of this obsession with Wolfe's weaknesses to come across a statement like: 'I am (I hope) a good Joycean.' Why? To keep in with whom? Coming from De Voto it's almost enough to make you hate Joyce. And indeed I do sometimes hate Joyce.

– Reason for Thomas Wolfe's lapses, De Voto himself probably analyzed perfectly elsewhere, about someone else he didn't hate, like De Voto: reason was Thomas Wolfe was in a hurry, knew he was going to die, like N., in same sort of hurry. And what about what *is* disciplined about him, his marvelous portraits, his humor, savagery, sense of *life*. There is far more sense of life actually felt in Wolfe than in all Joyce for that matter. I myself consider it unjust too to criticize Wolfe for seeming to have nothing fundamentally to say (as they say). He had not time to get a real view of life. A giant in body, he might not have really matured till he was 60. That he had not time was, for literature, a tragedy: and I myself feel that one should be grateful for what he has given us. Much to be learned in De Voto's articles however; agonizing about Mark Twain. Possibly De Voto had troubles of his own though, in that uneasy chair. Enough to give one delirium Clemens.

The sea is worse than before to me, its expanse, rough, gray blue or rainy, and without seabirds, says nothing to me at the moment: though well do I understand now Joyce's fear of the sea: (who knows what lives in it? Don't want to think about this — frightening thought occurred to me last night, when Primrose says I woke her up saying: 'Would they put Mother back in the sea?' What awful thing did I mean? Belief in mermaids?). It seemed to Martin he had offended some of the good Frenchmen too — both the second engineer and the third mate stern to him, curiously more formal: La Mer Morte, a sea that comes following a day of high wind when the wind has dropped, leaving behind the great dead swell of the day before: hangover within and without.

POSITION REPORT

S.S. *Diderot*

Date: 5 Dec. 1947
Latitude: 27° 24′ N.
Longitude: 54° 90′ W.
Course: Rv. 45
Distance: 230 m.
To go: 2,553 m.
Length of Day: 23H. 40M.
Average Speed: 9nds 7

Wind : N. 6
Sea : Houleuse, du vent
Signed : CH. GACHET 1st Lieut.

Two squalls : cobalt thunderstorms. Wind catches spray and blows it across the sea like rain, a tiny squall of rain.

Martin was gloomy and savage, lying all day in his bunk predicting death and disaster.

During these last days, since going through the Anegada Passage, have been through some important spiritual passage too – what does it mean ?

Afternoon squall hit suddenly with a million hammers. The ship shakes, shudders. The sea is white, sparkling, sequined – it is over in a flash.

Terrific squall toward sunset. Thunder. Cobalt lightnings reveal a sizzling sea . . . *vision of creation*.

For some reason this made Martin happy. He rose from his bunk and went down to dinner in a jovial mood. He even played games afterwards with the Mais, Andrich and Gabriel.

– am glad to be welcomed by skipper again – really believe I have now got through some spiritual ordeal . . . though a little hard to see what.

Dec. 6. My mother's birthday. In getting out of bed this morning I seemed to be edging out of the table after dinner.

– utter forgetfulness whether one had gone to lavatory or not.

– finally one doesn't bother; for 5 whole days – result : a pain in back : no wonder : forgetfulness of teeth, hatred of teeth, continually muttering little phrases like – I wonder . . . couldn't have been as if . . .

– Tragedy of someone who got out of England to put a few thousand miles of ocean between himself and the non-creative bully-boys and homosapient schoolmasters of English literature only to find them so firmly entrenched in even greater power within America by the time he arrived (Martin thinks), and responsible for exactly the same dictatorship of opinion, an opinion that is not based on shared personal or felt experience or identity with a given writer, or love of literature, or even any intrinsic knowledge of *writing*, and is not even formed independently, but is entirely a matter of cliques who have the auxiliary object of nipping in the bud any competitive flowering of contemporary and original genius, which however they wouldn't recognize if they saw it. What! A person like myself – Martin went on to write – who discovered Kafka for himself nearly 20 years ago, and Melville 25 years ago, when about 15, and went to sea at 17, becomes disgusted in a way not easy to explain. Kafka meant something spiritually to me then: no longer. Melville likewise: I find it almost impossible to share what they meant to me with these people. They have ruined these writers for me. In fact I have to forget that there is such a thing as so-called 'modern literature' and the 'new criticism' in order to get any of my old feeling and passion back. How can I help remembering that no fewer than seventeen years ago it was I myself who had to *point out* to one of the editors of the *Nouvelle Revue Française* that they actually *had* published Kafka's *The Trial*. On reading it – for no, of course he hadn't read it – the fellow said to me: 'Did *you* write that book?' 'What? Didn't you like it?' 'Not much – the bar part was quite funny – but I got the feeling I was reading about *you*.' (His boss made a play out of it fifteen years later.) Then again, fifteen years ago, I couldn't find a single book of Kierkegaard's in the New York Public Library save *The Diary of a Seducer*. (Some years later we found this book in the market in Matamoros, Guerrero, Mexico.) Now he is all the rage and there is probably even a waiting list in the best-sellers department for *Fear and Trembling*. And yet what right have these English junior housemasters of American literature to Kafka and Melville? Have they been to sea? Have they starved? Nonsense. They probably haven't ever even been drunk, or had an honest hangover. Nor did they even discover Kafka and Melville themselves . . . etc. etc.

A brilliant piece of scorn, thought Martin (who suffered slightly from paranoia), regarding what he had written, and with his mouth almost watering. Then he added:

Now you see how easy it is to be carried away by an impulse of hatred! There is some truth in what I say (that is, it is certainly true that I hate these people) but what of this whole thing, read aright? What a testimony to my inadequacy, my selfishness, my complete confusion indeed! Worse than that. Suppose we take it to pieces, starting at the end, and see what our persistent objective self makes of such a thing. First it seems apparent that the writer feels that literature exists for his personal benefit, and that the object of life is to get drunk, to go to sea, and to starve. (As well it may be?) Moreover we feel sure that the writer wants us to know he has *had* many hangovers, *been* drunk very often, and *has* starved. (Though this last is doubtful because it is immediately qualified by the word Nonsense.) Certainly we must feel, if we read him aright, that he is a most unusually dog-in-the-manger sort of fellow, because for some undisclosed reason, among other things, he wishes to prevent the 'English junior housemasters of American literature' from reading Kafka and Melville. Perhaps the writer wanted to be just such a curious junior housemaster himself, and failed (either in England, or in America, or even in both)? Mystery. Mystery too clothes the mention of *Fear and Trembling* and the *Diary of a Seducer*, though that the author evidently feels himself to be singularly misused (to the extent that it even causes him to have some sort of mystical experience in the New York Public Library), at the same time feels himself to be some sort of unrecognized pioneer, who maybe even lives himself in a state of Fear and Trembling, perhaps even is undergoing some sort of Trial at the moment, seems manifest here too. And how proud he is of being mistaken in his youth for the author of *The Trial*, though this little story looks like a lie. (Or does it? The little story in question is not a lie, Martin knows, the trouble is that he has told so many lies now he has become incapable of making the truth not look like a lie.)

— Alas, before we can arrive at any real view of the undoubted truth that seems shadowily contained in some of these damaging phrases, certain syntactical deficiencies in this first paragraph oblige us to question the writer's own 'love of literature' (it looks as though it isn't very wide — perhaps he has only read the three books he mentions, though we may doubt even that) — we may wonder why, if he despises these schoolmasters so much he bothers himself about their 'power,' wonder too if he has not even secretly thought of himself as being 'a non-creative bully-boy and homosapient schoolmaster,' at which rate we may feel that it is no wonder if he has failed to put a thousand miles of ocean between himself and himself (however schizophrenic) and come down finally to what seems to be the one undoubted unequivocal brute fact in the whole thing, which is that it looks indeed as though some sort of tragedy were involved.

What? Neurosis, of one kind and another, is stamped on almost every word he writes, both neurosis and a kind of fierce health. Perhaps his tragedy is that he is the one normal writer left on earth and it is this that adds to his isolation and so to his sense of guilt. (But without Primrose he wouldn't be a writer of any kind, or normal either.)

Just the same it is necessary for people to stand in judgment every now and then, and not allow themselves to be crippled by such smashing self-criticism as the above, or all talent – though we note with a smile he called it genius – would be 'nipped in the bud' and the world get nowhere. And this brought Martin to the business, the question rather, of equilibrium.

No one likes it (indeed it seems so intangible how can you discuss it?) and the people who recommend it, if one can so phrase it, are nearly always bastards who have never known what was more than enough anyway – (there Martin went again). And yet there has never been a time in history when there was a greater necessity for the preservation of that seemingly most cold-blooded of all states, equilibrium, a greater necessity indeed for sobriety (how I hate it!). Equilibrium, sobriety, moderation, wisdom: these unpopular and unpleasant virtues, without which meditation and even goodness are impossible, must somehow, because they are so unpleasant, be recommended as states of being to be embraced with a kind of passion, as indeed passions themselves, as the longing for goodness itself is a passion, and thus invested somehow with all the attractions and attributes of qualities rare and savage (though you personally can be as drunk as a cock on blackberry brandy for all I care, albeit your chances of equilibrium, unless you are a veritable Paracelsus, become increasingly fewer in that state).

Without such equilibrium, be it then only mental, Martin thought, all reactions, public and personal, will tend to react too far. Whereas before we had sadism in literature, for instance, now an equal kindness, a distaste for cruelty in any shape or form will be envinced: but we shall not believe it presages a universal change in man, because this apparent kindness will be allied with other qualities in themselves dull or wicked – albeit so far as cruelty is concerned this is one point upon which man should allow the pendulum to swing to its furthest reach of compassion for all God's creatures, human and animal, and there remain.

And yet one should be able passionately to impugn the wanton slaughter of wild creatures as something essentially cowardly, unworthy, contemptible and even suicidal without at the same time feeling bound in the same breath to attack your Hemingway; one should realize that your Hemingway has a right to shoot wild creatures and while he is engaged in that dubiously masculine occupation he is not, at least for the moment, shooting anyone else.

Bully-boys and schoolmasters now go to church, instead of Communist meetings, and obediently popular opinion follows, prayer book in hand. Into the church of myth go the other bloody lot – Oh shut up.

But the people really responsible for the spread of interest in Kierkegaard, stemming out of the interest in Kafka, for which they are equally to be thanked, Edwin and Willa Muir, the brilliant translators of Kafka, responsible by virtue of the preface to *The Castle*, have never received the credit. Since but for that preface Kierkegaard would no doubt have remained in oblivion, and the bully-boys and – Oh shut up. Shut up. Shut up.

When Martin starts to study French, after a difficult period of abstinence, but still with a hangover, he is confronted, to say the least, in his French grammar, with the following phrases:

Traduisez en français:

1. The man was not dead but his wife told him that he had died two days ago.

2. She dressed herself as the Goddess of Death.

3. She opened the door and offered to the drunkard a dinner that was not very appetizing – (all this stemming from a lecture on the page headed *L'Ivrogne Incorrigible* ... and beginning, Un homme revenait tous les soirs à la maison dans un état d'ivresse complet – below this was a photo of La Bourse, Paris, taken circa 1900).

4. You must suffer for your vice, said she. I shall come each day to bring you the same meal.

5. The meal does not matter, but I am suffering from thirst, you must come every hour to bring me 3 glasses of wine. – On the back of this rusty-colored book an embossed cock (perhaps the one I mentioned earlier as being drunk on blackberry brandy) greeting the dawn, beneath it the words: *Je t'adore, ô soleil,* in gilt letters ... *What does this portend?*

Kindly remark of Lorca's: I'd like to pour a river of blood on her head.

Dec. 9. Bloody weather! Slow, dark daylight. The salle-à-manger is depressing, porthole covers down and electric lights going at noon, and noisy, with sea thundering tons of water across foredeck.

The poor little Mais, who've huddled, arms entwined, on deck, chattering like little gibbons, are now sad and sick; they could not eat lunch and finally all lay down on bench behind table.

Only Gabriel is still gay: 'I have been eating 5, 6 and 8 because I am always hungry when the sea is bad.'

Crash! Coffee, milk, etc. falls into Primrose's lap and on floor. I fear she will be scalded (she was too) but she is wailing because her pretty new red corduroy slacks are stained.

Godawful storm is on the wing (a good line) unless I have been a seaman for nothing. As a matter of fact I was a seaman for almost nothing, as wages go these days.

King Storm whose sheen is Fearful.

Huge seas, snow-capped mountains, but a south wind en arrière so that the sea is following us; the *Diderot* riding it wonderfully (but rolling so everything in cabin is banging about) like a Nathaniel Hawthorne blowing along in the wind to see the devil in manuscript, or windjammer running before the wind : passed another Liberty ship, going in the opposite direction, pitching away up in the skies, could not be making more than 20 miles per day.

Our rescue ship – coming to meet us.

The crew, in oilskins and sou'westers, battling the driving rain and wind, stretch lifelines on the after deck, terrific seas beyond and astern. Beyond and astern of time.

At sunset, tremendous sight of sprays and seas breaking over ship, black smoke pouring out of galley chimney straight to bâbord shows, however, that wind has gone to west ...

Dec. 10. Gale increasing. And in fact what we seem in for is one of those good old Conradian Southwesterlies, dreaded by sailors, first read about at school by torchlight, where the moon, sun and stars disappear for 7 days, and oneself finally beneath the blankets.

Primrose says: well, this is the Atlantic, the Western Ocean as I always imagined it.

He heareth sounds and seeth strange sights and commotions in the sky and the element. Low, wild sky with now and then a muted sun; gray, gray sea with a huge roll (grosse houle), but confused and breaking in every direction, some waves breaking like combers on a beach with a crash, with curving snowy crests from which the wind lifts the spray like a fountain. Some waves collide, rising to jagged peaks high above the ship, where the top breaks, and even spouts. Most weirdly beautiful of all, once in a long time a light comes through the top: beneath the spray appears a pale luminous brilliant green like phosphorescence, as though the wave were lighted from within by a green flame.

Standing on the passerelle, Charles tells us the wind was Force 8 at 1 a.m. but has now dropped a little. There is a bad storm ahead all right but traveling faster than we are. We are making 11 knots.

Later, near sunset, the wind has risen, is still rising, and radio reports it is shifting to a southwesterly quarter. The radio operator and the 3rd engineer, on passerelle with us, obviously don't like it and mutter together, predicting a dirty night.

They have posted an extra lookout on the bridge.

Gabriel points to the #3 hatch just below, over which waves are constantly breaking (they are almost breaking over the bridge) and says: 'Flour! But ze cover eez waterproof.' 'Why?' says Primrose. 'What does he mean?'

The Commandant scampers up and looks around: 'She isn't rolling – not too much. A good ship, eh?' Good, fine, we say, and he is pleased.

Le vent chant dans le cordage.

Later. The wind is now Force 9 and still rising, also has shifted, and is abeam. Wind flickering the spray like smoke along the face of the water. We are making 9 knots.

Rilke comes to Martin's aid, via *The Kenyon Review*: 'The experience with Rodin has made me very timid toward all changing, all diminishing, all failure – for those unapparent fatalities, once one has recognized them, can be endured only so long as one is capable of expressing them with the same force with which God allows them. I am not very far off work, perhaps, but Heaven forbid that I should be called upon (right away at least) for insight into anything more painful than I was charged with in Malte Laurids. Then it will just be a howl among howls and not worth the effort . . .'

But Martin has not, as a matter of fact, read a line of Rilke, and the whole thing, on his part, is simply an illusion of grandeur.

And, 'Things must become different with us, from the ground up, from the ground up, otherwise all the miracles in the world will be in vain. For here I see once more how much is lavished on me and just plain lost. The Blessed Angela had a similar experience – "quand tous les sages du monde," she says, "et tous les saints du paradis m'accablereraient de leurs consolations et de leurs promesses, et Dieu lui-même de ses dons, s'il ne me changeait pas moi-même, s'il ne commençait au fond de moi une nouvelle operation, au lieu de me faire du bien, les sages, les saints et Dieu exaspéraient au delà de toute expression mon désespoir, ma fureur, ma tristesse, ma douleur,

et mon aveuglement !" This (says Rilke) I marked a year ago
in the book, for I understand it with all my heart and I cannot
help it, it has since become only the more valid . . .'
Frère JACQUES – Frère JACQUES –
Sonnez les MATINES ! Sonnez les MATINES !

Dec. 11. Gale still worse. Poor Salvadoreans and Dutchmen
stuck in their cabins on after-deck : seas breaking right over :
they can't get to salle-à-manger. Try to help but turns out
couldn't matter less, they are all seasick and it's impossible to
eat anyhow with dishes jumping off table onto floor – nearly
impossible to drink too, should one want to : have to brace back
against wall, clutch bottle in one hand and glass in other and
pour teaspoonful at a time, for Primrose too. Have to write
standing up too.

STORM OVER ATLANTIS

Martin had a dream of seeing mad pictures of Bosch, in Rotterdam. Probably I have seen them somewhere, or reproductions
of them, particularly the dreadful St Christopher. Real dream
was preceded by a vision of a gigantic cinema, also apparently
in Rotterdam, otherwise catastrophic ruin, a great queer slim
tower, at the top of which church bells were ringing ceaselessly.

Then barrel organs as big as shops, and cranked with the
kind of energy one associates with a coal trimmer, i.e., myself,
winding up ashes from the stokehold on a winch . . . I once
knew a man, who in thus dumping the ashes overboard, went
overboard himself with the ashcan. That chap not unlike me
either.

Then the St Christopher, carrying Christ on his back, and
a fish in his right hand, a dog barking on the opposite bank,
old women, cocks, and a sort of gnome house up a tree where
the gnome has hung up washing in near background, someone enthusiastically hanging a bear, on the other side of another
kind of river, with a background of castles, old Rotterdam, etc.
(will we make it ?), but rather modern ; some sort of naked
fiend apparently dancing by his clothes, preparing to bathe from

the river bank – the general effect one of the inerrable horror, and Satanic humor. But why should Martin be dreaming about it ? perhaps clairvoyant –

The Beast

– The abomination of desolation, standing in the holy place.

But the Bosch picture of most importance to *La Mordida* I might describe as follows : in the foreground there is the same detailed figure, to whom I will return, in the background is a house, with some rafters missing from the roof, panes missing in the windows, etc., but giving a sense of even greater inerrable evil and horror and at the same time poverty and utter debauchery : in the doorway a man and a woman are discussing some matter that one knows is gruesome and terrible, without being able to say quite why : on the right of this house, which also on examination shows some signs of having been recently partially burned, an old man is peeing lustily ; to return to the figure in the foreground : he has the air of a pilgrim, his goods slung over his shoulder, cadaverous he is likewise, and one leg is bandaged (like Death in my other dream) ; up a rather nice-looking tree between him and the man peeing are various objects that turn out upon close inspection to be demons of one sort and another, the most remarkable being an extremely wide, cat-like of visage, yet seemingly bodiless creature a bit like the Cheshire Cat in the illustrations to Lewis Carroll. This should occur in *La Mordida* in Trumbaugh's dream : for the meaning of this horror – a horror this time almost without humor unless it is the pissing man – is indeed that of the Pilgrim – even Bunyan's if you like, though the imagery is far more deeply religious, the man in the foreground in fact is the Protagonist, turning his face from damnation, as he thinks, and limping off into the unknown, and leaving his poor house, though he is making a great mistake as it happens, for his poor house was his salvation – like an image of his niche in the next world he was presented with in advance – and his business was to purify it and rebuild it, before setting forth ... To hell with this ... I think the trouble with Martin is that Hieronymus Bosch is literally the only painter he can appreciate at all, and at that not much, because he seems vaguely to recognize – well, whatever it is he does recognize, poor devil. Or was it because he was a pre-Adamite?

– What I'm really getting at with Martin, is to try and plot his position of isolation, not merely in society, but from all other artists of his generation. Though an Englishman perhaps, in reality he belongs to an older tradition of writers, not English at all, but American, the tradition of Jamesian integrity and chivalry, of which Faulkner and Aiken, say – though both Southerners, which raises other questions – are about the last living exponents, albeit their subject matter might sometimes have scared their elders. However, Martin is quite incapable of their kind of chivalry and tolerance toward writers of that same generation, of whose souls the cover on *Esquire* might be considered the outward semblances, and who tend to divide mankind into two categories: (a) those who are regular, (b) the sons of bitches, the bloody bully-boys, who –

Bah, but what I mean is something like this. I am capable of conceiving of a writer today, even intrinsically a first-rate writer, who *simply cannot understand*, and never has been able to understand, what his fellow writers are driving at, and have been driving at, and who has always been too shy to ask. This writer feels this deficiency in himself to the point of anguish. Essentially a humble fellow, he has tried his hardest all his life to understand (though maybe still not hard enough) so that his room is full of *Partisan Reviews*, *Kenyon Reviews*, *Minotaurs*, *Poetry* mags, *Horizons*, even old *Dials*, of whose contents he is able to make out precisely nothing, save where an occasional contribution of his own, years and years ago, rings a faint bell in his mind, a bell that is growing ever fainter, because to tell the truth he can no longer understand his own early work either. Yet he still tries, for the hundredth thousandth time, to grasp *The Love Song of Alfred Prufrock*, for the nine millionth time to grapple with *The Waste Land*, of which the first line – though he knows it by heart of course! – is still as obscure to him as ever, and in which he has never been able to understand why Christ should have been compared to a tiger, though this has caused him to read William Blake (he had really been drawn to William Blake in childhood because he'd read in his

84

father's London *Times* that Blake was cuckoo) whose poem about the little lamb is perhaps the only thing in all literature that he has thoroughly grasped, and even in that case maybe he's fooling himself. I am partly joking, for in fact my writer has a thorough grounding in Shakespeare. H'm. Anyhow, when he really faces up to matters, he finds his taste has been formed not necessarily by things that he has liked, but by things that he has understood, or rather these are so pitifully few that he has come to identify the two. Is this a fantastic portrait? Because it isn't that this man is not creative, it is because he *is* so creative that he can't understand anything; for example, he has never been able to follow the plot of even the simplest movie because he is so susceptible to the faintest stimulus of that kind that ten other movies are going on in his head while he is watching it. And it is the same way with music, painting, etc. At the age of 37, having acquired a spurious fame for various pieces that, as I say, he has long ceased to understand himself, he wakes up to the fact that he has really only enjoyed with aesthetic detachment four things in his life. A poem by Conrad Aiken, a performance of *Richard II* when he was 10 years old at the Birkenhead Hippodrome, a gramophone record of Frankie Trumbauer's with Eddie Lang, Venuti and Beiderbecke, and a French film directed by Zilke (rhymes with Rilke?) called *The Tragedy of a Duck*. Despite this, he still heroically reads a few pages of William Empson's *Seven Types of Ambiguity* each night before going to sleep, just to keep his hand in, as it were, and to keep up with the times ...

There is a truth contained in this portrait, for this man, while a genuine artist – in fact he probably thinks of nothing but art – is yet, unlike most artists, a true human being. For alas this is the way the majority of human beings see other human beings, as shadows, themselves the only reality. It is true these shadows are often menacing, or they are angelic, love may move them, but they are essentially shadows, or forces, and the novelist's touch is missing in their human perception. Nothing indeed can be more unlike the actual experience of life than the average novelist's realistic portrait of a character. Nonetheless Martin's blindness, isolation, anguish, is all for a reason. I can see that on that road to Damascus, when the scales drop from his eyes, he will be given the grace to understand the heroic strivings of other artists too. Meantime he must slug it out, as they say, in darkness, that being his penance.

(Note: it must be said somewhere that Martin had been on this planet for so long that he had almost tricked himself into believing he was a human being. But this he felt with his deeper self not to be so, or only partly so. He could not find his vision of the world in any books. He had never succeeded in discovering more than a superficial aspect of his sufferings or his aspirations. And though he had got into the habit of pretending that he thought like other people, this was not the case. It is thought that we made a great advance when we discovered that the world was round and not flat. But to Martin it was flat all right, but only a little bit of it, the arena of his own sufferings, would appear at a time. Nor could he visualize the thing going round, moving from west to east. He would view the great dipper as one might view an illuminated advertisement, as something fixed, although with childish wonder, and with thoughts in mind of his mother's diamonds. But he could not make anything move. The world would not be wheeling, nor the stars in their courses. Or when the sun came up over the hill in the morning, that was precisely what it did. He was non-human, subservient to different laws, even if upon the surface he was at best a good-looking normal young man with rather formal manners. How else explain the continual painful conflict that went on between him and reality, even him and his clothes. 'There is a continuous cold war between me and my clothes.' Like a man who has been brought up by apes, or among cannibals, he had acquired certain of their habits; he looked like a man, but there the resemblance ended. And if he shared some of their passions, he shared these equally with the animals. Describe The Getting Up of Martin Trumbaugh, in the complications, futility, complications with clothes, reality, etc. And yet, also, in his deepest self, he possessed aspirations that were neither animal, nor, alas, any too commonly human. He wished to be physically strong, not in order to defeat people, but in order to be more practically compassionate. Compassion he valued above all things even though he saw the weakness in that desire. In fact anybody who said anything like this would immediately seem to be condemned for some sort of hypocrisy in his eyes just as he felt himself condemned at that moment. That weakness of self-pity he wished to correct too. He valued courtesy, tact, humor. But he wanted to find out how these could be put into practice in an uncorrupted form. But above all he valued loyalty – or something like loyalty, though in an extreme form – loyalty to oneself, loyalty to those one loved. Above all things perhaps he wanted to be loyal to Primrose in life. But he wanted to be loyal to her beyond life, and in whatever life there might be beyond. He wanted to be loyal to her beyond death. In short, at the bottom of his chaos of a nature, he worshiped the virtues that the world seems long since to have dismissed as dull or simply good business or as not pertaining to reality at all. So that, as in his lower, so in his higher nature too, he felt himself to be non-human. And he was in general so tripped up by the complexities of his own nature that too often he exhibited no virtues whatsoever, and all the vices, once glaring but now obscure; sins, that for all her victory, Protestantism is responsible for rendering less deadly than they in fact are. And he had good cause –)

Another dream of a huge desolate cathedral, yet involved marvelously with life, pissoirs underneath it, shops living within its very architecture, the great unseen triptychs of Rubens in the gloom, and the gigantic tinkling of a huge bell ... The peace, and the distant bowed priests in white, carrying ingots.

The wireless operator praying lonely in the church: and I too, am he.

– Delirium of sea under moon –

Dec. 11. Night

> Al stereless within a boot am I
> Amid the sea, betwexen windes two
> That in contrarie standen evermo

Chaucer's comment is to be taken seriously: something has gone west in our steering gear. That is what I think at least,

though I can gain no information and to my humiliation I have
no knowledge of the hydraulic contraption we're dependent on.
But the ship did not answer her helm from the upper bridge
earlier, and there is something evilly wrong. Nearly all hands
seem working down blow, and I suspect the second mate of
having gone down the propeller shaft, which is a bad sign ...
All stereless within a stormboot are we.

– Tonight, in a full gale, off the Azores, our cabin – the Chief
Gunner's – being on the lee side and the wind from the south-
west, with tremendous seas, but being driven down wind, it was
possible to leave our porthole wide open, through which one
could see, as the ship lurched down to leeward, great doctor of
divinity's gowns of seas furling to leeward,
the foam like lamb's wool: the wind rose
to a pitch of wailing in the cordage so extreme that it sounded almost false, like
movie wind about a haunted house: and
indeed the whole ship sounded like an immense exaggeration of the same thing:

*The Mariner hath
been cast into a
trance; for the
angelic power causeth
the vessel to drive
northward faster than
human life could
endure.*

clankings of chains, unearthly chimes, inexplicable tinkerings
clinkings and chatterings and sudden horrid whistlings: from
down below in the engines, there issued an unimaginable noise
of battering, whistling and thumping, accompanied too, for
whatever reason, and at regular intervals, and as if were con-
cealed down there some of mystic Ahab's secret harpooners
engaged in forging their weapons, a tremendous sound of
hammering that always ceased after a while, and doubtless was
concerned some way with the propeller but so fearsome that I
could explain it to Primrose only by saying that indeed it was
the custom during gales for the chief engineer to keep his intran-
sigent greasers employed in chipping rust (she didn't believe me
but nodded gravely), that they might not become discouraged or
bored and lose their nerve: on top of this, and also at regular
intervals, there was the noise that seemed to come out of the
wall between myself and the wireless operator's cabin, as of a
jack being cranked up, which Sacheverell Sitwell has taught us
to associate with the signing off or evening greeting of a poltergeist. Beneath one, lying in the bunk, when this was possible,

the ship squirmed and twisted, at moments of crisis, like a woman in an agony of pleasure, and looking out at the storm, and observing the gigantic seas, rising all above us as if we were in a volcano, it seemed impossible the ship could survive the punishment she was receiving; horrible detractable noises too came from the closed galley two decks below where that day the cook had been badly burned: and yet the sea never visited us through the porthole, we were safe in the midst of chaos, the wind rose to a howl of wolves as we plunged on, leaving me not merely a feeling that it was impossible to be experiencing this but, at every moment, the feeling that one had not experienced it at all.

> The supernatural motion is retarded; the Mariner awakes, and his penance begins anew.

We have had to change our course, the skipper says, and are going by dead reckoning.

Mad game of chess with skipper in his cabin; tables and chairs are mostly anchored to deck (nearly said floor), other chairs etc. and so on are lashed, so the cabin resembles escapologist's 'rumpus' room – how I hate that phrase! – everything goes over from time to time anyhow: giacomo piano opening: chessmen peg into board like cribbage board – bottle of whisky in skipper's furred sea-boot beside table, because sea-boot won't fall over, is for me, he scarcely touches it; this chess is his idea of an hour's relaxation instead of sleep – he has summoned me to play in the middle of the night as if I were a medieval courtier subject to the King's wishes : dash to the chartroom something like one of those dashes, when scrum half on opponent's twenty-five, over the try-line – opposing XV in this case being not human beings but objects, fortunately static: wireless operator hasn't turned in for three days, looks half dead, poor fellow, keeps fighting uphill into skipper's cabin every now and then with idiotic reports of fine weather and light winds in the Baltic, meantime the scene outside, when I can see it, is like a descent into the maelstrom. Other, more serious radio reports, to the skipper's sardonic amusement, are always accompanied by some such remark as 'These reports have nothing to do with navigation.' We are evidently in a bad way though skipper has no intention of telling me what is wrong, or at least not yet; anyhow we can't hear ourselves speak. Skipper looks damned grave, however; despite which, after a long game, he beats me very decisively. Grisette, the little cat, is delighted with all these escapologist's arrangements, 'for her benefit.' I was so concentrated on the game that I forgot to look on the bridge, which seemed unnaturally dark, to see if there was a man at the wheel. However I tell Primrose that there was. But so help me God, I don't think there was.

– Game of chess now seems to be utterly unreal and something like that eerie wonderful absurd scene in the French movie by Epstein of *The Fall of the House of Usher* in which Roderick Usher and the old doctor are reading by the fire, the house has already caught fire, not only that but cracks are opening in the walls and the house is in fact coming to pieces all around them, while flames creep toward them along the carpet, an insane electric storm moreover is discharging its lightnings outside in the swamp, through which Mrs Usher, née Ligeia, having just risen from the grave, is making her way back to the house with some difficulty; nonetheless, absorbed in the story, Usher and the good doctor go on reading: the unspeakably happy ending of that film, by the way, Martin thought, under the stars, with Orion suddenly turned into the cross, and Usher reconciled with his wife in this life yet on another plane, was a stroke of genius perhaps beyond Poe himself, and now it occurs to me that something like that should be the ending of the novel. . . .

> Roderick Usher rose at six
> And found his house in a hell of a fix.
> He made the coffee and locked the door,
> And then said, what have I done that for?
> But had poured himself a hell of a snort
> Before he could make any kind of retort,
> And poured himself a jigger of rum
> Before he heard the familiar hum
> Of his matutinal delirium
> Whose voices, imperious as a rule,
> Were sharper today, as if at school :
> Today, young Usher, you're going to vote.
> Said Roderick, that's a hell of a note.

So he packed his bag full of vintage rare,
His house fell down but he didn't care,
And took the 9 : 30 to Baltimore
And was murdered, promptly, at half past four.

– Three flying Dutchmen.

Later. In vain attempt to get some information I am informed by the fourth mate – the sort of information I might have given myself in a similar situation – that all hands are engaged in putting a ceinture around the ship to prevent its falling apart. (Indeed this is not so funny as it sounded – get from newspaper cuttings Pat Terry's story of the ship that used chains in this regard : also it is an electric welded ship ; danger of breaking in two or cracking hull very real.)

Charles says, smiling, 'These Liberty ships, you know, Sigbjørn, they all fell in two in the Atlantic, in the war.' Then, seeing Primrose's face, he added, 'Do not worry, Madame, we have put a ceinture around its middle.'

Later. – My sailor's instincts tell me, all of a sudden – and it is amazing with what suddenness such a crisis is upon one – that it will actually be an unusual bloody miracle if we pull through. The worst is being able to do nothing. Worse still, can't tell what they're doing, or if they think they are doing anything, what they imagine it can be. Despite the fourth mate's joke, there is an actual sound as of the ship breaking up. On an old type of ship such as I knew, if the steering gear went, there was still an old-fashioned windjammer wheel on the poop that could go into direct action. On top of that – believe it or not – even as late as 1927, we carried sails on board ; and the lamp-trimmer, one of the petty officers, and a rating they seem to have no longer, corresponded to the old sailmaker. Here there is no windjammer-like wheel, and as certainly there are no sails. But there are two wheels, one above the other, on the upper and lower bridge, and so far as I can gather, both of these are out of commission. Yet we still have steerage way, of a kind, and are not hove to. The thing to be thankful for is that we haven't lost our propeller. Yet.

– Martin took his ignorance of the nature of the crisis to heart, telling himself that it was because these Liberty ships were not like the old ships where you could see what was going on, that there was an almost Kafka-like occlusion, everything closed, ghastly, so that in the Chief Gunner's cabin, while it connected with the bridge, you might as well have been hidden away on the upper deck of one of the Fall River Line paddle-steamers for all that you were in contact; but no matter what he told himself, it seemed all part and parcel of his wider isolation, and in fact like the ultimate ordeal of —

Primrose is assured, whenever she washes up against any-one, that everything is all right and there's nothing to worry about. She can't possibly be fooled but pretends she is. She's a good sailor, spends her time eating sandwiches, for there's been no hot food for two days, and watching the storm from the lower bridge. What else to do? Can't get into bunk or you're thrown out. The poor Salvadoreans, the Hungarian sports-man, and the Mynheer Peeperhorns are all half dead of seasick-ness and there is nothing anyone can do to help them. Our store of liquor, however, takes on a dimension of social utility for once. Second mate reports all lifeboats to starboard smashed. You'd think one would notice this, but somehow one didn't. One lifeboat to port is still possible — Côté à l'Abri du vent ... etc. While wheel is functioning again on the lower bridge.

Later. The wind is now 100 miles an hour. Seems unbeliev-able but I've forgotten whether this is Force 10 or 12. Wireless weather report: overcast sky, some rain.

Dec. 12. Position Report. S.S. *Diderot.* There is no position report. (As Stephen Leacock would say.)

Dec. 13. 3 a.m. Wind is now Force 10-11. On lower bridge with Primrose and Commandant, who says to Primrose, laugh-ing:

'Well, there is now nothing I can do. But if you like, Madame, you can pray.'

— The storm, paralyzing scene from bridge, of the ship in anguish shipping sea after sea of white drifting fire, after each smash the spume smoking mast high above the foremasthead light.

Later. We have now had no sleep for 2 nights – I think it has been 2 nights – impossible to lie down, or even sit down. We stand, bracing ourselves and holding on. This desk thank God is strongly anchored, so I hang on with one hand to desk, write with other. Hope I can read this scrawl later. Primrose spends most of her time on lower bridge. I know she is frightened but she won't say so. She comes staggering in every so often to re-assure me, or give latest report. Primrose . . .

She tells me: Everyone is on duty except 1st mate, who is asleep! Skipper sends man to wake him. Impossible. Finally skipper himself stamps down in a rage. They shout and shake him, but, says André, 'He was like a dead corpse.'

Absolute blackness and wild water all around. Our rudder trouble has started all over again. Uncanny scene of completely useless wheel in bridgehouse spinning round, with the ship going like a bat out of hell. Or did I dream it?

Ship seems to jump out of water, shudder from end to end.

Sonnez les matines!

Sonnez les matines!

Back in Chief Gunner's cabin I remember Gerald once saying, 'when in doubt make a memorandum.' So I do . . . Death compared to a rejected manuscript. Am my grandfather's son, who went down with ship – do I have to do that? Ship not mine anyhow . . . Seems unnecessary. Would be downright awkward, in fact. Embarrassment of skipper. A short story: 'The Last Apéritif.'

Martin reflected that these kind of idiotic thoughts were simply a mechanism in forced inaction to short-circuit anxiety about Primrose. This anxiety, when one gives way a bit, seems less anxiety than an inoculation against intolerable and appalling grief, a grief indeed that seems exactly like this sea . . .

Primrose, laughing, manages to shout to me: 'Do you know, I just had the most idiotic thought, if we have to take to the life-boat I mustn't wear my beautiful fur coat – I don't want to ruin it!'

But, as a matter of fact, there are now no lifeboats.

No use trying to get into bunk – we are pitched out on the floor.

Another way of confronting death is to conceive of it as a Mexican immigration inspector: 'Hullo. What's the matter with you, you look as though you'd swallowed Pat Murphy's goat and the horns were sticking out of your arse.'

(That is what the Manx fisherman admirably observed to the skipper of the liner, who not only nearly ran his boat down, but started yelling at him apoplectically for not keeping out of his way. So I tell Primrose this story which diverts her a lot. In fact, it is enough to make God laugh, that story, I always think. Possibly something like this anecdote – which I had from a Manx fisherman – is the origin of someone's threat – Bildad's? – in *Moby-Dick*: 'I'll swallow a live goat, hair and horns and all.')

Our house. Incredible jewel-like days in December sometimes. Such radiance for December. Celestial views. Then a bell ringing in the mist. Would like someone to have it, live in it, without fear of eviction.

> – Thou god of this great vast, rebuke these surges
> Which wash both Heaven and Hell: the seaman's whistle
> Is as a whisper in the ears of death,
> Unheard.

But one should be grateful that there are not 6 *short* whispers followed by one *long* whisper.

In fact, as I surmise, many lives have been saved by the weather's being too bad to abandon ship.

Sonnez les matines!
Sonnez les matines!

Three S.O.S. going at once. Radio next door crackling like small storm within a storm inside. Operator tells me – how many hours ago? – Costa Rican tanker has been sinking for three days. A Greek and a Finn also in distress. And now a Panamanian. Greek ship is called ΑΡΙΣΤΟΤΕΛΗΣ just to give us our unities presumably, since Aristotle's personal destiny is not much help. (Note: Aristotle drowned himself.) We are all too far away from one another, all too far down the drain ourselves, to do any good. Still, it is a comfort to each other to know we are not alone. This is apparently one of the worst storms in living history in the Atlantic. Though messages still come through, 'having nothing to do with navigation.'

Ventilators singing in wild organ harmony: Hear us, O Lord, from heaven thy dwelling place!

– No ship would stand many more seas like that – in old type of steamer half crew would be cut off in the fo'c'sle. Now it is the poor passengers, the Salvadoreans, etc., who are cut off.

Popular illusions to spike about French, officers and crew of this ship anyhow (message in a bottle):

That they are predominantly homosexual. (There are seemingly none aboard this ship. Though a Frenchman is capable of living a balanced and even chivalrous life with a female giraffe, without inflicting it on you.)

That they are predominantly unfaithful to their wives. (There is one longing in common among all the married men, officers and sailors to whom I have spoken, to be home with their wives for Christmas. Though this may be a virtue peculiar to married sailors.)

That they are mean. (Your concierge may be so. Madame P.P. is so.)

No matter what yoke they were reeling under, no matter how starved, I believe you would never see in France, or among Frenchmen, the appalling sights of despair and degradation to be met with daily in the streets of Vancouver, Canada, where man, having turned his back on nature, and having no heritage of beauty else, and no faith in a civilization where God has become an American washing machine, or a car he refuses even to drive properly – and not possessing the American élan which arises from a faith in the very act of taming nature herself, because America having run out of a supply of nature to tame is turning on Canada, so that Canada feels herself at bay, while a Canadian might be described as a conservationist divided against himself – falls to pieces before your eyes. Report has nothing to do with navigation. Instead of ill this very extremity in Canada probably presages an important new birth of wisdom in that country, for which America herself will be grateful.

That they are not good sailors. (Even Conrad, in his most

whiskery mood, admitted in *The Rover* that they were among the best.)

That they have no, or a prissy, or a precise or merely urbane sense of humor. (Rabelais' 'roaring arm chair' has never been vacated.)

Prosper Mérimée writing on the Scots. And on the Americans placed at different tables on the Riviera (during the American Civil War) 'to prevent them eating each other.' Similiar illusions should be spiked re Americans, English, Jews, Mexicans, Negroes, etc., etc. An example of humor to be appreciated in any language: Grisette is now in heat.

Greatest fault of the French is that they do not listen to what each other say. No wonder their governments fall – or rather they are talking so much all at once they can't even hear them fall, perhaps.

Prayer to the Virgin for those who have nobody them with.

For she is the Virgin for those who have nobody them with.

And for mariners on the sea.

And to the Saint of Desperate and Dangerous Causes.

For the 3 El Salvadoreans. For the 1 Hungarian sportsman. And for the 3 Mynheer von Peeperhorns.

Plight of an Englishman who is a Scotchman who is Norwegian who is a Canadian who is a Negro at heart from Dahomey who is married to an American who is on a French ship in distress which has been built by Americans and who finds at last that he is a Mexican dreaming of the White Cliffs of Dover.

Mystical objection to changing one's religion. But let the whole world make a fresh start. A universal amnesty (extending even to the bullies, the Mexican immigration inspectors, the schoolmasters, and finally myself, who have never lifted a finger to speak against the death in life all about me till this moment). Society is too guilty in the eyes of God to hold any man permanently to account in a larger sense for a crime against it, no matter how wicked: collectively, who have always – these donkey, these man – done something worse.

The day in Bowen Island we found the bronze bells and saw the harlequin ducks.

Prayer for Einar Neilson, who saw us off, singing 'Shenandoah.'

'And from the whole earth, as it spins through space, comes a sound of singing.' (C.A.)

Sonnez les matines !

Sonnez les matines !

¿Le gusta esta jardin? ¿Que es suyo?

Vanity of human beings is terrific, stronger than fear, worse than that story in Schopenhauer.

S.O.S. going on next door. Battement de tambours !

God save the Fisher King.

Can't tell what's happening on deck at all. And there is absolutely nothing, for the moment, that can be done, which is never how you visualize it. Nevertheless, Martin reflected, this is a position all novelists find themselves in eventually. Put on your life jacket, your arms through the shoulder straps. Damned if I will. Couldn't if I tried. Have always had trouble with things like that. Put life jacket on Primrose, Martin thought. But Primrose, eating a sandwich, has already decided she wants to return to the bridge. So meanwhile we manage a drink. It is a rather good, strange drink.

à ce signal :

– Go to your cabin.

– Cover yourself warmly.

– Put on your gill-netting of sauvetage, and letting yourself be guided by the personnel render yourself at the Bridge of Embarcations, on the side secluded from the wind . . .

The signal of abandon . . . Couldn't hear it given in this noise.

Chief Gunner's cabin.

Martin swore that if he survived he would never willingly do another injurious action, or a generous one for an ulterior motive, unless that were an unselfish one. But the thing to do was *not to forget this,* like the character in William March's story, if you ever got out of the jam. God give me, he asks, a chance to be truly charitable. Let me know what it is You want me to do . . .

– Wish old Charon was here . . .

Through the Panama

*The whole is an assembly of apparently incongruous parts,
slipping past one another –*
Something like our steering gear in fact.
– law of series.
Sonnez les matines !
Sonnez les matines !
Miraculous such nights as these . . . etc.
Great God – we seem to be steering again.

And the ancient Mariner beholdeth his native country.

The second mate says to Primrose, laughing, 'All night we have been saving your life, Madame.'

And to teach by his own example, love and reverence to all things that God made and loveth.

Dawn, and an albatross, bird of heaven, gliding astern.

À 9nds. arrivée Bishop Light, Angleterre, le 17 dec. vers 11 H.

– S.S. *Diderot*, left Vancouver November 7 – left Los Angeles November 15 – for Rotterdam.

Frère Jacques
Frère Jacques
Dormez-vous ?
Dormez-vous ?
Sonnez les matines !
Sonnez les matines !
Ding dang dong !
Ding dang dong !

STRANGE COMFORT
AFFORDED BY THE PROFESSION

SIGBJØRN WILDERNESS, an American writer in Rome on a Guggenheim Fellowship, paused on the steps above the flower stall and wrote, glancing from time to time at the house before him, in a black notebook :

Il poeta inglese Giovanni Keats mente maravigliosa quanto precoce morì in questa casa il 24 Febbraio 1821 nel ventisessimo anno dell'età sua.

Here, in a sudden access of nervousness, glancing now not only at the house, but behind him at the church of Trinità dei Monti, at the woman in the flower stall, the Romans drifting up and down the steps, or passing in the Piazza di Spagna below (for though it was several years after the war he was afraid of being taken for a spy), he drew, as well as he was able, the lyre, similar to the one on the poet's tomb, that appeared on the house between the Italian and its translation:

Then he added swiftly the words below the lyre:

The young English poet, John Keats, died in this house on the 24th of February 1821, aged 26.

This accomplished, he put the notebook and pencil back in his pocket, glanced around him again with a heavier, more penetrating look – that in fact was informed by such a malaise he saw nothing at all but which was intended to say 'I have a perfect right to do this,' or 'If you saw me do that, very well then, I *am* some sort of detective, perhaps even some kind of a painter' – descended the remaining steps, looked around wildly once more, and entered, with a sigh of relief like a man going to bed, the comforting darkness of Keats's house.

Here, having climbed the narrow staircase, he was almost instantly confronted by a legend in a glass case which said:

Remnants of aromatic gums used by Trelawny when cremating the body of Shelley.

And these words, for his notebook with which he was already rearmed felt ratified in this place, he also copied down, though he failed to comment on the gums themselves, which largely escaped his notice, as indeed did the house itself — there had been those stairs, there was a balcony, it was dark, there were many pictures, and these glass cases, it was a bit like a library — in which he saw no books of his — these made about the sum of Sigbjørn's unrecorded perceptions. From the aromatic gums he moved to the enshrined marriage license of the same poet, and Sigbjørn transcribed this document too, writing rapidly as his eyes became more used to the dim light:

Percy Bysshe Shelley of the Parish *of* Saint Mildred, Bread Street, London, Widower, *and* Mary Wollstonecraft Godwin *of* the City of Bath, Spinster, a minor, *were married in this* Church *by* Licence *with Consent of* William Godwin her father *this* Thirtieth *Day of December in the year one thousand eight hundred and sixteen.* By me Mr Heydon, Curate. This marriage was solemnized between us.

PERCY BYSSHE SHELLEY

MARY WOLLSTONECRAFT GODWIN

In the presence of:

WILLIAM GODWIN

M. J. GODWIN.

Beneath this Sigbjørn added mysteriously:

Nemesis. Marriage of drowned Phoenician sailor. A bit odd here at all. Sad — feel swine to look at such things.

Then he passed on quickly — not so quickly he hadn't time to wonder with a remote twinge why, if there was no reason for any of his own books to be there on the shelves above him, the presence was justified of *In Memoriam, All Quiet on the Western Front, Green Light,* and the *Field Book of Western Birds*

– to another glass case in which appeared a framed and unfinished letter, evidently from Severn, Keats's friend, which Sigbjørn copied down as before:

My dear Sir:

Keats has changed somewhat for the worse – at least his mind has much – very much – yet the blood has ceased to come, his digestion is better and but for a cough he must be improving, that is as respects his body – but the fatal prospect of consumption hangs before his mind yet – and turns everything to despair and wretchedness – he will not hear a word about living – nay, I seem to lose his confidence by trying to give him this hope [the following lines had been crossed out by Severn but Sigbjørn ruthlessly wrote them down just the same: *for his knowledge of internal anatomy enables him to judge of any change accurately and largely adds to his torture*], he will not think his future prospect favourable – he says the continued stretch of his imagination has already killed him and were he to· recover he would not write another line – he will not hear of his good friends in England except for what they have done – and this is another load – but of their high hopes of him – his certain success – his experience – he will not hear a word – then the want of some kind of hope to feed his vivacious imagination –

The letter having broken off here, Sigbjørn, notebook in hand, tiptoed lingeringly to another glass case where, another letter from Severn appearing, he wrote:

My dear Brown – He is gone – he died with the most perfect ease – he seemed to go to sleep. On the 23rd at half past four the approaches of death came on. 'Severn – lift me up for I am dying – I shall die easy – don't be frightened, I thank God it has come.' I lifted him upon my arms and the phlegm seemed boiling in his throat. This increased until 11 at night when he gradually sank into death so quiet I still thought he slept – But I cannot say more now. I am broken down beyond my strength. I cannot be left alone. I have not slept for nine days – the days since. On Saturday a gentleman came to cast his hand and foot. On Thursday the body was opened. The lungs were completely gone. The doctors would not –

Much moved, Sigbjørn reread this as it now appeared in his notebook, then added beneath it:

On Saturday a gentleman came to cast his hand and foot – that is the most sinister line to me. Who is this gentleman?

Strange Comfort Afforded by the Profession

Once outside Keats's house Wilderness did not pause nor look to left or right, not even at the American Express, until he had reached a bar which he entered, however, without stopping to copy down its name. He felt he had progressed in one movement, in one stride, from Keats's house to this bar, partly just because he had wished to avoid signing his own name in the visitor's book. Sigbjørn Wilderness! The very sound of his name was like a bell-buoy – or more euphoniously a light-ship – broken adrift, and washing in from the Atlantic on a reef. Yet how he hated to write it down (loved to see it in print?) – though like so much else with him it had little reality unless he did. Without hesitating to ask himself why, if he was so disturbed by it, he did not choose another name under which to write, such as his second name which was Henry, or his mother's, which was Sanderson-Smith, he selected the most isolated booth he could find in the bar, that was itself an underground grotto, and drank two grappas in quick succession. Over his third he began to experience some of the emotions one might have expected him to undergo in Keats's house. He felt fully the surprise which had barely affected him that some of Shelley's relics were to be found there, if a fact no more astonishing than that Shelley – whose skull moreover had narrowly escaped appropriation by Byron as a drinking goblet, and whose heart, snatched out of the flames by Trelawny, he seemed to recollect from Proust, was interred in England – should have been buried in Rome at all (where the bit of Ariel's song inscribed on his gravestone might have anyway prepared one for the rich and strange), and he was touched by the chivalry of those Italians who, during the war, it was said, had preserved, at considerable risk to themselves, the contents of that house from the Germans. Moreover he now thought he began to see the house itself more clearly, though no doubt not as it was, and he produced his notebook again with the object of adding to the notes already taken these impressions that came to him in retrospect.

'Mamertine Prison,' he read ... He'd opened it at the wrong place, at some observations made yesterday upon a visit to the historic dungeon, but being gloomily entertained by what he saw, he read on as he did so feeling the clammy confined horror of that underground cell, or other underground cell, not, he suspected, really sensed at the time, rise heavily about him.

MAMERTINE PRISON [ran the heading]
  The lower is the true prison
of Mamertine, the state prison of ancient Rome.

The lower cell called Tullianus is probably the most ancient building in Rome. The prison was used to imprison malefactors and enemies of the State. In the lower cell is seen the well where according to tradition St Peter miraculously made a spring to baptise the gaolers Processus and Martinianus. Victims: politicians. Pontius, King of the Sanniti. Died 290 B.C. Giurgurath (Jugurtha), Aristobulus, Vercingetorix. – The Holy Martyrs, Peter and Paul. Apostles imprisoned in the reign of Nero. – Processus, Abondius, *and many others unknown* were:

> decapitato
> suppliziato (suffocated)
> strangolato
> morto per fame.

Vercingetorix, the King of the Gauls, was certainly strangolato 49 B.C. and Jugurtha, King of Numidia, dead by starvation 104 B.C.

The lower is the true prison – why had he underlined that? Sigbjørn wondered. He ordered another grappa and, while awaiting it, turned back to his notebook where, beneath his remarks on the Mamertine prison, and added as he now recalled in the dungeon itself, this memorandum met his eyes:

Find Gogol's house – where wrote part of Dead Souls – 1838. Where died Vielgorsky? 'They do not heed me, nor see me, nor listen to me,' wrote Gogol. 'What have I done to them? Why do they torture me? What do they want of poor me? What can I give them? I have nothing. My strength is gone. I cannot endure all this.' Suppliziato. Strangolato. In wonderful-horrible book of Nabokov's when Gogol was dying – he says – 'you could feel his spine through his stomach.' Leeches dangling from nose: 'Lift them up, keep them away . . .' Henrik Ibsen, Thomas Mann, ditto brother: Buddenbrooks and Pippo Spano. A – where lived? became sunburned? Perhaps happy here. Prosper Mérimée and Schiller. Suppliziato. Fitzgerald in Forum. Eliot in Colosseum?

And underneath this was written enigmatically:

And many others.

And beneath this:

Perhaps Maxim Gorky too. This is funny. Encounter between Volga Boatman and saintly Fisherman.

What was funny? While Sigbjørn, turning over his pages toward Keats's house again, was wondering what he had meant, beyond the fact that Gorky, like most of those other distinguished individuals, had at one time lived in Rome, if not in the Mamertine prison – though with another part of his mind he knew perfectly well – he realized that the peculiar stichometry of his observations, jotted down as if he imagined he were writing a species of poem, had caused him prematurely to finish the notebook:

On Saturday a gentleman came to cast his hand and foot – that is the most sinister line to me – who is this gentleman?

With these words his notebook concluded.

That didn't mean there was no more space, for his notebooks, he reflected avuncularly, just like his candles, tended to consume themselves at both ends; yes, as he thought, there was some writing at the beginning. Reversing this, for it was upside down, he smiled and forgot about looking for space, since he immediately recognized these notes as having been taken in America two years ago upon a visit to Richmond, Virginia, a pleasant time for him. So, amused, he composed himself to read, delighted also, in an Italian bar, to be thus transported back to the South. He had made nothing of these notes, hadn't even known they were there, and it was not always easy accurately to visualize the scenes they conjured up:

The wonderful slanting square in Richmond and the tragic silhouette of interlaced leafless trees.

On a wall: *dirty stinking Degenerate Bobs was here from Boston, North End, Mass. Warp son of a bitch.*

Sigbjørn chuckled. Now he clearly remembered the biting winter day in Richmond, the dramatic courthouse in the pre-

cipitous park, the long climb up to it, and the caustic attestation
to solidarity with the North in the (white) men's wash room.
Smiling he read on :

In Poe's shrine, strange preserved news clipping: CAPACITY
CROWD HEARS TRIBUTE TO POE'S WORKS. *University student, who
ended life, buried at Wytherville.*

Yes, yes, and this he remembered too, in Poe's house, or one
of Poe's houses, the one with the great dark wing of shadow on
it at sunset, where the dear old lady who kept it, who'd
showed him the news clipping, had said to him in a whisper:
'So you see, *we* think these stories of his drinking can't *all* be
true.' He continued :

Opposite Craig house, where Poe's Helen lived, these words, upon
façade, windows, stoop of the place from which E.A.P. – if I am right
– must have watched the lady with the agate lamp: Headache –
A.B.C. – Neuralgia: LIC-OFF-PREM – enjoy Pepsi – Drink Royal
Crown Cola – Dr Swell's Root Beer – 'Furnish room for rent': did
Poe really live here? Must have, could only have spotted Psyche
from the regions which are Lic-Off-Prem. – Better than no Lic at
all though. Bet Poe does not still live in Lic-Off-Prem. Else might
account for 'Furnish room for rent'?
Mem : Consult Talking Horse Friday.
– Give me Liberty or give me death [Sigbjørn now read]. In
churchyard, with Patrick Henry's grave ; a notice. No smoking within
ten feet of the church ; then :
Outside Robert E. Lee's house :
Please pull the bell
To make it ring.
– Inside Valentine Museum, with Poe's relics –

Sigbjørn paused. Now he remembered that winter day still
more clearly. Robert E. Lee's house was of course far below
the courthouse, remote from Patrick Henry and the Craig house
and the other Poe shrine, and it would have been a good step
hence to the Valentine Museum, even had not Richmond, a
city whose Hellenic character was not confined to its architecture, but would have been recognized in its gradients by a Greek
mountain goat, been grouped about streets so steep it was painful to think of Poe toiling up them. Sigbjørn's notes were in the

wrong order, and it must have been morning then, and not
sunset as it was in the other house with the old lady, when he
went to the Valentine Museum. He saw Lee's house again, and
a faint feeling of the beauty of the whole frostbound city outside came to his mind, then a picture of a Confederate white
house, near a gigantic red-brick factory chimney, with far below a glimpse of an old cobbled street, and a lone figure crossing
a waste, as between three centuries, from the house toward the
railway tracks and this chimney, which belonged to the Bone
Dry Fertilizer Company. But in the sequence of his notes 'Please
pull the bell, to make it ring,' on Lee's house, had seemed to
provide a certain musical effect of solemnity, yet ushering him
instead into the Poe museum which Sigbjørn now in memory
re-entered.

Inside Valentine Museum, with Poe's relics [he read once more]
Please
Do not smoke
Do not run
Do not touch walls or exhibits
Observation of these rules will insure your own and others' enjoy-
ment of the museum.
– Blue silk coat and waistcoat, gift of the Misses Boykin, that
belonged to one of George Washington's dentists.

Sigbjørn closed his eyes, in his mind Shelley's crematory gums
and the gift of the Misses Boykin struggling for a moment
helplessly, then he returned to the words that followed. They
were Poe's own, and formed part of some letters once presumably written in anguished and private desperation, but which
were now to be perused at leisure by anyone whose enjoyment
of them would be 'insured' so long as they neither smoked
nor ran nor touched the glass case in which, like the gums (on
the other side of the world), they were preserved. He read:

Excerpt from a letter by Poe – after having been dismissed from
West Point – to his foster father. Feb. 21, 1831.
'It will however be the last time I ever trouble any human being –
I feel I am on a sick bed from which I shall never get up.'

Sigbjørn calculated with a pang that Poe must have written

these words almost seven years to the day after Keats's death, then, that far from never having got up from his sick bed, he had risen from it to change, thanks to Baudelaire, the whole course of European literature, yes, and not merely to trouble, but to frighten the wits out of several generations of human beings with such choice pieces as 'King Pest,' 'The Pit and the Pendulum,' and 'A Descent into the Maelstrom,' not to speak of the effect produced by the compendious and prophetic *Eureka*.

My *ear* has been too shocking for any description – I am wearing away every day, even if my last sickness had not completed it.

Sigbjørn finished his grappa and ordered another. The sensation produced by reading these notes was really very curious. First, he was conscious of himself reading them here in this Roman bar, then of himself in the Valentine Museum in Richmond, Virginia, reading the letters through the glass case and copying fragments from these down, then of poor Poe sitting blackly somewhere writing them. Beyond this was the vision of Poe's foster father likewise reading some of these letters, for all he knew unheedingly, yet solemnly putting them away for what turned out to be posterity, these letters which, whatever they might not be, were certainly – he thought again – intended to be private. But were they indeed? Even here at this extremity Poe must have felt that he was transcribing the story that was E. A. Poe, at this very moment of what he conceived to be his greatest need, his final – however consciously engineered – disgrace, felt a certain reluctance, perhaps, to send what he wrote, as if he were thinking: Damn it, I could use some of that, it may not be so hot, but it is at least too good to waste on my foster father. Some of Keats's own published letters were not different. And yet it was almost bizarre how, among these glass cases, in these museums, to what extent one revolved about, was hemmed in by, this cinereous evidence of anguish. Where was Poe's astrolabe, Keat's tankard of claret, Shelley's 'Useful Knots for the Yachtsman'? It was true that Shelley himself might not have been aware of the aromatic gums, but even that beautiful and irrelevant circumstantiality that was the gift of the Misses Boykin seemed not without its suggestion of suffering, at least for George Washington.

Baltimore, April 12, 1833.
I am perishing – absolutely perishing for want of aid. And yet I am not idle – nor have I committed any offence against society which would render me deserving of so hard a fate. For God's sake pity me and save me from destruction.

E. A. POE

Oh, God, thought Sigbjørn. But Poe had held out another sixteen years. He had died in Baltimore at the age of forty. Sigbjørn himself was nine behind on that game so far, and – with luck – should win easily. Perhaps if Poe had held out a little longer – perhaps if Keats – he turned over the pages of his notebook rapidly, only to be confronted by the letter from Severn:

My dear Sir:
Keats has changed somewhat for the worse – at least his mind has much – very much – yet the blood has ceased to come . . . but the fatal prospect hangs . . . *for his knowledge of internal anatomy . . . largely adds to his torture.*

Suppliziato, strangolato, he thought . . . *The lower is the true prison. And many others.* Nor have I committed any offense against society. Not much you hadn't, brother. Society might pay you the highest honors, even to putting your relics in the company of the waistcoat belonging to George Washington's dentist, but in its heart it cried: – *dirty stinking Degenerate Bobs was here from Boston, North End, Mass. Warp son of a bitch!* . . . 'On Saturday a gentleman came to cast his hand and foot . . .' Had anybody done that, Sigbjørn wondered, tasting his new grappa, and suddenly cognizant of his diminishing Guggenheim, compared, that was, Keats and Poe? – But compare in what sense, Keats, with what, in what sense, with Poe? What was it he wanted to compare? Not the aesthetic of the two poets, nor the breakdown of *Hyperion,* in relation to Poe's conception of the short poem, nor yet the philosophic ambition of the one, with the philosophic achievement of the other. Or could that more properly be discerned as negative capability, as

opposed to negative achievement? Or did he merely wish to
relate their melancholias? potations? hangovers? Their sheer
guts – which commentators so obligingly forgot! – character,
in a high sense of that word, the sense in which Conrad sometimes understood it, for were they not in their souls like hapless
shipmasters, determined to drive their leaky commands full of
valuable treasure at all costs, somehow, into port, and always
against time, yet through all but interminable tempest, typhoons
that so rarely abated? Or merely what seemed funereally analogous within the mutuality of their shrines? Or he could even
speculate, starting with Baudelaire again, upon what the French
movie director Epstein who had made *La Chute de la Maison
Usher* in a way that would have delighted Poe himself, might
have done with *The Eve of St Agnes: And they are gone!* ...
'For God's sake pity me and save me from destruction!'

Ah ha, now he thought he had it: did not the preservation of
such relics betoken – beyond the filing cabinet of the malicious
foster father who wanted to catch one out – less an obscure
revenge for the poet's nonconformity, than for his magical
monopoly, his possession of words? On the one hand he could
write his translunar 'Ulalume,' his enchanted 'To a Nightin-
gale' (which might account for the *Field Book of Western
Birds*), on the other was capable of saying, simply, 'I am perishing ... For God's sake pity me ...' You see, after all, he's just
like folks ... What's this? ... Conversely, there might appear
almost a tragic condescension in remarks such as Flaubert's
often quoted 'Ils sont dans le vrai' perpetuated by Kafka – Kaf
– and others, and addressed to child-bearing rosy-cheeked
and jolly humanity at large. Condescension, nay, inverse self-
approval, something downright unnecessary. And Flaub – Why
should they be dans le vrai any more than the artist was dans
le vrai? All people and poets are much the same but some poets
are more the same than others, as George Orwell might have
said. George Or – And yet, what modern poet would be caught
dead (though they'd do their best to catch him all right) with
his 'For Christ's sake send aid,' unrepossessed, unincinerated,
to be put in a glass case? It was a truism to say that poets not
only were, but looked like folks these days. Far from ostensible

nonconformists, as the daily papers, the very writers themselves – more shame to them – took every opportunity triumphantly to point out, they dressed like, and as often as not were bank clerks, or, marvelous paradox, engaged in advertising. It was true. He, Sigbjørn, dressed like a bank clerk himself – how else should he have courage to go into a bank? It was questionable whether poets especially, in uttermost private, any longer allowed themselves to say things like 'For God's sake pity me!' Yes, they had become more like folks even than folks. And the despair in the glass case, all private correspondence carefully destroyed, yet destined to become ten thousand times more public than ever, viewed through the great glass case of art, was now transmuted into hieroglyphics, masterly compressions, obscurities to be deciphered by experts – yes, and poets – like Sigbjørn Wilderness. Wil –

And many others. Probably there was a good idea somewhere, lurking among these arrant self-contradictions; pity could not keep him from using it, nor a certain sense of horror that he felt all over again that these mummified and naked cries of agony should lie thus exposed to human view in permanent incorruption, as if embalmed evermore in their separate eternal funeral parlors: separate, yet not separate, for was it not as if Poe's cry from Baltimore, in a mysterious manner, in the manner that the octet of a sonnet, say, is answered by its sestet, had already been answered, seven years before, by Keats's cry from Rome; so that according to the special reality of Sigbjørn's notebook at least, Poe's own death appeared like something extraformal, almost extraprofessional, an afterthought. Yet inerrably it was part of the same poem, the same story. 'And yet the fatal prospect hangs . . .' 'Severn, lift me up, for I am dying.' 'Lift them up, keep them away.' Dr Swell's Root Beer.

Good idea or not, there was no more room to implement his thoughts within this notebook (the notes on Poe and Richmond ran, through Fredericksburg, into his remarks upon Rome, the Mamertine Prison, and Keats's house, and vice versa), so Sigbjørn brought out another one from his trousers pocket.

This was a bigger notebook altogether, its paper stiffer and stronger, showing it dated from before the war, and he had

brought it from America at the last minute, fearing that such
might be hard to come by abroad.

In those days he had almost given up taking notes: every
new notebook bought represented an impulse, soon to be over-
laid, to write afresh; as a consequence he had accumulated a
number of notebooks like this one at home, yet which were
almost empty, which he had never taken with him on his more
recent travels since the war, else a given trip would have seemed
to start off with a destructive stoop, from the past, in its soul:
this one had looked an exception so he'd packed it.

Just the same, he saw, it was not innocent of writing: several
pages at the beginning were covered with his handwriting, so
shaky and hysterical of appearance, that Sigbjørn had to put
on his spectacles to read it. Seattle, he made out. July? 1939.
Seattle! Sigbjørn swallowed some grappa hastily. Lo, death
hath reared himself a throne in a strange city lying alone far
down within the dim west, where the good and the bad and the
best and the rest, have gone to their eternal worst! The lower is
the true Seattle ... Sigbjørn felt he could be excused for not
fully appreciating Seattle, its mountain graces, in those days.
For these were not notes he had found but the draft of a letter,
written in the notebook because it was that type of letter possible
for him to write only in a bar. A bar? Well, one might have
called it a bar. For in those days, in Seattle, in the state of Washington, they still did not sell hard liquor in bars – as, for that
matter, to this day they did not, in Richmond, in the state of
Virginia – which was half the gruesome and pointless point of
his having been in the state of Washington. LIC-OFF-PREM,
he thought. No, no, go not to Virginia Dare ... Neither twist
Pepso – tight-rooted! – for its poisonous bane. The letter dated
– no question of his recognition of it, though whether he'd
made another version and posted it he had forgotten – from
absolutely the lowest ebb of those low tides of his life, a time
marked by the baleful circumstance that the small legacy on
which he then lived had been suddenly put in charge of a Los
Angeles lawyer, to whom this letter indeed was written, his
family, who considered him incompetent, having refused to
have anything further to do with him, as, in effect, did the

lawyer, who had sent him to a religious-minded family of Buch-
manite tendencies in Seattle on the understanding he be en-
trusted with not more than 25c a day.

Dear Mr Van Bosch :

It is, psychologically, apart from anything else, of extreme urgency
that I leave Seattle and come to Los Angeles to see you. I fear a
complete mental collapse else. I have cooperated far beyond what I
thought was the best of my ability here in the matter of liquor and
I have also tried to work hard, so far, alas, without selling anything.
I cannot say either that my ways have been as circumscribed exactly
as I thought they would be by the Mackorkindales, who at least have
seen my point of view on some matters, and if they pray for guidance
on the very few occasions when they do see fit to exceed the stipulated
25c a day, they are at least sympathetic with my wishes to return.
This may be because the elder Mackorkindale is literally and
physically worn out following me through Seattle, or because you
have failed to supply sufficient means for my board, but this is
certainly as far as the sympathy goes. In short, they sympathize, but
cannot honestly agree ; nor will they advise you I should return. And
in anything that applies to my writing – and this I find almost the
hardest to bear – I am met with the opinion that I 'should put all
that behind me.' If they merely claimed to be abetting yourself or
my parents in this it would be understandable, but this judgment is
presented to me independently, somewhat blasphemously in my
view – though without question they believe it – as coming directly
from God, who stoops daily from on high to inform the Mackorkindales, if not in so many words, that as a serious writer I am lousy.
Scenting some hidden truth about this, things being what they are,
I would find it discouraging enough if it stopped there, and were not
beyond that the hope held out, miraculously congruent also with that
of my parents and yourself, that I could instead turn myself into a
successful writer of advertisements. Since I cannot but feel, I repeat,
and feel respectfully, that they are sincere in their beliefs, all I can say
is that in this daily rapprochement with their Almighty in Seattle I
hope some prayer that has slipped in by mistake to let the dreadful
man for heaven's sake return to Los Angeles may eventually be
answered. For I find it impossible to describe my spiritual isolation
in this place, nor the gloom into which I have sunk. I enjoyed of
course the seaside – the Mackorkindales doubtless reported to you
that the Group were having a small rally in Bellingham (I wish you
could go to Bellingham one day) – but I have completely exhausted

any therapeutic value in my stay. God knows I ought to know, I shall never recover in this place, isolated as I am from Primrose who, whatever you may say, I want with all my heart to make my wife. It was with the greatest of anguish that I discovered that her letters to me were being opened, finally, even having to hear lectures on her moral character by those who had read these letters, which I had thus been prevented from replying to, causing such pain to her as I cannot think of. This separation from her would be an unendurable agony, without anything else, but as things stand I can only say I would be better off in a prison, in the worst dungeon that could be imagined, than to be incarcerated in this damnable place with the highest suicide rate in the Union. Literally I am dying in this macabre hole and I appeal to you to send me, out of the money that is after all mine, enough that I may return. Surely I am not the only writer, there have been others in history whose ways have been misconstrued and who have failed ... who have won through ... success ... publicans and sinners ... I have no intention –

Sigbjørn broke off reading, and resisting an impulse to tear the letter out of the notebook, for that would loosen the pages, began meticulously to cross it out, line by line.

And now this was half done he began to be sorry. For now, damn it, he wouldn't be able to use it. Even when he'd written it he must have thought it a bit too good for poor old Van Bosch, though one admitted that wasn't saying much. Wherever or however he could have used it. And yet, what if they had found this letter – whoever 'they' were – and put it, glass-encased, in a museum among *his* relics? Not much – still, you never knew ! – Well, they wouldn't do it now. Anyhow, perhaps he would remember enough of it ... 'I am dying, absolutely perishing.' 'What have I done to them?' 'My dear Sir.' 'The worst dungeon.' And many others: and *dirty stinking Degenerate Bobs was here from Boston, North End, Mass. Warp son – !*

Sigbjørn finished his fifth unregenerate grappa and suddenly gave a loud laugh, a laugh which, as if it had realized itself it should become something more respectable, turned immediately into a prolonged – though on the whole relatively pleasurable – fit of coughing....

ELEPHANT AND COLOSSEUM

It was the early afternoon of a brilliantly sunny day in Rome, a young blue midsummer moon tilted down over the Borghese Gardens, and under the awning on the sidewalk terrace of the Restaurant Rupe Tarpea, crowded by men and women talking, a lone man named Kennish Drumgold Cosnahan sat drinking a glass of milk with an expression of somber panic.

'And this panic, Cosnahan, would you say that this is merely due to the fact that you don't know how to ask for a glass of wine in Italian?'

'Something like that, Drumgold, something like that.'

'Or rather, while you can manage a stern "vino rosso, per favore," in a wine shop or trattoria, you're afraid that in this place they'd bring you a whole expensive bottle you couldn't afford.'

True, Cosnahan did not know how to ask for a glass of milk in Italian either, for all that he'd had a grandmother born in Sicily, but there having appeared a homeless glass upon the tray of a waiter glancing about him, he had cleared his throat, taken his courage and murmured something like 'Nel mezzo del cammin di nostra vita mi ritrovai in –' which was about all the other 'Italian' he knew (and certainly all the Dante).

His presence upon the terrace validated in this curious fashion, Cosnahan sat waiting for the increase of confidence he felt it should bring about. But no, glancing from time to time at the novel he had laid rather consciously on the table, already he began to be afraid of finishing the wretched glass of milk, for that would bring the ordeal of payment that much closer, another ordeal, also linguistic in character, for it meant speaking to the waiter again, who even now was giving him a renewed fore-and-aft look.

Since it wasn't merely the milk he would be paying for (any more than anyone who bought that book would only pay for the spiritual nourishment it contained) but the commanding site of the Restaurant Rupe Tarpea upon the Via Veneto, to say nothing of the three other sidewalk restaurants on the other three corners created by the crossroads with the Via Sicilia and *their* rent, or their exquisitely dressed female occupants eating ices, to whose charming activities he felt he would be expected also, obscurely, to contribute; as naturally he would be paying also for the view, should he turn around, of the gateway of the Porta Pincia, and finally for the Via Vittorio Veneto itself, with its sidewalks ten feet broad, and its plane trees casting dappled shadows on either side as it swept in great curves down toward the invisible Piazza Barberini; the Via Veneto, which, with its ceaseless traffic of horsecabs and bicycles, combined with expensive American, Italian and English motorcars, gave one not merely the physical sense of its own spaciousness, but produced in him – when now and then he forgot his besetting unease – that expansive feeling of great riches and peace, that purring roaring feeling, yet somehow quiet as a Rolls Royce engine, of life being at a sort of permanent flood, as if there had never been a first world war, let alone a second one, which was like an evocation of 1913, of those truly pre-war days from which he retained only this curious yet powerful sensation, when with his parents he must have visited London or Dublin, or at least Weston-super-Mare, at the age of five.

'Yes this deficiency in even the first principles of most foreign languages, Cosnahan, in one whose unconscious mind must be a veritable treasure house of the literature of the Gael – do you not find it strange? – in one whose lineage, if it does not actually go back to Oshin, the –'

'I do, Drumgold! And it makes one wonder sometimes if I am human. Ta dty lhiasagh dty ghoarn !'

'Thy recompense is in thine own hand . . .' Cosnahan picked up the novel that had fallen to the sidewalk and then, with a covert glance at the waiter, the papers which had dropped out of it. He rearranged the wrapper of the novel, regarding as he did so with a suddenly assumed official air the photograph printed on the back; it showed the same face that was reflected in the window, only without the somberness or panic. Happy was the word, and the face appeared considerably younger, though the photograph had been taken only sixteen months before. *Ark from Singapore*. Not a very good title. Arthur should have thought of a better one. On the other side of the cover was pictured the captain of a merchant vessel with his pipe falling out of his mouth, taken aback – and no wonder – before the weathercloths of the bridge, over which spray was blowing, at the spectacle of a healthy young elephant emerging from his chartroom. High seas were rising about the steamer . . .

Cosnahan searched the face in the photograph. He was disconcerted slightly by the sense of difference, of no longer looking altogether at his own likeness. Yet what was uncanny was the way those eyes looked back at him. He might have been looking at the young Emmanuel Swedenborg, or somebody, in a lighter mood. Yet this afternoon Cosnahan could not wholly think himself back into the happy scene of that snapshot, nor into the whole person it portrayed, of the youngish man, perhaps thirty-five, bronzed, fit, and wearing bathing trunks, arm-in-arm with the pretty gay wild-looking girl wearing shorts and a jersey, smiling and holding up to the camera a tomcat of whiskerando mien, closely resembling Theodore Roosevelt . . . The Cosnahans in Nantucket, it said, beneath it, with Citron-le-Taciturne.

Published by Arthur Wilding and Co., 30th Thousand, the words were added on the flap.

That had been Arthur's idea too, that photograph, Cosnahan reflected, and Arthur who'd taken it, and Arthur also who had named their then nameless new cat, that time he'd flown down to Nantucket for the weekend to help them correct the proofs. At midnight, having mistakenly decided that some Danish beer would keep them awake, Cosnahan had said: 'For the Lord's sake, let's read something else by someone else!' so Art had picked a book at random, of ancient biography, from the shelves, and read aloud, in a sepulchral voice, some words to this effect: 'As a young man I had often brushed against the ghastly wig of the Duke of Brunswick, traversing the corridors of night restaurants, in the hot breath of gas, patchouli, and spiced meats; at Bignons, on the couch at the rear, Citron-le-

Taciturne had appeared to me one evening, eating a slice of foie gras . . .'

Whereupon their untitled cat had sprung through the half-open window onto Arthur's shoulder, and had ever after been called Citron-le-Taciturne.

And now a pang struck Cosnahan wondering where the little cat was. Perhaps at this moment, though it was hard to calculate what time it might be in Nantucket, he was having his afternoon snack, prior to making his evening inspection of the ropes and hawsers, and to dropping in, it could be, at the Tavern on the Moors, though they often invented feline hostelries for him, such as the Claw-bar and Grill, or the Ratskeller, or even, when it seemed he might have strayed as far as New York, the Mouseum of Modern Art. Or it could be, since he was devoted to Lovey, that he had followed her to the summer theater where she was playing, and had been adopted by the cast, was even performing in the play.

'Success ! –' Cosnahan lit his pipe.

There was something implausible and self-defeating about his particular brand of it, as if – he was thinking of the dream he'd had last night – a play should somehow run for three years on one Saturday matinee. But the rub was that Cosnahan's sales had remained within that inclusive figure of thirty thousand for half a year, most of the copies having been sold in the first few months, most of them actually in the first weeks. Such a success, resembling one of those earthquakes which, by the time one has got used to their roars and jolts, are already subsiding into their equating minor shocks and tremblings, might be all in the day's work to Arthur. Not so to Cosnahan. It had stopped his working altogether. He'd been stopped cold ever since those first few weeks, hadn't been able to do another stroke.

The first edition had contained some advance notices, some even by major writers who, engaged in gloomy and somber strifes of their own, often tend to turn a kindly eye toward humor, in many cases even bad humor, which they may well consider to be better than none. But for the fourth edition – and this was the fourth edition before him – Art's partner, who had not liked the book too well to begin with, insisted on a new idea: he wanted to give the impression that its reception had not been merely highbrow (this anomaly had been known to occur not merely in the realm of light literature but in the movie and the comic strip), but had been spontaneous from Honolulu to the North Pole. So he had quoted from a host of more popular eulogies.

Reading these later eulogies produced in Cosnahan a bizarre mental commotion as of some endless mirrored reduplication, as if it were not merely that all these reviews had been written before of countless other books, but that for a moment he felt like an eternal writer eternally sitting in the eternal city, eternally reading precisely the same sort of notices from which he always derived precisely the same eternal feelings of mingled pleasure, pain, gratitude, sadness, amusement, dismay and beautiful vain-glory; though in another way, of course, it could not at all feel like this because, satiated and indeed tottering with praise though he was, when he read any of his reviews, or even, as here, bits of reviews, it was always as if he were reading them for the first time: against this too, was it really possible that any such extraordinary observations as this had ever appeared of any book, possible that he was, after all, a unique case? 'Sheer joy' – he read; 'if you like a mixture of Conrad and Algernon Blackwood at his best, then Cosnahan's your man.' 'A mixture of early Conrad and Wodehouse at his funniest – sheer spoofery – I roared!' said another generous fellow. 'These bright and breezy pages,' another was content with. 'And if you can imagine a combination of Jack London, James Stephens and James Oliver Curwood – with a bit of roaring O'Neill thrown in for good measure, there you have Cosnahan!' added another. 'Elfin humor – with a robust touch – a miracle!' qualified someone else. While a last good-hearted chap, whom it was invidious to suspect of not having read the beginning either, observed, 'There is a passage of rare philosophy at the end.' Elsewhere attention was called to the impartiality of the publishers, either that, or it was a mistake, or Art's partner hadn't been able to resist it, by quoting merely the terse subscription to Cosnahan's photograph in the *Time* review, which stated bluntly and ambiguously, 'In the Arabian Sea, a Jumbo,' and redirected finally back to the author by means of a green detachable slip to the book itself on which was printed: 'The world is reading America's new and greatest humorist! Kennish Drumgold Cosnahan! *Ark from Singapore* has now been translated into Italian, French, German, Swedish, etc.'

Nor was this all.

Kennish Drumgold Cosnahan [Cosnahan was now informed] was born in Ballaugh in 1908, in the old Kingdom of the Isle of Man. He is a collateral descendant of the renowned Cronkbane family, and another forefather was instrumental in translating the Bible into Manx. Born of strictly Methodist parents, one of his brothers, Matthias Cosnahan, became a Catholic priest. One of his uncles, however, is a Mohammedan, and he finds the famous name Drumgold of obscure origin, though there was one other Drumgold in the Sicilian branch of the family. Another brother disappeared and is at present a member of the government of St Helena. Kennish he believes to be a more autochthonous Manx name than his surname, though not, he says, as indigenous as Quayne, Quaggan, Quillish, Qualtrough, Quirk, Quale or Looney. Young Cosnahan could only speak the old Gaelic until he was nearly nine, though he had visited England several times. Cosnahan was sent to a school in England when, in his own words, 'A Zeppelin dropped a bomb on me. This,' he adds, 'was the beginning and end of all my war service.' [In fact he had spent seven months in the American merchant marine during the last war, but had seen no action, save once when his ship ran aground off Venezuela, trying to ram a nonexistent submarine.]

In 1924 he went to sea before the mast, later serving as a carpenter's mate, and in *Ark from Singapore* he has reached back to this early experience, in 1927, on a sailing ship, with a deck cargo of lions, tigers, and elephants from the Straits Settlements bound for the Dublin Zoo –

Dear Arthur, Cosnahan thought. Tigers – there had been no tigers, or lions either. As if the company of one elephant, five black panthers, ten snakes, and a wild boar had not been enough! As for the sailing ship, it was just a British tramp steamer exactly like the one on the cover, save that this one had curiously acquired an American flag.

– two years after which he emigrated to the United States and settled in the island of Nantucket. It will be recalled that of Melville's characters in *Moby-Dick* one whaler, described simply as 'grizzled,' came from the Isle of Man.

Cosnahan is the recipient of an award for saving life at sea from the Japanese government, of which he will only say, 'Before the war, of course.'

(Yes, quite true. But it had been Mrs Cosnahan who gave Art that bit of information; he never would have – he hoped – himself. Just the same, he rather liked it . . .)

Cosnahan is also the author of several well-known Manx Gaelic poems, some hymns which are still played in church, and is highly regarded in jazz circles when he can be persuaded to play as a cool exponent of bebop upon the bull fiddle. He married Lovey L'Hirondelle, a young actress, in 1940. They have no children, and make their home all the year round in Nantucket, swimming, playing tennis, and in the company of their cat, Citron-le-Taciturne . . .

Cosnahan laid his pipe aside, took a sip of milk, threw away a crumpled Gauloise from Paris days he found in his pocket and discovered an American cigarette he could not light because he now had no matches. An Italian returning to the next table offered him one, and Cosnahan, bowing his thanks, fleetingly hoped he would somehow manage to identify his beneficiary with the photograph on the cover of the novel, which was lying on the table with that side up : but the man had stooped courteously to retrieve a newspaper clipping that had fluttered out, and himself bowing, turned away.

Cosnahan reseated himself and studied the clipping which, having a more genuine appearance than the others he possessed bearing the clipping bureau's letterhead – it had been culled by himself from a newspaper when in the Isle of Man, after long search – made it all the more painful that it should contain what it did. It was the solitary notice that had appeared on the English edition of his book in his old home, and beneath the pastoral caption, *The Browsing Manxwoman*, ran as follows :

This book, though bearing upon it the once distinguished native name of Cosnahan –

(Once distinguished, reflected Cosnahan. Who had undistinguished it? Himself? His brother John, in his Napoleonic haunts, or his brother Matthias, in his priestly vestments? The name was less natively Manx than Irish anyhow.)

– of Cosnahan, and which is reported to have had a considerable vogue in the United States, does not reflect credit upon the citizens of our island, and is of very little interest to our readers. Of a type of humour that was outmoded a dozen years ago, and dealing with the banal subject of a shirp carrying a cargo of wild animals that break loose from their cages, instead of being hilarious, it is just deadly dull. Definitely not recommended.

Cosnahan suddenly catching sight of his reflection in the window at this point as he looked up was rewarded by a glimpse of his face as it perhaps essentially was. That Swedenborgian look was still there, but of an elder Swedenborg this time, who worries whether the printer's got an angel in the wrong paragraph; and it had that decidedly Manx look, of the man who knows wood or boats, who wonders if he's made a mistake and if so is prepared to be angry with himself. Cosnahan turned the clipping over. LOCH PROMENADE CONVENIENCES UN-SIGHTLY, *Suggestion work be stopped. Town Council agrees to carry on.* What? He'd never noticed the reverse side of the clipping before.

Councillor Eccleshare [he read] declared that the building would have looked better if it were only a couple of feet high instead of forty, and similar to the conveniences on Queens Promenade. Councillor Timmons considered some machinery should be set in motion to enable the Council to discuss the matter and that now was the time to stop the building if the matter was going to be reconsidered. There was no point in finishing the building and then, on second thoughts, tearing it down. Alderman Shillicorn objected that the conveniences were not only ready to be opened but in fact had been in use for several months. The conveniences were second to none in the British Isles and were a tribute to the engineers who had been working against difficulties.

This indeed added up to a more sensible review of his book than the other, and he put the clipping in his pocket, feeling he might be able to use it, and oddly in a better mood as he brought out the letter written in pencil and begun that morning in the sidewalk café beneath his pension, over a cup of coffee: the letter was to his wife, and reading it over his face reflected in the window became gentle and composed.

What a beastly disappointment she couldn't have come to Europe with him. And yet had she come it would have involved only a worse disappointment for her. Lovey (her nickname came from Lovey Lee, an old recording by the Memphis Five, that she and Cosnahan used to play when they were first in love: first it was only her nickname, then nobody ever called her Margaret, now it was her stage name too) was an actress, who had almost stopped acting after she married him. It was one of those inexplicable runs of bad luck: she was too young, she was too old, the show folded before it reached New York, or once, agonizingly, after weeks of rehearsals, excitement, congratulation, the 'chance of a lifetime,' after the play opened in Boston the author rewrote the whole thing and changed her part to that of a ten-year-old boy. But now, at the last moment, after all their plans had been made for the trip to Europe they could at last afford, she'd been offered the lead in this show at the Nantucket summer theater. Whether he had his own success partly to blame, or to thank for this, he didn't know, but Cosnahan, seeing her delight outweighed her dismay, would have put off the trip. He hated travel for its own sake, especially without his wife, they could always go next year, whereas the show, if it succeeded, would go on to New York. Cosnahan had stayed long enough to see from the rehearsals there was every indication the play was going to be a hit, but meantime his brother Matthias had cabled to say that their mother, who was very old, was seriously ill in the Isle of Man. And so, after all, he had come over alone, and left three days before the opening night of Lovey's show. And since his own health forbade him to fly he had arrived too late. His mother – a Methodist to the last, to Matt's disappointment – was dead and buried before he even arrived in Liverpool.

Cosnahan wrote his wife a note every day: this was one of his longer letters, though the only one he'd written with any family news other than the sorrowfully inexpressible, or to say how much he regretted his mother had never known her. First he told her, as always, how much he loved her (one proof of which lay in his writing at all, since even the composition of a letter had become difficult) and missed her, congratulated her on the continuing success of the play, answered a few minor questions, asked after the house, and, naturally, Citron-le-Taciturne.

Then he informed her that he still hadn't seen his brother Matt, who had already been obliged to depart for a Catholic congress in Bruges by the time he, Cosnahan, arrived in the Isle of Man. Matt's position as a priest in the island was a bit embarrassing under the circumstances, which had not been made any easier by the antics of their eldest brother John, who, a politician of the extreme left wing, or no wing, some kind of anarchist of the ancient gentle Proudhon persuasion, had just tried, as she had possibly read in the papers, gently to overthrow the government of St Helena where he was at present incarcerated – unless to say that in regard to St Helena at all was an overstatement. Matthias could not be visited at present where he was (as for that matter neither could John) but was coming to Rome where he had business and Cosnahan expected to meet him at any moment now. Nor had he seen Art yet, who'd written him from Paris, so Cosnahan knew he was in Europe at least, that *he* would be in Rome at any moment too; anyway Cosnahan was continually on the watch for them both. Then, because he didn't want to say that if Matt didn't show up, he wouldn't have met anybody in Europe he knew who'd ever heard of his great American triumph, and because he thought it might amuse her, he told her about the Pensione Borgnini where he lived . . .

But quite suddenly he laid his letter aside with a sigh. His first thought when he'd received Matt's cable on the ship: *Deeply regret Mother died June sixth writing Matt,* and the cable sent from Bellabella (its little railroad station full of fuchsia !) – Cosnahan's first thought had been : I'll write Mother and explain why I couldn't write her before she died; how my every breath hung on my success – on news of more success, on news of my book, now a best-seller in Dallas, now in

Tombstone, and now, God knows, in Eclectic, Alabam! And then on less success, and then on no success, but yet to be translated into Italian, Sanskrit, Esperanto, English! That was the reason I couldn't write you, dearest Mother, why I couldn't find time to send a word, and now I understand that all this I took to myself and wallowed in, you would have transmuted into true gold with the alchemy of your love, and read in it your own simple pride in your son. And then he realized: I'll never write to Mother again, never, never, write that letter I always put off, nor send her a lapis lazuli elephant again, nor tell a lie, nor boast to her, and what shall I do now when that emptiness comes round, the remorse for not having written, what shall I do without staying that remorse, and if I should lose even that remorse, what then?

As a matter of fact it was just such a thought that had stopped him going on with his letter. For the sudden reflection: I haven't written Mother this month, had come to him, quite consciously, before the augmenting and tragic reality had had time to banish it: she'd been dead a month, he'd scarcely written for a year ... Well, he loved his mother, and there was no sentimentality about it, she was a large-hearted and humorous woman, never mind how eccentric. The practical side of him considered his mother well out of it, since his father was dead too; though she had all of her senses, indeed more senses than she should have, she was fabulously old, there was little to hope for in the world left to her, and she would certainly be better off in the beyond with the old man: that was exactly how Cosnahan phrased it to himself: 'in the beyond with the old man.' But was she in the beyond, or, rather, the right sort of beyond with the old man? For the uncomfortable thought lingered that Matt might be right – that in any case it was not surprising he was anxious for his mother's soul, which anxiety had a sounder and rather more complex basis than that she happened to be a Methodist. For the curious thing about all this was, to tell the truth, Cosnahan's mother was a witch ...

Doubtless the literature is not large regarding the operation of the dark powers among the converts of John Wesley, Cosnahan thought, staring blankly into the orthodox depths of Rome.

But he was afraid that what the neighbors said had a foundation in fact. Actually his mother never used these powers save for good and he did not think she could help herself. And, unquestionably, she did not regard them as dark. As for the eerie reputation it gave the Cosnahans in Ballaugh, her gifts were also, in their wry manner, a social asset. Common sense suffered his mother not only to live, but to thrive. From as far back as Cosnahan could remember she was considerably in demand, for in Cosnahan's day poltergeist phenomena were fairly common in the Isle of Man and his mother had the capacity, more properly the attribute or the duty of a Catholic priest, of being able to halt these manifestations. And it was hard in one way to imagine anything more full of profoundly comic possibilities than this: an island beset by the diabolic, in which the phenomenon of coals hurtling out of the kitchen stove to hang in the air and drop one by one at leisure was no unusual occurrence, yet where they had driven out the very force that was capable of canceling the evil: the Catholic priest. Naturam expellas pitch-fork, something or other recurret! Throw out nature with a pitchfork but back she always comes! It was much as if God, with that all-wise sense of humor that Cosnahan respected increasingly the longer he remained as a guest upon His earth, had kept Mother Drumgold (as he feared they called her, though she rarely gave any tangential exhibition of her abilities more disturbing than keeping the kettle off the boil on Michaelmas Eve, and this only under extreme social pressure) up His sleeve, an heresiarch so extreme as to function almost like an outsister within the stern enemy camp, a Methodist most wonderfully Methodistic. Though only a Manx Methodist perhaps would be able to see nothing contradictory about it all.

Cosnahan was aware that the subject of witchcraft and the supernatural, by no means always the same thing, had suddenly undergone a startling recrudescence of popularity with the public mind within the last few years, and to him at least this was not strange, that admirable comedian Dostoievsky — for Cosnahan was a well-read man — having long ago hit upon what was, for him, a satisfactory and common-sense solution, at least of the latter, that would have been appreciated by any Tourist Trophy motorbicycle racer in the Isle of Man, briefly that the nearer you approached the goal, the nearer that goal, viewed from another angle (no matter how many circuits of the island you had to make first), approached you; which was to say that so long as man was crouched headlong on his handlebars toward death, the nearer death, and the world of ghosts, approached man: in short, to mix his metaphors with clichés, as his mind always did whether he liked it or not, if man was intent on having one foot in the grave, he must take the consequences. These consequences had been reflected in literature by a preoccupation with the next world, and hence with 'dark forces,' so enthusiastic that it seemed almost to adumbrate a kind of imminent doom which, on second thoughts, either had already come to pass, was impossible, or unnecessary, and in any case if you believed in the Resurrection and the Life didn't matter so much – unless it was to prophets with a stake in the business. But between merely writing about supernatural or unlawful powers and actually being in possession of them was, to speak literally, a world of difference. And Cosnahan was only too well equipped to say this because he possessed unlawful powers himself, or at least powers not above suspicion. Both Matthias and he had inherited within limits, with Matt it was innate before he found divine ratification, the power to put a stop to the same phenomena, though they discovered this by merest accident when they were quite young. Since the results of these phenomena are sometimes serious (and there is always the poltergeist to be considered) Cosnahan often thought it was this that sent Matt into the Church, though his father had felt differently, maintaining it had something to do with his joining the navy.

For himself Cosnahan found it hard to get away from the suspicion that he was a sort of demon, or a demon in reverse. Ever since that Christmas morning long ago when his mother, with whatever motives, profound, or endearing, or occult plans for his future, had presented him with a gray suède elephant – a trifle large for a periapt – he'd been conscious of something peculiar in his nature. Odd things happened to him. Inexplic-

able coincidences, and at school geometrical problems beyond
his power he had often found solved as by another intelligence,
on those occasions, that was, when another human intelligence
was not available. True the ineradicable beliefs held to this day
upon his island, in the all-dreaded Buggane for example, or the
sweet fancy that at the new moon the sea birds that rode the
ninth wave from the shore were the souls of the dead, did not
exactly tend toward the mundane. 'The supernatural,' as even
the Browsing Manxwoman would admit, 'must always be the
deepest part of any Manxman's nature . . .' But it was the aroma
of frying Cosnahan that more than once had risen to his nostrils
during his dreams that sometimes gave him cause for alarm. In
ancient days he had comforted himself by the reflection that his
expurgatorial talent, inherited as it was from a God-fearing and
tender-hearted woman, was of heaven rather than hell. No
sooner had he at last found consolation along these lines, however, than the power seemed to fade, to be replaced by another
curious faculty, of an almost flawless and Homeric uselessness,
when it was considered that soon after it took possession of him
he set out on another voyage to sea: Cosnahan discovered he
was a water-diviner. He almost still was. Indeed he still felt the
tug sometimes, even without a wand, though much more rarely,
for it was as if ever since his book's publication – albeit he
wouldn't put it to himself quite like this – 'his powers had
been falling off,' so that he hadn't known whether to be glad
or sorry when he experienced that old uneasiness again only
the other day in St Peter's, where they were making excavations
in search of St Peter's tomb, and he had thought of asking a
priest were they looking for water too there underground, because in that case he felt he knew where it was. But he had been
too shy to do this . . .

Cosnahan sent a mute prayer to heaven for Mother Drumgold's soul and went on reading what he'd written about his
pensione; his room, large, clean, airy (the Pensione Borgnini
was only a hundred yards from where he sat, in the Via Sicilia –
so near, yet in terms of expensiveness and décor, so far), but so
noisy he was kept awake half the night. No running water,
and the Mexican plumbing a mile away between the dining

room and the kitchen. Lack of conveniences didn't bother him much, they were used to that in Nantucket, it was the combination of discomfort, lack of privacy and noise that distracted him: no locks on the doors, and no numbers, so that one was constantly wandering into the wrong room and surprising people: the massive Swedish woman, who worked for an airplane factory, saying: 'He said my heart was a fortress,' the Englishwoman she lived with, who always wore slacks and couldn't be left alone since her breakdown and who kept trying to make purchases with English money . . . Cosnahan glanced away from his letter down the Via Veneto up which a horsecab, containing Nikolai Gogol, with tragic beaming nose, and smoking a cigar, seemed eternally plodding . . . (But how cruel to make fun of the poor Swedish woman, the consciousness of whose massiveness perhaps stabbed her to the heart, or the poor Englishwoman whose breakdown could not have been any fun for her! No wonder writers stopped writing. Better to make fun of Drumgold Cosnahan, at those times when inscribing his unlikely name for the police in every such pension he had visited in Europe, a species of absolute torture to him, and his flawless incompetence as a linguist, and the unhappy fact of having forgotten so much of the old language, while being condemned half to think in it all the while. Better to write about animals, you could be funny about them without hurting anyone's feelings, not even your own – or could you? Better still not write at all . . .) And the woman who, after supper, he had overheard saying, 'My sweet sugar duckling waggle-tailed plum!'

Next he was trying to describe for his wife, because she particularly liked this kind of thing, the atmosphere of Rome: the peculiar flavor of the Roman mornings, the fresh cool air and hot sun, and the afternoons hot, and the 'unique golden quality of the Roman sunlight.' 'And the Corso Umberto, narrow, with screaming jammed trolley-buses, for the Via Veneto, where traffic is limited, is an exception, and the sidewalks only two feet wide that you can't stay on because of the crowd, and can't step off either, or you step under one of the buses, driven at terrific speed, one right behind another!' What on earth was this? Certainly this wasn't the way to keep Lovey's mind at

rest about him, the poor girl would be worrying enough abou
his fear of traffic as it was, and he was about to cross the sentenc
out when he saw the next one was even worse: 'The Piazz;
Venezia is an inferno, with twelve different kinds of buse
coming at you from every direction, and swarms of motor
scooters hurtling at you!'

Cosnahan crossed out both these sentences in such a way
that the 'Unique golden quality of the Roman sunlight' man
aged to flow with reasonable excuse into a description of the
Forum, with its white marble steps leading to nothing, anc
broken pillars among which the grass was green, and anothe1
sentence where he became rather grandiose about the 'sweep
and grandeur of the Eternal City,' which was nonetheless 'prouc
and cruel as it was beautiful,' and the tall dark columns, anc
dark red brick arches, and here were the broken pillars again
on the ground this time, like fallen trees, and the lovers among
the flowers, lying or sitting on the ground in the sunlight, jusl
as he would have liked to be lying or sitting on the ground with
her. Finally, since it didn't seem a particularly thoughtful idea
to describe the remarkable beauty of Italian women, he described instead the young monks, if they were monks, to be
seen everywhere, with their brown eyes and beards and saintly
faces, in their coarse brown robes, striding down the avenues
in their sandals, not failing to add that his identity with them
could not have been more complete . . .

After this he abandoned such descriptive flights and tried to
tell her what he'd been doing: sitting in Keats's house, sitting
in the dungeon once graced by the person of Vercingetorix,
and what was worse, for him, sitting every day in the American
Express. This was because Lovey's letters would arrive in a
bunch; only once in Rome had he received any mail from her,
and these letters mostly antedated the ones he had already received in Paris. Though in any event he would have hung
around the place, feeling in the American Express a certain
connection with Arthur, or even his anything but American
brother, Matthias, either of whom might turn up there. And of
course he'd been to the Colosseum, which reminded him of
Androcles and the Lion and also of the Albert Hall in a dentist's

nightmare. – At this point Cosnahan said how odd it felt to
have been once a European immigrant yet this to be his own
first visit to Rome. But he added that for the rest his visitations
must seem singularly pious to her. For, thinking of his mother,
and missing his wife as he did, it gave him a great deal of comfort to wander into the Roman churches, and even to light
candles within them ... This was about as far as he'd got in
the letter. It was a bit hard to explain that with no inbred belief
in the power of masses and holy water, he nonetheless seemed
to have a magical belief in the power of holy water and candles
to insure him, as well as Mother Drumgold, against the possible
consequences of their unorthodoxy. It was too complicated,
whereas what he felt was simple.

But he had somehow to tell his wife, which would delight
her, how, more impiously, he'd lain on a bench and gazed at the
roof of the Sistine Chapel, and otherwise unimpressed by
Michelangelo's muscular comic strip (though it was always possible that the introduction of Noah had afflicted him with an
obscure form of professional jealousy) he had thought of the
time they whitewashed the ceiling of their cottage in Nantucket,
and of the dreadful mixture running down their arms and dripping into their eyes. He might report too that in Raphael's
tapestry of the Supper at Emmaus he'd noted that the artist
with fine human foresight had provided an item which Rembrandt, in his incomparably greater interpretation, had over-
looked: a spare carafe of wine cooling by the disciples' side, an
observation he hoped would not be considered irreverent, anyway the Pope hadn't considered it irreverent to have the work
in the Vatican Museum.

And he could conclude by remarking that neither his besetting heresies, his Protestantism, nor the knowledge that there
were few Manx Catholics left – as he made out Matt intended
to shepherd most of them to Rome himself next year, Holy
Year, which was part of his business here now – had prevented
his taking it as a personal injury when he noticed that upon
the innumerable confession boxes in St Peter's almost every
known and unknown language was represented except Manx
Gaelic.

Which had seemed, Cosnahan laid down his letter and rested his chin on his hand, all the more reason why then and there he should say his Ayr ain t'ayns niau, Casherick dy row dt' ennym. Dy jig dty reeriaght, Dt' aigney dy row jeant er y thalloo myr te ayns niau. Cur dooin nyn arran jiu as gagh laa. As leih dooin nyn loghtyn – just as he had learned, God rest her soul, at Mother Drumgold's knee.

As we are forgiving to those who are committing trespasses us against, said the Manx. Assuming that there they were, those enemies, and, right at that moment Cosnahan looking away from his table and down the Via Veneto again, up which a huge new Cadillac the size of a conservatory was advancing soundlessly, should they recall all the beautiful old cobbled streets and ancient houses of Douglas that were still being destroyed or pulled down, and beautiful St Matthew's pulled down and the countryside ruined to make a Liverpool holiday. Yet perhaps this kind of assumption was the great fault of the Manx. And his great fault too. The entire population of the Isle of Man seemed to be trespassing against him, for one thing, because nobody recognized him at home now that he'd become so successful in America. By which he didn't mean merely on the plane of the Browsing Manxwoman. He hadn't even seen a familiar face in Douglas, unless you counted Illiam Dhone, a man, it was true, so unique now he thought of it he might be considered a civic welcome in himself.

For Illiam Dhone had been hanged half an age ago on an open plot of ground where St Barnabas' Church now stood, and by a freak turn of fortune's wheel, survived this unpleasant ordeal.

Later he had been pardoned, and later still proved innocent, which naturally was considered reason enough for his having survived, and this more than Lazarus of a man he'd met out-side Derby Castle and they went into a pub and drank a pint of Castletown Manx oyster stout together. But so long had Cosnahan been a stranger to the old ways and the old speech that – standing under the familiar sign *Castletown 1st prize Ales* and regarding over the bar one of these Manx calendars of singular composition for the previous November that said

24th, Last Norse King of Man died 1205, 27th, Nobles Hospital opened 1906, 30th, Winston Churchill born 1874 – he had all but forgotten that Illiam Dhone was not his companion's real name, that it was a nickname meaning sandy or fair-haired, to which the companion himself, now bald, gave no clue; all but forgotten too that this nickname wasn't strictly his own but derived, with the quirky sardonic humor of the Manx, from that other Illiam Dhôan, their own monarch martyr and rebel hero, once collogued into cruel death, in fact, which no Manxman ever really forgets, shot, successfully, before his pardon arrived, Illiam Dhôan who was forefather of that famous navigator and mutineer of the H.M.S. *Bounty*, that later founder of another remoter Isle of Man, Pitcairn, and the bearer too of the great and simple name of Christian. But no relative at all of the only fellow in Europe who'd recognized Cosnahan on his first trip home in twenty years, and even this Illiam Dhone, who was an engineer's artificer and whose hands were covered with pitch, had not congratulated him, and he had been of two minds, under the circumstances, whether to congratulate Illiam Dhone.

Though in fact the latter (who had doubtless not read the Browsing Manxwoman) *had* paid him a sort of back-handed compliment:

'I heard roundabout, Cosnahan, you know, you had been doing quite good work.'

And Cosnahan had almost thought of also saying to him:

'Good work, Illiam Dhone –'

So true it was that these dreamed-of moments of recognition never come off, back from the wars, back from sea, famous or in disgrace, the reception at your source was always the same; there was none –

But what did he expect? Had success on another continent really made him such a swellbox, he wondered, putting away his letter in his pocket with an important air, as though it were a sheaf of diplomatic papers (the huge Rupe Tarpea, he decided, was too public a place to finish it, moreover he had plenty of time to add to it for the airmail he aimed to catch didn't go till midnight), so vain that he quite seriously expected to be recognized everywhere he went, quite seriously expected to be recognized here, in the Rupe Tarpea, so infatuated, that in the same breath he cursed that success, such as it was, he lamented it was not enough, or had passed?

Was he really such a preposterous swellfish as all that? . . . Or was it all, just simply, honest-to-God loneliness? That seemed more like it, the endemic affliction of great cities. Europe was the place where he had his connatural being, this its center, and he would have liked to talk to someone he knew of old. That was understandable, if it did not explain his whole feeling.

But looking down the Via Veneto again, for him there was no one save Gogol, in his hansom cab, clopping eternally up the street, with his eternally beaming nose, and his cigar, and that Rolls-Royce-like purring between the trees, and the same Cadillac the size of a conservatory, and behind him the old gateway the Porta Pincia, and before him the bicycles and tricycles and a few priests and many Americans going up and down through the dappled shadows between the plane trees of the avenue sweeping down to the Piazza Barberini, which he couldn't see, and the striped awnings on the four cafés at the four corners of the crossroads, like the sails of yachts at a regatat ruffling at this moment in a catspaw of breeze, lazily lifting too the caparisons of the horses . . . Cosnahan wondered if this was the very place where, if you sat long enough, so they said, you were *certain* to meet someone you knew. Perhaps it was not a café they meant but just some Roman square. Or perhaps not even a square but just Rome itself, or possibly not Rome either, but Paris, or Budapest . . . Come Arthur, come Matt, he thought . . . And now every other person who passed down the Via Veneto seemed to be a priest or an American publisher. Other people were certainly experiencing better luck: he had observed a'hearty greeting only a few tables away on the terrace between two folk from Twin Falls, Idaho. Yes, he had read that there'd never been a time in history when, with this flood of tourists, so many encounters between friends and acquaintances were taking place in Rome

Yet it didn't seem that even that more romantic encounter with somebody already fallen in with in Europe was in store

133

for him, nothing for example – had his loyalty not been complete – like that felicitous meeting in Rome by the hero of a book he'd been reading with a girl named Rosemary. He remembered the name because it was the same as the original of one of his own, though very different, characters in the Ark, so different that as a matter of fact, she was an elephant ... (It was she upon the cover of his book, being, in a manner of speaking, its heroine.) But failing Matt or Arthur, how he would have loved to see, still somehow by some miracle half expected to see, one of the faces from his island, to speak one of the old names again from Laxey or Ballaugh, or Derbyhaven. Where were they? For they could not all have died, or been killed in the war, all their adventurousness subsumed in that. He would have given anything to meet one of those old friends with the crooked, harsh, twiggy names, the marshy, crazy names, craggy souls like tough wildflowers that rooted themselves on rock like eryngo root: where were all those old purists, the carpenters and ship-builders he knew, whose religion had been handicraft, 'to do their best and no shucking on the job' but whose real conformity ended there. Their fathers would be dead, but where were those of only thirty or forty when he'd known them, who would now be three score and ten, men yet of another age, like Quayle, who smuggled a whole hogshead of rum through the Liverpool customs on a bet. Their sons, his boyhood friends, were scattered, but where had they all scattered to? And now to Cosnahan half closing his eyes it was as if he were sitting once more on the esplanade in Douglas, watching, his more distant view blocked no doubt by the finest conveniences in the British Isles, the people pass, all with the same faces of the same capitulated sleath, all wearing, it seemed even, the same sleathy clothes nowadays, saying to himself: where is Quayne, and where is Quaggan? where is Quillish? where is Qualtrough? where is Quirk and Quayle and Looney? And Illiam Dhone, who had been hanged? And yet lived, because he was innocent ...

'That will be a hundred lire, sir,' said a new waiter in English, smiling and coming up to him.

'Lhiat myr hoilliu!' Cosnahan laughed, rising to his feet so grateful for the smile and the English words he didn't think of the hundred lire.

Quocunque jeceris stabit. That was something he knew how to say too, much good it would do. Cosnahan, stick and book under his arm, and lighting his pipe, walked down the Via Veneto in the direction of the Piazza Barberini. He was glad the waiter, who'd ended by tipping him with the matches, had disturbed him, for paradoxically enough, considering the trend of his thoughts, he had an appointment. Sort of appointment.

For Cosnahan's presence in Rome was not altogether without purpose. Not merely according to the blurb, but to the terms of a contract drawn up in America, an Italian translation should not only have been made, but be upon the Italian bookshelves by now, though he had so far failed to find it. Similarly with those other countries. Just as it was implied in the blurb again, not only Italy but France too, and even Sweden had leaped at the reviews in the New York papers hailing him as America's newest and greatest humorist, leaped, but without of course looking first at the book itself – how could they since their publishers were dependent on their New York agents, who looked solely at the reviews? – nor calculating the difficulties involved in translating a writer who still half thought in Manx Gaelic, yet wrote in English, into Italian, French, Swedish, etc. The result was that his French publishers when he finally found them in Paris, which was not so easy as one might think, having at last to their distress actually read the work, regretted their hastiness and despite having beforehand remitted him a ruinous advance in dollars (spent long ago in America) were still more than willing to suffer this and let the ill-considered thing drop. He was bound to feel that if the book were eventually translated into French his sudden presence had turned the matter into a point of honor. Sweden meantime preserved an arctic and impenetrable silence, as of the Pole. In England, that had not had to translate it exactly, its praise in America had for some reason prejudiced the publishers, who had let it drop silently and stealthily down the drain, which of course accounted for what had happened in the Isle of Man, while his

'German' publisher, who'd signed a contract for the largest advance of the lot, and lived in Switzerland – though there was a chance now an honorable firm in Western Germany itself would take it – had decamped to South America without paying a cent. With all this, Cosnahan could not help wondering sometimes what had caused his novel to succeed in America to begin with. It couldn't be entirely because contemporary literature had reached such an absolute nadir of badness that his own book glittered on high by comparison like the Circlet of the Western Fish ... No, a mystery remained, there was something about the *Ark*, whatever it was – Cosnahan couldn't help hoping his Italian publishers might have at last seen it, now they'd had time to read the thing, though it happened Casnahan hadn't heard from them directly, but from Arthur himself, in a postcard only the other day from Paris:

Am now over on this side and will try to get to Rome quam celerime if you are still there. I heard via the St Germain grapevine your Italian publishers would be glad of more biographical material – details of family, streets, houses, ancestors – they go in for that kind of thing in Italy – and could use it in publicity apparently – Arrivederci and congratulations on Lovey's hit – ARTHUR. P.S. Hope you are working.

Which seemed to suggest that the book *was* out here after all, although – Cosnahan's heart missed a beat – he didn't dare count on it ... And naturally Arthur hoped he was working! But had Art considered those very distractions he implied? Had he himself? Considered that Cosnahan's presence in Europe at all was due to his obscure but huge longing *to* find himself, after so much former failure, actually translated (the very word 'translated' had a mystical tinge to him) into other European languages. This was partly due to the small curious linguistic recess in which he had dwelt during early years. Primarily, of course, this recess had insulated him from the English language. But this wasn't the half of it. Nearby Wales confronted him with a language Celtic indeed, but incomprehensible as it was magnificent, savage, bass-toned and druidical, and with words as long as its railway stations. And English once learned, a speech greeted him in Liverpool, that somber and neighboring city, that no familiarity with its caught accents in his invaded island itself could prevent sounding more foreign and harsher to his ears than the language of Tibetan priests, twirling prayer wheels. Yet while it saddened him to conform and learn their language to the point of adoption, to that extent too it had represented so much more of a victory for him, not merely to have mastered English, but to have done this so masterfully the result could be translated into – What? into French? Cosnahan and Flaubert! That was great, heroic. But Italian: that had grandeur and nobility too. Drumgold Cosnahan translated into the language of Dante, Garibaldi and Pirandello! Thus it was possible to say that he was actually *in* Europe because he had expected to find himself translated here, and had looked forward beyond words to enjoying the thrill of this realization with his wife.

So it had been, in some measure he allowed himself to remember, in Paris, where, wrongly directed to his French publishers at the top of some fifteen flights of stairs without an elevator, upon each floor of which, no sooner had he put a light on than the lights of all the floors savagely went off, until groggy with weariness, and afraid of falling seventy feet into a courtyard in the dark, for there was no railing, he had knocked and knocked at a door from behind which came a sound of crime, or stifled laughter, to ask for help, whereupon five minutes of darkness later that could be compared only to the anguished moments of a mountaineer caught in a storm upon an unnegotiable overhang, all the lights in the building went on again with a crisp crash, whistles wailed, and fifteen armed and bewhiskered gendarmes out of Zola came clattering and clanking up the stone stairs, arrested him and took him away in a Black Maria, where, soon discovering a common interest in rugby football, and the gendarmes that Cosnahan had once played scrum-half against the Racing Club de France, they all became the firmest of friends in no time. At last Cosnahan not only had felt a certain reluctance to leave the Bastille of the Seventh Arrondissement, which seemed to him much cheerier than his hotel room, but had decided that in no country in the world was it such a privilege to be arrested.

And so it almost was, what was unseemly about this incident, and the special disappointment it presaged, having been forgotten in the meantime, here in Rome. He had felt, his first day as he walked down this same sunlit street toward the Forum, that a Manx author such as himself should be translated into Italian, and that this author should himself be in the Eternal City, constituted a phenomenon so remarkable it should have been greeted by the firing of cannon from the monument of Vittorio Emmanuele!

But it so happened that though he possessed a copy of his French contract, and the Swedish one, and his German one, he had omitted to bring a copy of his Italian contract with him, so that not remembering the address of his publishers here, nor for the moment their name, and having his own peculiar difficulties about making inquiries, he had allowed himself to be directed at first to the wrong offices, which were housed by the Tiber, and proved a sort of distributing house, like a huge shed or storeroom, but the machinery of whose presses shook the whole building, as if it were an American newspaper office; such was one's impression, or perhaps it was merely the titanic thunder of the tramway outside, the Circolare Sinistra; and the difficulty of finding this place at all, together with the extraordinary complexity of explaining what his business was — which when he at last made contact was instantly and secretively assumed to be connected with the black market, so that he was beckoned out to a back room where he stood among the piles of other American translations being continually carted away in great blocks, among which at any moment he kept expecting to see his own work disappearing, even as he ever more faint-heartedly tried to explain what now several Italians, including a poor old beggar and somebody strayed in from the street trying to sell him a lottery toicket, were assuring him was quite impossible, as did a child, who picked his pocket — had left him so discouraged finally that when he saw that just outside the door over the way was the Palace of Justice, an apparition carrying with it a reminiscence that at this moment retained only its threatening aspect, he had all at once felt utterly exhausted and allowed three days to elapse before trying again.

Meantime, walking down the Corso Umberto, it had come to him that his publisher's name was Garibaldi, a name not to be forgotten, one would have thought; they were the only other publishers in Rome who published translations, and, it devolved, were now in the Via Officino del Vicario, where they must have moved from the Corso Umberto; this name he also recalled from his contract; it had taken him the half-hour before his early lunch this morning to locate them by phone with the aid of his kindly padrona di casa, who had been strangely informed that they were not open again till four o'clock this afternoon.

That was some time hence, it was now one, but the fulfillment of even a half-appointment was for him a circumambient operation, the more so when he imagined he had something to prepare for it.

'And so there you are, Cosnahan, my boy –'

'*Where* am I, Drumgold? The book has died, hasn't it?'

'Died, Cosnahan? What! When the Italian translation may be out, a sensation for all you know!'

Rome, he thought, with mild paranoia ... How right was that historian he must one day read: success invites self-neglect; by means of self-indulgence. For what did he imagine he was doing this afternoon if not still pursuing the uneasy glimmer of this evanescent sprite of yet more fame? What was behind that 'further biographical material' of Arthur's that he was already in his mind seeking to prepare for Garibaldi, had given himself three hours to prepare, long enough, more or less, to plot out a *War and Peace*? At this rate he could see another self of his wandering after this will o' the wisp, this ignis fatuus, all over Europe, to Finland, Germany, to Sweden, perhaps, God knows, end up by stalking his German-Swiss translator all the way to South America and never get home at all.

What on earth *was* he after? Was what he really wanted the kind of recognition no one would suspect? A word would do, or not even a word, but some sign, a kindly look, the look that told him, that had told him in America, what workmanship, what craftsmanship there might be in his confounded book. Was that what he was waiting for here? And was the final joker this, that he, a Manxman, was being compelled at first hand to endure, and as a 'successful American,' a 'bloated capitalist,' and before the scornful judiciary of his own European kin stuffing their eyes full of Spam while Coca-Cola ran out of their nostrils, that treatment known as the 'European cold shoulder'?

Perishing Moddey Doo! Yet for what else but that kind word was he waiting? Certainly he'd experienced almost every other benefit to be derived from it all in America, at that moment of 'instantaneous success' (and as if an 'English' immigrant could be quite without former knowledge of the *American* cold shoulder!) – the people who wouldn't lend him any money when he was poor who now all at once started ringing him up at every hour to borrow some, the people who spoke to him who wouldn't speak to him before, the people who sent him telegrams from Hollywood saying 'This is money and I mean big money, Cosnahan,' and when they saw there was no money in it or not enough for them, and that his fame was not so great as they had at first supposed, dropped the whole thing, the people who having found out he was going to Europe insisted they were befriending him by giving him five-thousand-franc notes in exchange for dollars, which notes were taken away from him at the customs as illegal tender, and never returned, thus leaving him broke over the week-end in Paris, those writers who would never have spoken to him before either, but now just wanted to *look* at him, or wanted him to contribute without payment to their magazines, the thrice-blasted Canadian writer conversely who went out of his way to say 'Of course I haven't read your book, Cosnahan,' the lady, also a writer, and with far more money than he, he'd met once in a bar before he was married, who seriously put in a legal claim for twenty-five per cent of the profits from Arthur, because he'd remarked jokingly on that occasion ten years before that if he ever wrote a successful book at all, which at that moment seemed most unlikely, by crikey he'd give her a quarter of the proceeds, and what was worse produced an unsteady yet ruthless witness to his rashness, his own handwriting – all this he had experienced, and, moreover, forgiven, or tried to, for what, after all, is more irritating and disturbing than a personal acquaintance who suddenly becomes famous? Hasn't he done that in a way just for *us*? Didn't he ask us to have a drink with him ten years ago, and though we refused, didn't bother to answer his letters, isn't it just like taking things up where we left off? Sure, hasn't he justified, or expunged, in the twinkling of an eye, all we *haven't* done with our lives meantime? And indeed, hadn't we better go and see him for *his* sake, for we know *him*, what a spendthrift he is, and if we don't get there first he'll be ruined again just like he was when we met him, before you can say knife, and besides we have just the kind of work for him that will make *our* name, but at the same time *his* name shine brighter – all this then he had known, as well as that true generosity of the few people who believed in him, the handful of reviewers who meant what they said, and the people like Arthur and Seward and Bill. But the people who believed in him were all American, and over here in Europe – once more came that inexplicable childish pang, yet so deeply he couldn't believe its cause was mean or unworthy – he'd received no word from the heart, no word at all, unless (not counting his civic reception by Illiam Dhone) it was what his brother Matt said over the phone during that one long-distance conversation, mostly taken up after the first two serious and clear minutes by their saying 'What!' 'I can't hear you' – which was besides disrupted by a mysterious German voice from somewhere that kept repeating through the continental brouhaha something like 'Nicht so besonderes schlecht!' or 'Hamburger Beefsteak mit zwei Eier und Kartoffelnsalad' – oh, to hell with it all!

And how in the old days they had prayed for his success – his mother and father and Matthias and his brother John, now in durance vile in St Helena (to whom, he wondered, pausing by a kiosk, should he not send a picture postcard with the Mamertine Dungeon upon it, if that would cheer him up, or hurt his feelings, or a Christmas card, perhaps a Christmas card, if he could get one, would arrive in time for Christmas), hoping that he 'had something good in him,' and that he would 'make good over there.' Ah, this was what hurt, that his 'making good' had come too late; his father was dead, his mother was dead, and though he had at least sent her a copy of *Ark from Singapore* with its glowing advance notices upon it, followed by a lapis lazuli elephant he'd bought for her in Provincetown, it miserably turned out that the copy, being American and new, had somehow been held up, then lost. It could be Mother Drumgold, not knowing what it was, had even refused to pay duty on it. He still hadn't found out why she didn't get it. Matt was a dreadful letter writer. In fact, though a priest, he was almost illiterate. When the English edition, a flat failure, came out a little later, his mother couldn't even have been aware of it. But why go on torturing himself? What a shopworn tradition the dramatics of even this version of a success story belonged to. Yet ungrateful as it sounded, how could the European help looking upon America, under certain circumstances, as primarily his sounding board, his test of strength? If the opportunity was greater, so was the competition. And having at last become 'something,' not infrequently he would depart back to his native land with the substantial gains earned at the expense of his magnanimous opponent, and never a backward look. Now Cosnahan had become an American, married an American, sent down his roots in American soil. He had not the slightest desire ever to live again in the Isle of Man. But there was still this much of the European left in him, that he could ask the old question: how can a European feel himself American without first making his peace with Europe, without becoming, however deviously, reconciled with his home?

All of which made Matthias' having said, his voice reaching him at intervals with brotherly and secular extravagance over the telephone in Douglas, 'No, old man, I didn't say it wasn't funny, because it is. I said . . .' and after a catastrophic whingdinging in several keys, a voice abruptly, 'Hamburger Beefsteak mit zwei Eier und Kartoffelnsalad! –' '*What?*' and then his voice clear and laughing again, 'I said it reminded me of the times we used to sing "Hear Us O Lord from Heaven Thy Dwelling Place," reminding him of the old Manx fishermen's hymn, more important to him perhaps than anything, though said faintly, and at long distance, and from Bruges.

Deciding not to cross here he resumed his walk on the same

side of the Via Veneto, still in the direction of the Piazza Barberini. Cosnahan was not exactly a man who walked without thinking where he was going. On the contrary, he often thought so intensely about it that every time he approached what, to another, would have seemed a logical crossing, his direction was modified by the decision at all costs, if possible, to avoid that crossing. At the same time he liked to drift, steering as by dead reckoning. Cosnahan had met other men who lived in the country, nearly always ex-sailors or prospectors, who combined this love of walking for its own sake with this same invincible suspicion and fear of traffic. With him this fear had become a far more positive thing in Europe, largely, he suspected, because he didn't have his wife with him. And he remembered how she used literally to pilot him across the streets on their rare trips to Boston or New York: 'Hurry up, Drumgold,' she would say, 'there goes a nice perambulator we can get behind.' Or, 'Here's a dear old lady with a ducky little three-year-old child who'll run interference for us.' Lovey's laughter rang clear as a merry bell.

What really made it worse was that he was now deprived of all the fun they used to get out of it, for he liked to exaggerate the whole thing a little, or conversely, have conscious and terrifying bouts of heroism and pilot *her*.

– Cosnahan knew he was absent-minded, and that his absent-mindedness in combination with this Roman traffic scared him out of his wits ... Meantime, enjoying the sidewalks of the Via Veneto, generous in width and shady beneath the plane trees, he appropriately thought also of the award for bravery the Japanese government had given him.

It was twenty-one years ago, in the typhoon season, at sunset. His ship was lying peacefully in Yokohama harbor when a storm came darkening around the point. Half the crew were ashore, nearly all the rest had turned in, and the second steward, a fireman, and himself were standing outside the second steward's cabin amidships having a drink of Chinese samshaw and watching, amused because it was equipped with a motor horn it proudly tooted at intervals, a Japanese fishing boat, now about a cable's length away, that had been puttering into port for some time, its dinghy behind. At once it was dark, and rough, with a howling wind and rain; then a collision of thunderclaps crashed almost on top of a gigantic discharge of lightning, in whose brilliance the fishing boat seemed pinned against the night; the lightning blazed a little longer, and they saw the vessel break in half like a stick, and as the two halves sank its crew scramble over the stern into the dinghy, which as they cut adrift was instantly half swamped.

Then in the tumult the heartrending wail downwind for help went up, and one seemed to distinguish a woman's voice among those others, rising and falling, of the shipwrecked.

Cosnahan's duty was more properly to stand by the lifeboat's falls, rather than be a saving member of it, but both he and the fireman climbed into it anyhow, an old-fashioned boat with oars, as would have the steward, had he not been ordered below by the captain to warm up blankets, in case they saved anybody, and get whisky, which in his case was redundant.

What seemed most likely was that they'd never get the lifeboat launched and away, and if they did would need saving themselves, for the sea was running so preposterously high that their freighter, tied to buoys fore and aft, was nearly rolling her bulwarks under. Cosnahan smiled at the memory of how important they'd all at once become, that skeleton crew of lonely men, with the captain yelling against the wind, and the wireless operator running up and down companion ladders saying 'Aye aye, sir!'

They got all the Japanese, however, taking the dinghy in tow, though they had to cut it loose finally, transferring its shipwrecked occupants to their lifeboat which had become in charge, at last, of a fat quartermaster named Quattras, a cowardly braggart, everyone thought, and the possessor of a Portuguese wife in Surabaya he was reported to mistreat. For this reason his shipmates rarely cared to admit afterwards the heroism of this man. Since, while the Japanese men were all behaving with the stoic courage of their race, a woman is a woman in any language, and nothing could induce this one, who weighed two hundred and fifty pounds, and was besides in hysterics, to leave the dinghy – perhaps courage in itself, for it was all the little family had left in the world. Despite the awe-inspiring sea, and above all the dreadful din, to which the poor woman added her frenzied bellows, making of the whole one esemplastic miserere, wailings from heaven and earth commingling in a single howl, then exploding in livid light, to be resumed into the same uproar once more, Quattras, who could not swim, sprang unhesitatingly into the scending dinghy, and from that position hurled his ponderous and operatic cargo into the lifeboat, itself in danger of capsizing.

Now the quartermaster was also a Manxman, and like all Manxmen imagined he was a writer or a poet, though in English, and every watch below after that incident was to be seen, to the crew's saturnine relish, working on a story which he entitled tersely, on Cosnahan's advice – this was its sole concession to economy – 'The Dinghy.' But that nobody should make any mistake about his vocation, the quartermaster worked standing up with the door to his room wide open, his papers spread out on the vacant upper bunk, and his hair falling wildly over his face in a tangle of inspiration.

In this story, 'The Dinghy,' though, there was no hint of the drama of what had occurred. There wasn't enough romance in that for Quattras. There was nothing of the Japanese family who'd lost their possessions, their little boat, even their bloody little motor horn, nothing, to speak fact, of the leachy dinghy itself, that had stayed in sight half that night, lit by intermittent flashes, and drifted under the lee the next morning when Cosnahan himself, who'd been haunted by it and hadn't slept, dived down the gangway and tied it up; nothing of their tragic joy then, nor their gratitude at having been saved by a handful of barbaric foreign seamen: a quartermaster who on duty behaved as though too fat to move, two scared apprentices, and a fireman and a carpenter's mate both of whom were half-cockeyed, scarcely knew what was up, only obeyed instinct and knack and were actually, at the worst point, laughing their heads off. Quattras, his heroism, neither was anywhere to be found. Not from modesty, nor any aversion to the subjective, or even because he had some sage notion the truth wouldn't sell. On the contrary he felt that what he had written *was* the truth, that it *would* sell, but only to a 'high-class audience.' And if it did not, he was artist enough to admit, that would be only because it was *too* truthful, *too* realistic, too 'art for art's sake,' and in short, too much like that Sagami Sea of Japan that had all but engulfed them all, 'over their heads.' So for the sake of this art, this truth, he introduced pirates, opium runners, a beach-comber in decaying white flannels, while the poor old mother aged seventy, whom he himself had rescued, became a pretty American, fleeing from her brutal father, at the connivance of a tall, dark, and slim Frenchman, who had no part in the dashing proceedings, with a fortune in Shanghai.

– What did man know of his own nature? How many people went through life thinking they were other than they were? Not even the evidence of his own essential being right under his red nose would convince him. How many lives were necessary to find out? Heroic old Quattras, now a Canadian, had never lost the illusion that he was a writer – and who was Cosnahan to say him nay? – at long last had even succeeded in getting something published in a Montreal newspaper, a martial item he'd sent in about butterflies, in which, feeling this time a little propaganda might be in order, he had in all seriousness de-scribed the insects as 'Butterflies manly and strong ... Righting the wrong.' And 'fighting the foe' and 'about they go' it seemed, triumphantly, right smack into the Kremlin ...

Yet what did he, Cosnahan, know of himself? Was he a writer? What *was* a writer? Was any clue to what he was to be gained by giving Garibaldi some more elaborate biographical notes as suggested by Arthur, when finally he saw his Italian publishers? There was some sense in it, to be sure, but what would it help to explain of Cosnahan, should he say: My great-great grandfather, Cronkbane, late of Cronkbane ...

Cosnahan found himself in a long narrow labyrinth of cob-bled streets without having come to Barberini at all. It was a region of underground restaurants, sinister steps leading down-ward to padlocked grottoes, to just the kind of place where he'd have liked to think out his notes over a brandy or a grappa, only none seemed open. Nocturnal haunts. 'And as a young man I had often brushed against the ghastly wig of the Duke of Brunswick, traversing the corridors of night restaurants – ' It seemed to him too that the other evening at dusk he had come home this way, barred to motor traffic, in a horsecab, and how beautiful it had been, first with the spectacular sunset behind the Arch of Constantinople, and the light fading from scarlet to rose, and from rose to violet, and the lights beginning to flash on. Clipperty-clop, in the sideslipping cab over the cobblestones, clipperty-clop, by these narrow alleyways and by-streets, and then suddenly coming upon the Trevi Fountain – how he loved fountains! which was perhaps natural since they were the city cousins of springs and wells – the cool waterfalls and clear green pool seeming to wash away all the dust and heat of the day, and the people, just gazing into it, sitting round the semi-circular low wall.

And then later that night, he had taken another horsecab through the park, and down through the avenue of magnolias, their leaves glittering hard and carved under the lamplight and a deep gold young moon, larger than he ever remembered having seen a new one before (it was the same one that, a little older, was still going strong in mid-afternoon over the Borghese Gardens), hanging beneath black cypresses. And a few little bars with their lights and flowers shone out as he drove by, the cab feeling so undated and impersonal he could imagine himself in any century at all, save when he remembered he was Drumgold Cosnahan . . .

He came out into the heat and light of one of the indeterminate and dangerous streets in the approaches to the monument of Vittorio Emmanuele, and paused before the titanic thunder and confusion of the traffic. How did you go, how did you begin to go? Yet this momentous traffic was scarcely a symptom of the age in which he lived: in the second century, his guidebook had told him, the traffic was so heavy deliveries had to be made at night to avoid congestion, and was even forbidden in certain streets, as in part it was still forbidden in the crepuscular region he'd just traversed, because of the racket on the cobbles. Cosnahan could see the Colosseum from here – it was just over there he got the horsecab. And the moment before he got the horsecab (and this was not getting across the street) a scene had taken place that caused him to feel his loneliness most of all –

Truckloads of Italian soldiers had been coming down the street toward the Arch of Constantine waving branches of green leaves, singing and cheering, truck after truck of them against the spectacular sunset sky, the continually reclouding heavens. And then, as they passed Cosnahan standing there, catching sight of him they waved at him: he waved back, the soldiers in the next truck behind saw and waved too, more and more enthusiastically till all were yelling and waving wildly, and one soldier ripped all the green leaves from his branch and threw them at Cosnahan with both hands upthrown –

What a joyous and heartwarming scene was that, how deliciously ironic this triumphant recognition of Cosnahan for what he was not, or had not participated in, nor could his absurd consciousness of being a 'Manxman of distinction' altogether resist this reception as something obscurely purporting to recognize that too, for to his vanity it did not seem extravagant, just for a moment, to imagine that in this way he was being welcomed to Italy, Lovey and himself; then he remembered Lovey was not there, though how could they be waving like that unless they had seen her so prettily standing beside him? And how delighted she would have been by this. 'See, they've brought out the army to welcome you, Drumgold,' she'd have said. And they would have laughed all the way home.

Cosnahan eyed the chaos of the road, and somehow attaching himself to a sudden excited gaggle of priests careening out of an alleyway, made the awful and dangerous crossing toward the Forum.

Inside the Forum, to which he had to buy a ticket, and into which he was preceded by the same priests who, all unknown to them, had shepherded him across the road, and two jolly monks, or so they seemed to him, he breathed more easily. Here at least there was no traffic. And how many priests there were! He had no idea of the different orders, and of the two whom he'd put down as 'jolly monks,' one was wearing a white robe with a black cape over it, upon which, seen from behind, was the emblem of the cross, the vertical arm in red, the horizontal in blue: the other, obviously standing him an afternoon treat, was wearing just a dark gown. But there were all kinds of other priests. There were priests clomping along in heavy boots, in shoes and black socks, in shoes and white socks. And here were majestic priests with cobalt blue sashes and cobalt blue buttons marching down the front of their jet black robes, imperial ones in scarlet robes, and tall solemn ones carrying their hats behind their backs. There was every kind of priest, in short, except the priest Cosnahan wanted to see. Father Matthias Cosnahan, who was his brother. Yet it did his heart good to see them. He reflected that those were unusual thoughts for someone to have who had been born in an atmosphere where Catholics were vilified and priests still scaldingly demeaned as pot-bellied parasites – Matt's faith had to survive a day when if a priest could be sneaked in at all he came from Liverpool and had to hold a service in a stable. It gave him the feeling too that Rome, whether it bore out its legends or not, was one place where you didn't really need to be alone. On the other hand the very staggering multiplicity of these men of God came close to unnerving him again: it was almost hallucinatory, so that, advancing slowly, his stick under his arm, toward the Basilica of Constantine, he imagined he saw Matthias everywhere, and he began to feel there must be some mistake, that Matt had already left some later message for him that he had not received. So much had happened, for good or evil, since the brothers had last seen each other, and even so there was not going to be time to go into half of it.

Cosnahan watched the black swallows, or swifts, like bats playing round the Basilica. Like bats? He hoped the Laurentian thought wasn't a bad omen. Lovey's name, L'Hirondelle, meant swallow. And he remembered how they'd grown quite fond of bats ever since during a heat wave they'd found one stranded on a dusty path in the sunlight, with its little hands, and face like a tiny kitten, and he'd put it in the cool deep shade on a branch where it clung upside down hissing at him . . .

And the swallows, black as they might be, seemed to fly out of love, tossing in the summer air like children's darts, about the evocations of vanished splendor, about the Basilica, in which

he was now half ashamed to be less interested than in the white
convolvulus and morning bride and wild geranium growing
everywhere that you didn't read about in the guidebook.

Isle of Man wildflowers! Eryngo root in the north, samphire
at St Anne's Head; pennyroyal in the marlpits at Ballaugh, and
sea kale near Peel –

And there in front of him, examining some kind of spiked
and hooded flower, blue and white, stood Matthias again,
though Matthias would not have been wearing a long brown
corded robe with sandals. That a monk had seemed the same
thing as a priest, that he couldn't distinguish in his mind between the numerous denominations and orders, that he'd have
to go to his dictionary to discover the difference between a priest
and a friar, and could confuse a partial dedication with a complete withdrawal from the world of flesh, reminded him nonetheless at what a distance he stood from Matt.

He could see him now, though he had not seen him, his
strong and humorous face with the two front teeth broken in
an unhieratic fracas at a rugby match, and hear his voice,
though he had heard it only on the phone, deep, certain, rich,
and full of mischief and unpriestlike comfort. This clear sense
of his brother's dedication and belief had the effect for a
moment, as it might with a person who has never loved or been
loved, of making him think that some great purpose and meaning in life had passed him by. And for a while, not really having
any definable religion himself save a belief in its freedom and
an appreciation of the prejudices of other people – or was it
because he seemed to detect once again, from afar off, that faint
but unmistakable odor of frizzling Cosnahan? – he felt ex-
cluded, by that very all-embracing tolerance that a moment
since was making him appear such a benign and condescend-
ing fellow, as from the great circle of religion altogether, and
more lonely than ever.

Cosnahan strolled up the Palatine Hill and, tired, sat on a
bench halfway up. My great-great grandfather Cronkbane,
should he say? was hung for stealing a sheep. Though the
sheep itself had not been harmed it appeared in a vision to the
next of kin, demanding further revenge. And immediately

afterwards the law that required hanging for theft was repealed. What happened then? . . . Did my great-great grandfather start haunting the sheep?

Two lovers were sitting on the grass under the House of Flavia and he could not help watching them; every now and then they would gaze long in each other's eyes, then look away again, then laugh. The boy took a wisp of grass and began to chew it, the girl took it away from him, and then she laughed. Then they took to looking in each other's eyes again. But such notation of these absurd actions, crude as in an old silent movie, did not describe how beautiful they looked, or *how* they looked, or what it said to him.

My great-great grandfather Cronkbane was not only a poet but a successful inventor and engineer. (Up the eternal Palatine Hill more eternal lovers were walking past more eternal monks and eternal smiling priests.) He surveyed the Isthmus of Panama and submitted to the United States, in 1855, a scheme for a canal without locks, for he was the first to assert that the Atlantic and Pacific Oceans were on a level ... Cronkbane's poetry is admittedly rugged, but it is vigorous ...

After a while Cosnahan, like a snag of driftwood caught in a current following some colorful boats downstream, found himself joining in the procession. Onid aalid ben. Ah yes, everybody in Rome seemed to be in love or a priest and all the girls were pretty. Pretty? Almost all these Italian women were exquisitely beautiful, and watching them pass, with that slow, heartbreaking saunter, grasses between their lips, with their lovers, these girls picking their feet off the ground and placing them down again so daintily, as if dancing some slow love dance (but always accompanied by some lover), their hair so glossy and silky, or fair as angels, and their long, slim, almost painfully beautiful legs, and their shy glances, you might wish the girl whose hair and whose carriage or whose hands you had already fallen in love with from behind, to turn round and prove ugly; that, you felt, would at least relieve your heartache. And yet – continuing to indulge, half abstractedly, in these pseudo- or rather contra-Proustian reveries – comparison was the only human relief there was, for having already fallen in love with

and lost one such exquisite phantom, it was almost necessary
to imagine that the next one that passed was more beautiful
still, if only not to think of one's wife. So that one was able to
say to himself: well, it was not that other one who was destined
for me but this one, and take comfort even in this thought from
the reflection that one is going to pass who is more lovely still,
the one who would say, or would never say, 'My sweet sugar
duckling waggle-tailed plum,' or whatever that was, translated
into Italian.

A Negro stood looking somberly at the Temple of Venus, and
Cosnahan wanted to speak to him and say something cheerful,
though he did not do so; and Cosnahan went back two hundred
feet to give a poor beggar woman with one leg (having passed
her meanly at first), at whom he smiled, fifty lire; half the price
of his milk, and he went on, feeling meaner than he had before
giving it to her.

How hot it was, too hot to smoke his pipe; Cosnahan, turning, made for the river where it might be cooler. And here was
the yellow, low Tiber with brown people bathing and playing
on the sand. Romans were diving off the top of a sort of houseboat in the mud below the bank. Cosnahan would have liked a
swim but probably you had to belong to some kind of club. By
the riverside the traffic was even more intense and noisy,
though the street was narrow and at least defined, with a dividing refuge, and he was not obliged to cross it yet: plenty of time
before his publishers opened: just the same, it might be more
sensible definitely to locate them well in advance, because he
wanted to find a quiet cool pub in which to sit an hour now and
try to write down his ideas for those 'further biographical notes,'
and, as all writers know, 'where is the publisher, there too is
the pub.' Some writers never get any further than the pub.

Over the bridges or along the embankment plunged red, glistening motorbicycles with pushbike-sized wheels, all with the
same exquisite girl on the pillion, each one a Beatrice, or a
Laura; and how reckless were these Romans, people steering
naked-wheeled bicycles at full speed without their handlebars
through this traffic, more fellows with girls on the crossbars of
pushbikes with mudguards whizzing along, and then more

priests: mobile priests this time, the most carefee and reckless of the lot, and here was a goggled old priest going hell for leather down the Lungo Tevere, and again Cosnahan mingled in the procession of priests on foot going and coming, priests with bowler hats, with flat-topped hats, with briefcases, with no hats at all, bearded priests carrying brown paper parcels, black-velvet-hatted priests carrying slim briefcases, more tall solemn ones carrying their hats behind their backs, good little priests reading their breviaries along the embankment, prancing priests, almost defrocked by a sudden wind and dust hurling down from St Peter's. A motorbicycle like a red gnat flashed over the Garibaldi Bridge. And this too was piloted by a priest with an expression he'd seen only once before, upon the countenance of the great George Dance, as in the Isle of Man he negotiated Ballig Bridge, when it seemed he was going to win the Senior Tourist Trophy motorbicycle race upon a Sunbeam with one cylinder. And now there were more priests: priests in rubber soles, in worn-out soles, blue-fringed, scarlet, and even a poor priest who limped and spat, and why shouldn't he, just like anyone else? And here came three more, dressed in white robes with black capes and hoods and wool stockings and black shoes, joking along – ah, he really loved all these priests, especially these three, not because they were funny, but because they seemed to take such a childish delight in making fun of themselves – they were the same ones he'd seen yesterday in the Vatican, he thought, in the mummy room, the eldest lecturing the other two on the glories of ancient Egypt, and Cosnahan bowed and smiled, though they did not recognize him, and he felt momentarily sad; besides, this might augur some worse disappointment ... Still, surely enough priests altogether there were to waft Mother Drumgold's soul to heaven, and as he walked on alone he prayed they might. But at the sight of a little procession of smiling priests on gray motor-scooters Cosnahan purred to himself: mechanized priests! Good Lord. Matthias must not be allowed to return home without one of those gray motor-scooters. He would insist upon it.

Ha, there was the Palace of Injustice again. Cosnahan remembered his publishers and began to be nervous, wishing he had

Arthur with him. Good, good old Art ... And Cosnahan now imagined that, instead of Matthias, he saw everywhere this man to whom he owed so much; a tall, rangy, cheerful yet sad-eyed Texan, of unending patience, but who always walked as if advancing toward the net to make a forehand drive at tennis. There were benevolent young-looking businessmen on motor-scooters too who might have been Art, and even passengers sitting bolt upright on the carriers of these motor-scooters that might just have been Arthur, nor did he fail to scan the faces of the passengers in the huge green tram-buses, with their sinister antennae aloft charging along on the overhead net of wires.

Cosnahan was thinking so hard of Arthur he somehow survived another crossing; the Tiber left behind, he found himself gratefully in another labyrinth of cobbled streets forbidden to traffic, stumbled upon the antique court that housed his publishers almost immediately, and observing at the same time, just as he had suspected, a place of seclusion, as if put there for the consolation of anxious or rejected authors, he continued toward the almost empty little bar with low benches and tables, sat down and ordered a large grappa, which was something he knew how to order.

By the door facing him was a sign: *Chi ha Ucciso Il Pettirosso?* beyond which in a tiny square two tootling street musicians were wrestling with what looked like ophicleides. That was good: it was as if the band had come to meet him already. They soon went away, however.

'Who killa the cock-a robin?' the barman explained what the sign meant, though why it was there remained a mystery.

Aye, that was a sad piece indeed, it made him cry with anguish when he first learned it. In his youth he had read a queer story by the same name, something about natural beauty and how man had killed it with ugliness and machinery and with his own spirit. Something like that. It had struck him as sentimental then, like a bit he'd written himself about the factory chimneys of Eleusis. But now Cosnahan, drinking his grappa, found himself thinking of the old lines: 'I am thy dying mother tongue, the first speech of this island race. 'Twas I who kept the strangers out ...' And Cosnahan took his pen and wrote:

'My great grandfather, Cosnahan Curghey Cronkbane, of Ballabeg, was born in 1816, in Cronkbane Street, Douglas ... Also a poet he developed a love ... of natural history pursuits. At sixteen he entered Edinburgh University ... In 1832 he investigated the natural history of Man ... A thoroughly patriotic Manxman who took pride in having only Manx blood in his veins ... he visited France, Switzerland, Germany, Algiers, always studying natural history ... he was appointed Government Palaeontologist in 1844 ... His memory is commemorated ... a marble bust. His poetry is admittedly rugged, but it is vigorous.'

And now, the next moment, his great grandson, with a feeling of genuine relief, and none of the nervousness that Cosnahan expected, with serene confidence indeed, found himself waiting in the enormous silent coolness of his Italian publisher's offices in Rome in the Via Officino del Vicario. Well, he was here, wasn't he? Or was he? For though he hadn't noticed this before, now that a little hard liquor had ascended to his brain, he had become aware that the fumes of unsullied renown must have been lying there dormant all afternoon simply waiting to be aroused again by this pleasant company, and to take full effect themselves, so that while no one could say that he was tight, in terms of quiet elation it was more as if he'd had seven drinks, not just two. Gone was his memory of France, of his disappointment in England, the silence in Sweden, of the abdication of occupied Germany for parts unknown, of his neglect in the Isle of Man itself – it was as though he had never left Arthur's office that extraordinary morning in New York, when he had said deprecatingly: 'Arthur, are the reviews good?' And Arthur had replied: '*Good?* Read that, man! I've been up all night ...' He was even almost oblivious, so entranced by himself was he, that he had been standing absolutely alone in the offices for nearly ten minutes, the American edition of *Ark from Singapore* in hand, half in readiness, to present to the senior representative of the firm, whose appearance would shortly no doubt be the result of the hidden activities of the pleasant young

Italian with the open shirt and loose tie, who was now tele-
phoning in a recess on his account, or to present to this young
man himself, should he wish to consult the American copy of
his book again, which, at this moment the youth smilingly re-
entered, he apparently did – he took it away with him this time
thoughtfully tapping the cover.

Perhaps the young Italian was even speaking to the translator
himself. Drumgold Cosnahan, at last translated into the language of Boccaccio and Manzoni, and Croce, and Pirandello,
who'd written a story about a poltergeist! Quite forgotten was
his sadness about the old language in the little bar with the
ophicleides playing outside, that he could hear dimly now, as
from another world, playing somewhere else. It was overwhelming. And Garibaldi's offices were as overwhelming as the occasion. The walls, hung with paintings in great gold frames, were
of dark crimson satin: the ceilings, of some carved polished
wood embossed with narrow gold designs, must have been
thirty feet high. Sumptuous chairs were arranged around a
huge oak chest, while the office beyond, with walls of jade
green satin damask, seemed the size of a small railroad station,
and was all done up in red and gold too, with carved chairs up-
holstered in satin about a carved circular table. And all around
Cosnahan, in the private office, were arranged the books of the
firm, which like those other unfortunate offices near the Palace
of Justice, specialized in translations, only instead of being just
bound in paper, these were all sumptuously bound. And among
these books, if he could but find it, would be his book, only this
was what he hadn't quite been able to make clear to the young
Italian. Cosnahan had, true, discovered one book with a ship
upon its cover that might have been *Ark from Singapore*, but on
closer investigation this proved a translation of a volume containing Conrad's *Typhoon*: and he'd just seen another cover
that might have been his, unfortunately it was André Obey's
Noah, when the young Italian returned.

Afterward it seemed their conversation went something like
this:

'I'm afraid we don't know your name, I can't find out
whether we're publishing your book or not, Signor.'

'But I told you – it's Kennish Drumgold Cosnahan – there it is, on the cover of that book you're holding.' Cosnahan took *Ark from Singapore* as the other now handed it back to him. 'And *this* is the book you've published. This very one!'

'I'm sorry, Signor – what is it again?' he said, screwing his head around and looking at the cover once more, interested and half-deprecative at once, as if the title were slightly beneath his notice, but at the same time, though he spoke excellent English, he were not averse to adding a new word to his vocabulary. 'Ark? Ark?'

'Yes, *Ark from Singapore*. You've published it – you, Garibaldi and Company.'

'Ah, but we don't have any such *Ark* in stock, no.'

'In stock! But you are publishers, Signor, not a bookshop, aren't you? Or have I made some mistake again?'

'Yes, that's it, a mistake,' said the young man. 'We do publish translations, only the very best – perhaps you are looking for another publisher – Piccoli, down by the Tiber, yes, opposite the Palace of Justice.'

Cosnahan winced. 'I am *your* author, and in fact you wanted further biograph – but never mind that. Here I am – look, this is me, on the back of the cover. This is my wife, my cat –'

'Yes, but we don't have you *here*, Signor.'

'But you've paid for me in dollars!'

'Ah, you want to change American dollars! How much is it you want to change?' said the young man courteously.

'I don't want to change – Tusen tak – muchas gracias, señor,' Cosnahan explained patiently. 'You've already paid for my novel in dollars. According to my contract the book should not only have been translated into Italian but have been out for a month. Of course I can understand it may have sold out. What I can't understand is that you should never've heard of me or the book either. And what I can understand least of all, Signor, is why in hell if that's so you should have paid any dollars for the goddamn thing in the first place –'

'Do you have a copy of your contract with you, Signor?' said the Italian, patiently too, for his part, and putting on a pair of spectacles.

'That's what I tried to explain before,' Cosnahan replied. 'I didn't bring my contract to Europe and I couldn't remember your address. It was a little harder to forget your name, and when I found one day I was in the Corso Umberto I recognized the address too. It's true I discovered you were in the Via Officino del Vicario, so I supposed you must have moved.'

'No, we haven't moved. But you see, Signor, we're only the sub-office.'

'The sub –'

'Yes, you see our main office is in Torino. I think that is where you made your mistake. On the Corso Umberto, Turin . . .'

'In Turin . . . I beg your pardon. Raad erbee cheauys oo eh, hassys eh!'

Kennish Drumgold Cosnahan was walking down the unfortunate, the illusory Corso Umberto that was not in Turin, the Corso Umberto – narrow, with screaming jammed trolley-buses, and the sidewalk two feet wide that you couldn't stay on because of the crowd and you couldn't step off or you'd step under one of the buses driving at terrific speed, one behind the other, that he'd written about to Lovey – though he hadn't noticed it till this minute. For once in his life, Cosnahan had not only lost his sense of humor but felt really desperate.

In a way, he supposed, after what had already happened, he had been prepared for it. He might have been prepared for it anyway by the ophicleides players who moved away as soon as he arrived at that bar, the priests of the mummy room who hadn't recognized him, his thinking that swallows were like bats, and much besides. And yet this was almost worse than anything, worse than not having met anyone he knew, while it extended the feeling unbearably, that in this place of all places where he might have expected at least his name to strike, they hadn't known either him or his book from Adam's off ox. Yes, and now this ridiculous incident – and a sub-office! what pleasure dome of Kubla Khan, what Doges' palace, must house then that main office in Turin? – had upset him so by its very crowning and cunning futility that he wasn't watching where he was going, had even forgotten to bother about traffic.

'Cosnahan?'

'Yes, Drumgold.'

'It is vanity, Cosnahan. The incident is without point, or at least the point you see in it. But that you're not looking where you're going is not without point...'

'– And it doesn't seem likely I'm being published in Turin either, whether they've paid me or not.'

'What does it matter? You're not going there anyhow. Go and look at the peacocks –'

'No peacocks, Drumgold. I don't want any more bad omens!'

'– so that you may see how vain some of God's creatures can really be!'

Nel mezzo del cammin di nostra vita mi ritrovai in ... And here was the bosca oscura, the obscure boskage. It was the Borghese Gardens, or perhaps this section was called the Park of Umberto, a spacious park of dark cypresses, dark evergreens, and brittle-leaved trees that looked as though they never shed their leaves, and where the sunlight and shadow were intense. Cosnahan had made almost an exact circuit from the point where he started, and he was not five minutes' walk, possibly, from the Porta Pincia and the Restaurant Rupe Tarpea again, but it had never occurred to him to come to the Borghese Gardens before. A wonder he hadn't, for he soon began to lose his gloomy thoughts. A few lovers were twined in the deep grass among flowers and poppies. Mounted policemen, like equestrian statues in slow motion, lingeringly paraded the transverse streets of the park under the trees, where a few motor-scooters scooted, though there was little cross traffic. The shadows cast by the cypresses were intensely black, not light and airy as he had noticed the shadows in the Bois de Boulogne, and this green grass full of poppies, for there was nothing like a lawn here, was wiry, and in patches grew a foot high. And above still palely tilted the afternoon moon. Vota Garibaldi, Vota de Gasperi, it said again on a wall. Garibaldi. H'm. Poor old John. He *would* send him a Christmas card. Cosnahan crossed a road. He had been looking for the peacocks strutting among the trees as he'd once seen them in Burton Woods, in England, though he hadn't seen any yet (he'd overheard the phrase 'such lovely peacocks in the gardens' at the pensione and surmised the famous Borghese Gardens were meant) and at that moment he felt a twinge, a sort of tug at his being, much as one felt divining water, not when the twig turned downward, but when he felt that water was near – not the same, yet like that. And here, all at once, as if in answer to it, beyond a Renaissance gateway like half a sphere that bulged out with iron spikes into a garden with a pretty lawn full of stone satyrs, was a zoo.

Cosnahan entered behind some nuns escorting a dozen little children. But undoubtedly it was *the* Zoo, and how stupid of him, and how unlike him, not to have known this, not to have found it out and come here before, for come he would have; as it was something unconscious, or even stronger and more mysterious, seemed to have propelled him hither, whereas normally a zoo, after a bar, was about the first place he made for when alone in any big city, upon which the zoo would be found to include most of the other's amenities too. For though Cosnahan was hurt by the idea of animals and birds in cages, their being captured or shot no less (and he himself was a first-rate shot who never hunted), his love of wild animals and everything wild, dating from his childhood upon a then wild island, was implicit and genuine. He acknowledged that there were wicked animals, as there were wicked people – yes, he would go that far – aye, and further maybe – with the Swedenborgians. Citron-le-Taciturne himself was a bit wicked, downright sinister in some respects, but that did not prevent one from loving the little cat, or from recognizing his lunar accomplishments, his nocturnal rituals and pomposities, as all representing the special magic of his moonkind ... But however that might be, or whatever, even some ironic sense of his own extraordinary rarity, had drawn his steps inexorably toward this place, what empathy, abysmal or divine or both, the zoo was evidently where Cosnahan was going and he was glad of it, to seek comfort, and who knows to give some comfort to the porpoise-playing seals, the searching bewildered polar bears, and perhaps even the poor endlessly pacing schizophrenic lions, within each of whom lay trapped, no doubt, the soul of a Manx-American author. And here were the peacocks. They were white ones, in two separate adjoining cages, with a pair of birds in each: alack, the wrong pair; it was an international cartoon, an imbroglio of pure peacock: for while the peahen in one cage and the royal peacock in the other exchanged arrant kisses through the wire meshes, the abandoned peahen cowered, and the corresponding alienated peacock now gorgeously crowding on full sail with a cry part bray and part meorw, screeched, the keeper all this time was quietly gathering up from their common roosting quarters the rival peahens' eggs . . .

ORARIO DEI PASTI

Antropomorfi	9.30	19
Scimmie	10	19.15
Carnivori	18.45	
Orsi Bianchi	20	
Elefanti	19	
Rapaci	18	
Foche	10.30	18.30

Having made out from this that it was too early to see any of the animals fed, Cosnahan, who had turned away feeling he was intruding on the peacocks' privacy, such as it was, followed the direction roughly indicated by two white signs placed one above the other, the upper saying *Rapaci*, the lower *Equidi*. Rapacious animals, he thought, and equus, equi, a horse; from this he deduced zebras and the like. Cosnahan smiled, was pleased by his intelligence, and felt much better already. He was looking at the lion over a carpet of wildflowers. For little white daisies and poppies and lilac-colored bellflowers were growing here sometimes right into the cages. Beyond the flowers, beyond the abyss, and within a scenical rocky lair, the lion lay asleep in the heat of the afternoon. Though it was nearly five by the clock on the façade of the restaurant the sun was scorching, and Cosnahan remembered his tropic days at sea, and how grateful he always was, being a carpenter and thus a day worker, to knock off just as the day was hottest, which wasn't midday, but anywhere between six and eight bells in the afternoon, or about an hour and a half ago – and at this moment he felt again,

more strongly, that same familiar twinge or pull at his being —
when, on that voyage he was thinking about, he would —
Elefanti, he read. Cosnahan advanced more rapidly through a
smell of elephants and roses. The walk to the elephants' cages
was shaded though the beasts themselves were moving in the
sun. And then, suddenly, marvelously — could it be ? — he saw —

Well, he saw that two elephants were being thrown hay by a
man outside their cages pitchforking the fodder from a pile over
to them. It was not their dinner hour but they were getting a
snack anyway, which was a good thing. The elephants stood in
two cages, roofless enclosures, well and sensibly built, with a
high stout iron fence outside, spiked on top, and separated from
the walk by a few feet. In unison they swung their trunks out,
down to the pile of hay, then up, with a benign and refined
gesture, feeding the fodder into their kindly, sardonic mouths.
Between times they would salute, through the bars, with a prac-
ticed intellectual twirl of their trunks, as though conducting, the
man with the pitchfork, or in a sterner but still friendly manner,
two children who, doubtless without intentional malignity,
were trying to feed them paper. Of this the two elephants appeared outwardly tolerant, but, disgusted, would drop the paper
and return to the hay. One of them now gently kicked over the
footstool with which he was provided, as to say : too bad you
weren't better brought up, little boy ! But even that silent rebuke
was administered with dignity, it seemed, and an extraordinary
patience.

The elephant! he thought. If ever there was a creation that
testified to the existence of almighty God, and His wide wild
humor, it was the elephant, that marvelous juxtaposition of the
grotesque and the sublime, even if, according to Victor Hugo,
that would make the Almighty a Romantic, as indeed one might
ask without offense, how could He help but be, among other
things ?

It was usual to sentimentalize about elephants, and much has
been written about their memory, longevity, fidelity, their patience and sapience, their enlightened compassion toward their
offspring, and their unlimited capacity as bond slaves, whether
in peace or war, in the service of man. Because in captivity they

Elephant and Colosseum

permitted year in and year out without complaining little children to ride on their backs, or to feed them paper – Cosnahan was glad to see the keeper had stopped these brats doing this for he was reluctant to fling them a punishing look in Italian – it was common to ascribe to them the virtues of patience and love and gratitude, in the human sense, as though the elephant existed for the benefit or amusement of man alone. Then when an accident happened, and someone was hurt or killed, the elephant was called a bad elephant and was shot, and his kind was discredited. And this was unfair.

Because an elephant, by the way, is an elephant, and, as with man, no one knows how or why he first came into the world, save that, in Cosnahan's opinion, one could be sure it was not as generally supposed. (For with our notions of evolution, was it not as with so many of our speculations, just as the great Manzoni said, that from the inventions of the common people, the educated borrowed what they could accommodate to their ideas; from the inventions of the educated, the uneducated borrowed what they could understand, and as best they could, and of all an undigested, barbarous jumble was formed of public irrationality that was called public opinion?)

And an elephant, as itself, within its own paradisal and thundery being as an elephant, among other elephants, in its own princely and poignant and oblique world, had its own elephantine virtues which, if they happened to resemble human ones, was an accident unless, as seemed the truth, it simply attested in this case to a common divinity. If it so happened then that an elephant showed you a love or an intelligence you were wont to say was 'almost human,' as usual you were flattering to yourself.

Since must there not have been some principle of goodness and sagaciousness first, existing in the elephants' perceptions, that the elephant was able to recognize too in the very different moral climate of captivity or slavery to man in which he found himself later obliged to live, some principle of tolerance, or above all pity, for his captor, who could not help himself, and a certain sense of interest in sportive adventure about whatever he was doing that he recognized as amusing and instructive to his elephantish faculties, monotonous though it might all seem to us?

In a human being this acceptance of slavery would be thoroughly ignoble, but there was no reason to believe an elephant saw matters that way, Cosnahan thought. The jungle is one thing, captivity another. Freedom was of the spirit. So reasoned the elephant, long before news magazines were invented, although Cosnahan, who liked to think he possessed a tragic sense, and in addition was incorrigibly on the side of bad behavior, would have liked to let out the elephant he was looking at, if that would have helped.

But perhaps he would have reckoned without the true nature of the elephant, which even in its wild state was a profoundly meditative animal. Like the sacred ibis who has the habit of standing on one leg for hours at a time by the Nile, in a manner which can only strike most human beings as idiotic, so, in its state of deep abstraction, with the elephant. Moreover watch elephants engaged in something calmly destructive in a movie, notice their faces closely, do we not observe that they are as if, ibis-like, smiling softly to themselves, enjoying at the same time some transcendental joke? And so perhaps they are ... Compassionate creature of titanic orisons! Who are we to say that the elephant does not have some higher comprehension of the will, as do those great mystics who inhabit some of the regions whence they come? To Cosnahan the kind of animism that could read such qualities into an elephant was not based on superstition, but on personal experience. An elephant may serve man, or as a spectacle for man, and as a friend of man, but what he really serves is elephant, his higher elephant.

But in order to understand these things it was perhaps first necessary to have loved an elephant, perhaps in a measure, more than oneself, to have shared, in a measure, the maelstrom, yet also the strange primal peace an elephant inhabited, even perhaps, as Cosnahan had once done, an elephant's very environment of imprisonment, if it can be true here, as it is said of human beings, that in certain common adversities the spirit of concord, comradeship and understanding is manifested at its highest. If you would know the elephant, therefore, O mahouts and maharajahs, try going through the tail-end of a typhoon with one upon a British tramp steamer capable of eight knots an hour in the year 1927, if possible at the age of nineteen, share also with the elephant the calms and the stupendous heat and the boredom, the unendurable monotony of the Oriental seas, the immeasurable length of that voyage over half the map of the world, over that endless desert of sapphire, on that ship capable of half the speed of a pushbike, whose engine's song is only Frère *Jacques*: Frère *Jacques*: Frère *Jacques*: – stand on the black-oiled foredeck with the lonely creature during the monsoon, in the tremendous shadow of the rain ... Then indeed, like some ocean-going Renan, you may find the elephant communing with you in regard to your origin and destiny !

And because it was precisely these incredible things that it occurred to him he had once actually done with an elephant, it was the elephant on the left, the one with more luxuriant ideas about the usage of her food apparently, who had taken Cosnahan's attention, though to say this is not to express his feelings: for Jung, Logic and Philosophy to the contrary, if Cosnahan was right, here was one elephant that was not merely true because she existed, not merely a phenomenon, but a conclusion, a statement, and a subjective judgment of a creator all at once. And how could that be? Yet, from time to time, while he watched, there ! she would pick up a wisp of hay from her food and place it accurately on the top of her head where, more refreshing wisps continually being added to the lofty pile – for their touching purpose was to cool her – something waggish sat finally like an exfoliating straw hat. Cosnahan advanced softly.

Could it be ? – it could – she was – it was, and he had no need to ask, if he could have asked, and he had meant to try, but the keeper had gone – yet how could he have forgotten ? And as it seemed now he never really could have forgotten. It took him back of course all those twenty-odd years to the experience that had informed *Ark from Singapore* itself, to a time when the British tramp steamer on which he was the carpenter's mate, the same voyage that had provided him with his meritorious adventure in the Yokohama harbor, only several ports later homeward bound, had loaded that freight as mentioned of heterogeneous wild animals at a Straits Settlement port, that is to say, it was not Malaya at all but Siam, at Bangkok: numerous black panthers, a quantity of snakes, a wild boar, and a young lady elephant. This unusual cargo which located itself on the foredeck, in the forepeak, and even on the fo'c'sle head, the fo'c'sle proper being aft, had been accompanied by a keeper, but the immediate problem was to find a seaman to help him. By British law it is possible to refuse such a job once at sea and despite the faint prospect of some extra cash in London, in addition to overtime at the rate of one shilling per hour, refused it was by the entire fo'c'sle after the first casualty; Cosnahan's senior, the carpenter himself, claimed that while he was lashing the cages, the elephant, with innocent eye, had deliberately tweaked him: thereafter few of the crew, plain superstition in Cosnahan's opinion, would venture forward beyond the rope barrier unless absolutely necessary, and the job of keeper's assistant devolved on Cosnahan alone. It occupied most of his time homeward bound.

Nearly all the other animals were going to the Dublin Zoo, but were to be unloaded at London, the chief exception being the elephant, who was lading for Rome. Since the ship didn't dock in Rome the beast was to be transferred to an Italian vessel at Port Said. But the ship very nearly didn't get to Port Said, or finally, anywhere else.

Yes, yes, yes, it could not be otherwise. It may be that many elephants have this habit of using their afternoon tea as head-gear, but there had only been this one elephant in Cosnahan's life. And what he remembered, or remembered again, was this very incident of the elephant's departure from them at Port Said, her destiny at length in Rome's Tyrrhenian port yet again to be transferred, from Ostia – was it? – to be transferred, where else but here? To no lesser place than the Rome Zoo. To this very place.

It was even so. And that parting had been executed in like, though reverse manner, to that of their first meeting, as with crushing indignity, harnessed like an infant and, alas, squeal-ing like one, she had been lowered into a lighter opposite the Casino Palace Hotel, while behind her in the wicked city of Port Said the advertisements for *Thé Lipton* winked on and off,

and up the slanting swaying planks from other lighters, up the
sides of a neighboring vessel, an endless procession of blackened
human slaves bearing baskets of coal had toiled all night, chanting from the Koran.

It had not been easy to forget, any more than how the search-
lights in the Suez Canal, where they had tied up eleven times
during the previous night, had bothered her before that, nor
how the cries of the panthers had maddened her with fright
during the tempestuous part of the voyage, nor how, only a
little while before Suez, they had looked at the moon hanging
in a sky of green above Mount Sinai together at five o'clock in
the morning, from the Bitter Lakes or wherever it exactly was,
knowing that their friendship would soon be at an end. Nor
how, several times, when the lifelines were stretched fore and
aft, and the battling scending steamer was working only three
knots against Himalayan seas, and not even a look-out would
venture forward, he had taken over from the keeper to sit up
with her all night – because though she was not too young to be
without her she still sadly, it seemed, missed her mother – Cosnahan having lashed himself to her cage at one point to prevent his being washed overboard, and at that both of them were
nearly drowned. And then – and might he ever be forgiven for
this? – he had but safely conducted her into slavery.

No, it was not something easy to forget, that parting before
the voyage was completed, but forget it he had – and the odd
thing was he never *could* have forgotten it had he not written
Ark from Singapore. For in order that his book should be
brought to a satisfactory close, or for the sake of unity, all the
animals without exception had to be manipulated, after their
brief hour of victorious and absurd freedom, successfully to
London. And what was the origin in fact of the escape, in
which the fictionalized Rosemary, having escaped herself, had
gone around kicking in the other cages, and letting the other
animals out? It was partly the fear of the other seamen that just
this would happen during the storm, and partly that Rosemary
had indeed escaped from her cage once, and had kicked in the
companion cage of the wild boar who had escaped too; but
Rosemary had heeded Cosnahan's voice and returned at last . . .

Cosnahan smiled. Unity, yes, but how much greater a unity was this! To think that all these years, the duration of a coming of age, Rosemary had been patiently waiting here, serving him in her way, going through her daily performances regularly as the pendulum of a clock, despite Mussolini, Fascism, wars, disasters, triumphs, Abyssinia, the Germans, Pirandello, Marinetti, the American liberation, Garibaldi, de Gasperi and Roberto Rossellini, eating her hay and then at seven o'clock drinking her buckets of milk, and munching her celery and carrots, gathering her strength and growing older unselfishly, as if just waiting for Cosnahan to find his way back to her, first in his mind, then, as if it were not enough that thus she had provided him for the first time with the basis of a living wage, in order that he might meet his benefactor in the flesh again, had actually paid his fare for him back across the Atlantic!

And had heeded Cosnahan's voice at last ... Cosnahan advanced softly, he patted that accurate questing trunk. 'Rosemary,' he said, 'how could I have forgotten you must be here? ... My lord, old girl, how you've grown ... Ah, well, no melancholy now. Jean traagh choud as ta'en ghrian soilshean!'

And Rosemary flapped her ears, which were not very large because she was an Indian elephant, and regarding Cosnahan with her shrewd small intelligent eyes, suddenly trumpeted

'–'

Cosnahan stood speechless.

Naturam, expellas, pitchfork. Nature! – talk about Nature coming back, there was the pitchfork too. Rosemary ... No preposterous recognition in literature, or fact, to ancient mahout, to John Carter after long jungle separation in *Tarzan of the Apes,* to Sabu – recognition, it was anagnorisis! – and now he knew why he'd thought of Androcles and the Lion – could have been more complete, or, he thought, as if more utterly in conscious defiance of those who would claim that after all the elephant's long memory, unless of injury, is a fable. Or more dramatic, in its way, for it seemed to him, didn't it even have a certain flavor of Aristotle about it?

– Ah, Rosemary, repository of my ancient youthful secrets, sharer of my dream in the violet Indian Ocean (in which you were violently seasick), how often, figuratively speaking, have I held your head, comforted you, while you announced your elephantine misery to the monsoon? How many times washed you, placed the huge soogie sponge full of water so that, when you became too hot, even as now, you could lift it with your trunk and give yourself a nice shower, how often fed you your afternoon hat – ah, dear Rosemary, what times we had! So as it were truncated our friendship, and yet so deep, so, as we see, irrefragable, almost eternal. And how will you fare, perhaps have fared already, translated into Italian? Who knows but that even now you are the rage of Turin, in the land of the Piedmontese! – Though for the moment the less said about that the better.

But now it was as if Rosemary was changing before his eyes into an elephant in a wooden cage, between the scuppers and the number two hatch, to port on the foredeck of that old merchantman. The deck after the storm was all a sleepy idle heave and susurration with intermittently somnolent flingings of spray through the scuppers. At the silently turning wheel above on the bridge a dilatory man stood with his eye on wilder tropes than that of the compass: Quattras. High up there too, pondered the officer on watch, a bored chin in a corner of the weathercloths. Somewhere the engine murmured to itself: *Frère* Jacques: *Frère* Jacques: *Frère* Jacques . . . One bell; and a flying fish, to Rosemary's grave inquiry, fell suddenly on top of her cage, and Cosnahan caught the quivering celestial thing swiftly, and choosing his moment, flung it far back into an ecstasy of its following brothers and sisters. Rosemary was changing into a lapis lazuli elephant. And the lapis lazuli elephant changing into a portrait of a young elephant, on the cover of a novel named *Ark from Singapore*, confronting a ship's captain at the entrance to his chartroom gazing at her with astonishment, much as the author gazed at the same portrait as, still laughing silently to himself, he sat once more under the awning of the Restaurant Rupe Tarpea on the Via Vittorio Veneto, in the twilight of Rome.

. . . Indeed, Cosnahan had changed himself, was aware, quite apart from the extraordinary sense of well-being he felt, of one of those changes which, fiction to the contrary, it is given to very few to remark exactly when they take place, for the good reason, he thought, that maybe they take place in sleep. And Cosnahan felt that he'd woken up. The waiter, the one he'd paid this noontime for the milk, advancing, had said with a welcoming tone: 'And where have you been all this beautiful afternoon?' To which he replied merrily: 'Cha bee breagerey creidit, ga dy ninsh eh y n'irriney!' a remark having nothing to do with credit but meaning simply, 'A liar will not be believed, even though he speak the truth!' And with complete confidence he had ordered, as suitable to the occasion, the bottle of spumante he was drinking with such consummate enjoyment. But first to give some report of all this to his wife, and Cosnahan brought out his letter again, no longer reluctant to finish it here, yet looking away from it down the Via Veneto wondering what he should say.

Still the same ceaseless traffic, yet still that same queer old feeling of riches and peace and grace about the flow of it within the Via Veneto itself, between the plane trees and the sidewalks ten feet wide: but why hadn't he noticed before that this was caused in part by the incidence that neither buses nor trams ran up or down the Via Veneto, they merely crossed it width-ways, as here at the Via Sicilia?

And now the heat of the day had gone and the light of the sky was fading from scarlet to rose and from cobalt to powdered violet and as the lights began to flash on Cosnahan asked himself: What was so theatrical about a swift flurry of figures or one lone figure under an arc light in a great city?

He would have liked 'to get it,' to capture too – he felt an almost passionate desire to capture – the beauty of the unending processions beneath Rome's high electric flambeaux. And now its marathon moon of tangerine. Arcturus. Spica. Fomalhaut. The Eagle; and the Lyre. But what to say to Lovey?

And Cosnahan glanced away from his letter again to where, the half-hallucination still persisting, a shadowy horsecab containing a twilit Gogol, visible now only as a cigar coal, seemed still plodding up the hill.

Yes, what should he say? That the discovery of Rosemary

(and of course, how could Lovey, since he had forgotten, know that their heroine's original had been going to Rome?) had reminded him – as if he needed reminding! – by bringing back those days of longing for home at sea, those more recent warlike days as well in the untenanted submarineless Caribbean, how he longed *now* to return to her, Nantucket, Citron-le-Taciturne? Or, which was true too, that had it not been for Rosemary he might never have met Lovey, since but for his duty to Rosemary he would have transferred in those days to a sister ship at Penang, whereas later it had been the animal's keeper, as he now remembered, who had first counseled him to emigrate to America? Perhaps he should mention in half-serious jest that Rosemary, other adolescent trivialities having passed his naïve soul by, was in truth his first great unselfish love, and hence perhaps responsible for who knows what qualities Cosnahan might in Lovey's eyes possess. Or – but what did it *mean*, his meeting with Rosemary? None of this was what he wanted to say, and some of it she already knew. No, it was all far stranger, more mysterious, more wonderful, more *miraculous* than this somehow! And far more complicated than anything he could so obviously say, even though the truth, about its having been a little like meeting himself. Suddenly Cosnahan, who would have had no difficulty at all in attributing the same faculty to an outside agency, felt as if there were some power deep within his own mind capable of thinking of a hundred things at once, each one of which was funnier than the last, more purely ludicrous, while at the same time more purely serious, even solemn, so that gripped at last by the huge comicality of the whole thing on the one hand, and on the other by the equally huge stateliness of its interlinked and profound counterpart, he felt, closing his eyes, that he was going to burst asunder from some attack of gigantic silent laughter. Moreover now a hundred ideas, a hundred meanings seemed spiraling up from the same depths, from the same source in his mind: like a concourse of irreverent angels they spiraled up as through a mental ether, on which he had turned his inward eye, and this no sooner imaged than angels in sort they were, and as though now the heavens without were drawn within him too, among these angels he seemed to detect Mother Drumgold floating upwards on her celestial journey. His mother? But the answer came before Cosnahan had time to question.

For was not Rosemary like a signal *from* his mother, nay, was it not almost as if his mother had herself produced Rosemary or at least guided his steps to her, his meek and impossible elephant, to a meeting in its gently buffoonish manner nearly sublime. And sublime because didn't it seem almost to tell him that life, all life, must have a happy ending, that it was our tragic sense that was the more frivolous, having been given us for aesthetic reasons alone, that beyond tragedy, beyond the world, if not altogether beyond art – naturally one hoped not too soon – reconciliation beyond our wildest dreams of optimism, that Cosnahan, though admittedly a lesser writer, was a more serious one than Shakespeare or somebody? And what was a further motive of this signal, this meeting, this guidance? Why to tell him that by accepting his mother's death, and now he had for the first time fully accepted it, he had released her, and he seemed to see her now flying up through the blue Roman evening clouds, beyond the young gold tangerine moon in the southern sky, ascending, accompanied by these angels of fact or thought, to be greeted by her St Peter with just a shade of a pained smile, in Manx Gaelic, at that gate ... Cosnahan lit his pipe. He was trembling a little. He was moved. And a moment later it did not seem that he had had these thoughts, which were a bit primitive even by primitive standards. Yet it was no less difficult to express in words for Lovey merely the mundane effect his encounter with Rosemary appeared to have had on him.

In a way, though it was hard to see why, it had been like one of those forgotten but universal aftermaths to some quarrel of early marriage, arising from having drunk too much at some stupid party, escaping from which into the inevitable bar one ran into some friend of one's youth, down on his luck perhaps, but who instead of borrowing money or showing signs of renewing the friendship beyond a point said, surprisingly and kindly, 'What sympathy do you expect to get in a place like this you can't get at home, you old bastard?' so that, although one didn't go home immediately, a little later one found that this advice, 'Why don't you go home, you can't handle the stuff,' must really have taken root on the spot: but in this case it was not alcohol he could not handle, it was – and so his earlier train of thought, like Cosnahan himself in his walk around Rome, came full circle –

It was success itself, oh, he'd known it, something about its effect he couldn't handle, and the futile search for which he must abandon, let them translate his wretched boook back into Manx if they wanted to: that is to say, it was just this vanity he had to abandon, for who wouldn't be honestly proud to be translated into Italian ?

And abandon for what? What but his work ! Yes, his precious, ridiculous, second-rate, and yet to him, and to his wife too if they must live, all-important work: it was this he had been missing all along, seeking some stimulus, somewhere, anywhere, to begin again, and in the act of seeking, the excuse to postpone that beginning; and now, at one of those rare points where life and poetry meet, Rosemary had appeared; for Rosemary, so to say, *was* his work – Cosnahan glanced down at the cover of his book again – Ah, Rosemary, unique elephant, certainly the only one who turned out to be the bluebird too.

Tomorrow, to that uniqueness of yours, I shall make an offering of the choicest Roman carrots, a bouquet of the freshest and crispest cisalpine celery. And sometimes it is true, so hapless does man seem to me, that I feel that if there is evolution, it must be to such as you. But great and wise though you are, Rosemary, I am bound to point out, our star being low, that man is more various.

Cosnahan took a sip of wine and watched the evening scene for a minute, feeling his sense of kinship deepening: the tricyclists, the bicyclists, the motor-scooters, the many tourists, the far fewer priests, the large number of Americans in uniform, the poor he could not succor, the diseased he could only direct a prayer at, the two carabinieri opposite who, with their eyes downcast, seemed intent rather on some invisible Mamertine scene beneath the earth, or as if brooding upon the multitudinous caryatids of human anguish that upheld the street at all, sealed away from the gaze of happiness and humor, the Swedish woman returning to the Pensione Borgnini, drawing back, half fearful too, before the mighty scission of a crossflowing bus ... Come Matthias, come Arthur ... But they would come in their good time, he would see them. He would introduce them to Rosemary, and how delighted they'd be. And he would ask Arthur which Huxley it was who wrote that men should not seek for their differences, rather that which draws them together, which of that very variousness, uniqueness, he'd just been thinking about; no matter, both were right, and which was the one who would have said: but can Rosemary laugh?

But it was not from the knowledge that he would now work again – though he would – that his deepest satisfaction sprang, that was now making him feel as happy as – why, as happy as some old magician who had just recovered his powers and brought off a masterstroke!

The words had almost slipped out of his mouth. And suddenly, at the realization of what he meant, a pure delight in all its renewed and ludicrous implications got the better of him, so that Cosnahan laughed aloud.

Good God, he really *was* a magician. Or this was the real wild fount of his feeling, shared suddenly, human (at the same time more than just universally ancestral), though it seemed to be; this was the real antique and secret source of his present pride, of his future salvation; this that would have caused his book to be translated, and by that, more than that, himself to be translated – his mother's son at last – into a conscious member of the human race.

And who might that be? Who was he? Who was anybody?

For the papers said that man was Smithers, they might even say that he was Drumgold. Cosnahan, they might say that man was. And somewhere they had got the notion that he was as common as the century ...

But man was Quayne, and man was Quaggan, man was Quillish, man was Qualtrough, man was Quirk and Quayle and Looney, and Illiam Dhone, who had been hanged. And yet lived – because he was innocent?

PRESENT ESTATE OF POMPEII

In thunder, at noon, in a leaden twilight, just outside the Pompeii station, a man said to them:

'Come to my Restaurant Vesuvius. The other restaurant is broken . . . in the bombardment,' he added.

Inside the restaurant during the thunderstorm, there was one moment of pure happiness within the dark inner room when it started to rain. 'Now thank God I don't have to see the ruins,' Roderick thought. And he watched, through the window, the dove in its little rainbeaten house, with just its feet peeping out, and then, the next moment, not a finger's breadth away, the same dove on the windowsill.

This happiness was spoilt for him by the proprietor's continued insistence on what he was going to eat – when he was perfectly content, after an antipasto, with bread and wine: moreover now the rain had stopped he knew he damned well had to see the ruins.

Still he could have sat with his wife forever in that dark deserted inner room at the Restaurant Vesuvius.

Yes, it was wonderful in the restaurant here at Pompeii, with the train whistling by on one side, and the thunder crashing around Vesuvius on the other: with the rain – liquid syllables of its epilogue – the pigeon, the girl standing under the garden trellis singing, and washing dishes in the rainwater, and Tansy happy, if impatient, he wanted never to go out, to leave this scene. But when the full bottle of vino rosso was depleted by as much as one glass his spirits correspondingly sank, and almost for a moment he did not care whether he stayed or left. He cared all right though: he wanted to stay.

If only that rich flagon of hope would stay too, undiminished with them ! Or if one could only go on looking at it as if it were some symbolic vessel of an unevictable happiness !

Roderick McGregor Fairhaven sat listening to his wife describe the scenes from the train yesterday (not this train, which was the Circumvesuviana, but the Rapido, the Rome-Naples Express), how fast it went, past the magnificent Claudian aqueducts, a station, Torricola – och aye, it was a rapido indeed, he thought, as once more in memory, bang: and they flashed through Divino Amore. (No stop for Divine Love.) And the white oxen and high tension lines, the lupins and hayricks, the bellflowers and yellow mullein, the haystacks like leaning towers of Pisa, a lone hawk fluttering along the telegraph wires, the rich black soil – Tansy had seen and recorded everything, down to the wildflowers whose name she didn't know: 'Lilac and gold, like a Persian carpet.' The precipitous, hilly country, and now on the narrow coastal plain the feeling of the shape of Italy: 'like a razor-backed hog.' Suddenly rain, and the castellated cities on the hilltops, a few dark tunnels, and beyond in the fields, in brilliant sunshine again, the men winnowing, the black chaff blowing from the wheat. And there had been nothing so beautiful, Tansy was saying, as the vermilion poppies blowing among the delicate tufted ivory-colored wheat. And then Formia, a dull station stop, but with a Naples-like town way off in the distance. They'd looked out of the window at more castellated towns built on gray rock, a blaze of poppies by a ruined wall, a flock of white geese waddling toward a pond where dark gray cows lay submerged like hippopotami. And 'You should have seen them, I thought they *were* hippopotami,' Tansy said, though now there were a flock of goats, rust-red, black and cream-colored, being herded up a steep hill by a skinny little boy with bare feet and bare chest and bright blue trousers. And the signs: *Vini Pregiati – Ristoro – Colazioni Calde* ... What did one want to look at ruins for? Why shouldn't one prefer the Restaurant Vesuvius to Pompeii, to Vesuvius itself for that matter? Roderick was now, in so far as he was listening, but delighted to hear her talk, vicariously enjoying the train trip in a way he hadn't at all in the howling electric train itself. Another brief stop: Villa Literno. And the sign: *E Proibito Attraversare I Binari.* These were the kind of things he'd planned to jot down for his students – but it was Tansy who turned out to be memorizing them. And as they approached Naples he thought, there is an anonymity in movement. But when the train stops, voices are louder, more searching it seems, it is time to take stock. To him of whom stock is being taken these are bad moments ... And there was an anonymity too in sitting still, in the dark restaurant at Pompeii, listening to one's wife talk so entrancingly. And he didn't want her to stop. Naples had been ruin enough in this year of 1948, and sad enough to have driven Boccaccio himself – Giovanni della Tranquillità indeed – right back to Florence without even having paid a visit to Virgil's tomb –

'Pompeii,' Tansy was reading aloud from her guidebook – as now thank God it started to rain again – 'an old Oscan town dating from the sixth century B.C., which had adopted the Greek culture, lay in the rich and fertile campania felix close to the sea, possessing moreover a busy harbor . . .'

'I know ... it exported fish sauce and millstones ... But I was thinking –' Roderick brought out his pipe – 'that I've read little about the malaise of travelers, even the sense of tragedy that must come over them sometimes at their lack of relation to their environment.'

'– what ? '

'The traveler has worked long hours and exchanged good money for this. And what is this ? This, pre-eminently, is where you don't belong. Is it some great ruin that brings upon you this migraine of alienation – and almost inescapably these days there seems a ruin of some kind involved – but it is also something that slips through the hands of your mind, as it were, and that, seen without seeing, you can make nothing of: and behind you, thousands of miles away, it is as if you could hear your own real life plunging to its doom.'

'Oh for God's sake, Roddy – !'

Roderick leaned over and replenished their wine glasses, at the same time catching sight of his reflection in a flawed mirror in which also appeared the rain barrel and the rain-dripping trellis in the garden and the dove and the girl washing dishes, where behind the word *Cinzano* and to one side of a card stuck in the frame which stated enigmatically *26-27 Luglio Pellegrinaggio a Taranto (in Autopullman)* he saw himself: beaming, merry, spectacled, stocky, strong, reflective, and grave, forceful yet shy, brave and timid at once, and above all patient, impatient only with impatience and intolerance, the liberal-minded and progressive Scotch-Canadian schoolmaster: he absolutely refused to credit himself the gloomy train of thought that had just been his, and indeed his mien contradicted it.

'... the eruption began on August twenty-fourth in the early afternoon with the emission of vast quantities of vapor, mostly steam, which rushed high into the air in a vertical shaft and terminated in a canopy of cloud ...'

Watching his wife, admiring her, touched by her enthusiasm, a great feeling of tenderness for her overcame him. And then it seemed to him for a moment that this was not unlike tenderness for himself. In fact half watching himself watch his wife in the mirror he could almost imagine he saw the brightness and generosity of his soul flashing off his glasses.

'Roddy, it does look a bit brighter, doesn't it? Well, if it doesn't stop we'll just go in the rain!'

And now, as the time drew closer to leave it, the Restaurant Vesuvius was already beginning to be invested with a certain nostalgia. And after another glass of wine he took delight in reflecting how something in the very depths of his wife's being seemed to respond to a moving fluctuant exciting scene: Tansy, pretty, a bit wild, delightful, enthusiastic, was a born traveler, and he often wondered if her true environment was not simply this moving ever changing background — he reached in his pocket for some matches and a news clipping fluttered out.

'Is that Dad's latest news report flying away?' Tansy said.

Roderick's father-in-law, who was a boatbuilder in British Columbia, near Vancouver, scarcely ever wrote his daughter at all and his correspondence with Roderick consisted of clippings from newspapers. Sometimes bits would be marked, sometimes not; very occasionally there would be half a page with some comment, in red carpenter's pencil. The enclosure Roderick had received at the American Express in Naples this morning was rather more fulsome, and consisted of half a page, mostly given over to advertisements for consolidated brokers, limited petroleum companies and drilling companies, and crowned by the

gigantic headline OIL! OIL! OIL! Subsidiary headlines
appeared: BRITISH COLUMBIA RIDING HUGE INDUSTRIAL
BOOM, OIL GAS ALUMINUM SPEARHEADING COLOSSAL INDUS-
TRIAL SURGE $BILLION PROGRAM.

At first Roderick thought this was an ironic reference to their
own small speculation, which had so astonishingly paid off. Then
he saw the item the old man had marked: a small 'filler' which
apparently had nothing to do with British Columbia at all and
ran:

SCARED TO DEATH

In Arizona, a 1000-acre forest of junipers suddenly withered and
died. Foresters are unable to explain it, but the Indians say the trees
died of fear but they are not in agreement as to what caused the
fright.

Eridanus. Now, in July, the forest, behind the pretty shacks
built on stilts grouped around the bay with his father-in-law's
boat-building shed in the middle, would be in full bright leaf,
celestially green and sunfilled, the winding path leading you
through scent of mushrooms and ferns and dark firs to airy
spaces where golden light sifted down through vine-leaved
maples and young swaying hazel trees. Tansy's rocky ten-foot
garden would be blooming with foxgloves and wild geranium,
marigolds and nasturtiums and sweet alyssum, fireweed and
hawks-beard would have sprung up on the bank, the sea (between visits of oil tankers to the refinery over the bay), cold,
salt and pure, would be glittering in the sun and wind below the
porch, and beyond, the mountains, still with high patches
of snow, would rise to heaven in a turquoise haze. The wild
cherry and dogwood blossoms would be gone now, the huckle-
berries and the blueberries would be ripe. Every day the mink
would emerge from the hollow tree where he lived with his
family and prance and dart secretively along the beach, or swim,
only a tiny vicious sleek brown head, importantly by. The
fishermen would all have sailed north to Active Pass or Prince
Rupert, and save at weekends there'd be nobody there at all
save the Wildernesses and perhaps the Llewellyns and his father-
in-law. And that was where he should be now – not in Paris
or Naples or Rome, in Eridanus, reading, correcting papers and

taking notes in the long summer twilight, chatting with Tansy's father or drifting down the inlet in their rowboat, or taking Tansy and Peggy on a picnic – watching the constellations; mens sana in corpore sano. Sailing boats would sweep downstream or tack across the bay, and at night the lights of the little ferryboat would move silently down the swift dark stream among the reflections of the stars. And at night, when Peggy was asleep, he and Tansy would argue, have a moonlight swim, talk some more over a pot of tea about *Time, Life*, Thomas Mann, Communism, the *Partisan Review*, the sthenic confusion of technological advance, the responsibilities of education, Peggy's future, Gurko's *Angry Decade* –

'In 79 A.D. the catastrophe occurred. For thirty-six hours Vesuvius poured down upon the town a rain of pumice stone followed by a rain of ashes and boiling water which mixture formed into a mass that covered the earth with a layer several yards thick. The survivors returned after days of terror.'

Suddenly Roderick remembered an evening last summer, remembered it with such intensity and longing he stared about him a moment as if seeking some escape from the Restaurant Vesuvius. A baby seal had come swimming up on the beach a few afternoons before, he and Sigbjørn Wilderness had picked it up, fearing it might be threatened or starve without its mother, and they'd kept it for several days in their bathtub. This particular day they'd taken the seal for a swim and suddenly, in a flash, it slipped away and was gone. They'd swum after it hopelessly, they walked along the beach, searching, and his father-in-law, who rightly considered the whole procedure puerile in the extreme, had annoyed him slightly by choosing this moment to mumble to them at length a story about a mermaid he claimed to remember some fishermen's having once picked up at Port Roderick in the Isle of Man and also put in a bathtub. (According to him they had boiled some eggs for the poor monster, but while they were doing this the mermaid escaped and he recalled distinctly that when they returned from searching for it along the beach, all the water had boiled out of the saucepan.) Because a killer whale – and not merely a killer whale but a white killer whale, an albino, the first seen in nineteen years – had been

sighted from the control tower of the Second Narrows Bridge
swimming their way into the inlet (one of a school, but it was
the Melvillean qualification that had supplied the menace) they
were anxious about the seal, cursed themselves for picking it up
at all, questioning too the humane paradox of the whole thing
since the seal was the greatest enemy of their friends the fishermen, and Roderick and Tansy had ended up sitting on the
Wildernesses' porch and talking ... Sometime later on – it
must have been nearly midnight for it was dark – Fairhaven
had gone back to his shack to get an ill-translated collection of
ancient belles-lettres published in the nineties, and a damned
stupid book too – Lamartine, Volney, God knows who – he for
some reason wanted to read from in answer to something Wilderness had said. And it was this walk through the woods and
back that he particularly remembered now: the stillness in the
forest, the absolute peace, the stars sparkling and blazing
through the trees (high on a cedar his flashlight gleamed on the
four watching shining timorous curious eyes of two racoons),
the stillness, the peace, but also the sense of hurt, the anxiety
because of the renewed talk that evening of the possibility of
the railroad's coming through, or that the forest would be
slaughtered to make way for auto camps or a subsection, so that
their troubles had seemed all at once, or once again, like those
of country folk in a novel by George Eliot, or Finnish pioneers
in the sixties (or, as Primrose Wilderness had remarked bitterly,
Canadians or human beings of almost any period): and the
sense too of something else topsy-turvily all the wrong way;
Roderick stood quietly on his porch a moment, listening to the
conversation of the tide coming in, bringing distantly, shadowily, more luminously, an oil tanker with it. To him, standing
on his porch, holding his book and flashlight, it was as if
Eridanus had suddenly become, like ancient Rome, a theater of
prodigies, real and imaginary. As though the white whale
hadn't been enough, the four o'clock news report from Vancouver heard over the Wilderness radio had related this in
renewed reports from 'several accredited sources' of the famous
'flying saucers' of that period which had been witnessed that
very afternoon from several different points traveling over

Eridanus itself, and a sworn statement by the Chief of Police
'now released for the first time to the public, that he had, while
fishing with his son beyond Eridanus Port the previous Sunday,
seen, cavorting there, a sea serpent.' Good God! This was all
hilariously, horribly funny, and Roderick could laugh again
thinking about it now. But the truth was he wasn't really
amused: these things taken together with his other deeper anx-
ieties, agitated him with that kind of dark conviction of the
monstrous and threatening in everything sometimes begotten
by a hangover. And unable to fit these matters comfortably into
the filing cabinet of a civilized mind it was as if willy-nilly
he'd begun to think with the archaic mind of his remote ancestors instead, and the result was alarming to a degree. More
alarming still was that with his civilized mind he had calmly
taken what might prove a threat to the whole world with far
less seriousness than he took a rumored threat to his home.
Roderick saw that the tanker had stolen silently right past the
refinery without his noticing it :

> Frère Jacques!
> Frère Jacques!
> Dormez-vous?
> Dormez-vous?

went the engines, if you listened carefully . . .
   And now, with an appalling chain-rattling, smiting and
dither of bells, hubbub of winches, submarine churning of propellers, and orders sounding as if they were spoken half a cable's
length away, though she was two miles distant, and besides by
now nearly invisible, all these noises traveling over the water
with the speed of a slingshot, she dropped anchor: a few final
orders floated across the inlet, then silence. Roderick stood gazing at the oil refinery, 'all lit up,' as Wilderness had put it,
'like a battleship on the Admiral's birthday . . .' But if the oil
tanker had seemed, for an inexplicable moment, to threaten the
refinery, the refinery, with its hard brilliant impersonal electric
glitter, seemed at this instant suddenly to threaten him. In a day
of prodigies, the refinery, though as an anything but absurd
one, now also took its place in the series. As if he had never seen

the place before at night, or as if it had just materialized, electrified with impersonal foreboding, it seemed now a sinister omen.

The light was on in his father-in-law's house next door, and he could see the old boatbuilder through the window, sitting in the warm soft golden light of his oil lamp that cast gentle shadows over the hammers and frows and adzes, the tools all sharp and oiled and lovingly cared for, smoking his pipe, but with his three other pipes ready filled for the morning beside him on the table, sitting under the oil lamp with his spectacles on, reading the *History of the Isle of Man* –

'The ruins are open to visitors daily, free of charge, from nine to seventeen o'clock. At the entrance, and even at the station, Italian, French, German and English-speaking guides (tariff!) press their services on the tourists.'

'*God* damn it, yes, what?' Fairhaven sighed, smiling at Tansy.

'The time required for a conducted round is from one and a half to two hours, but to view the place properly, four or five hours are necessary. Visitors are not allowed to take food in with them. Do you know, when I was a very little girl, my mother had a stereopticon,' Tansy said, 'with pictures of Pompeii. Really it was my grandmother's.'

'Hoot toot!'

'Oh, I wonder if it'll look like those pictures! I remember them perfectly . . . You haven't heard a word I said.'

'Och yes . . . they're going to rain ashes and boiling water on us, and we can't take any food in,' Roderick said. 'But what about wine?'

– 'All kind of different bird here,' said the guide, 'snail, rabbit, ibis, butterfly, zoology, botanic, snail, rabbit, lizard, eagle, snake, mouse.'

There was no one else in the city of Pompeii (which at first sight had looked to him a bit like the ruins of Liverpool on a Sunday afternoon: or supposing it to have suffered another, latter-day catastrophe since the Great Fire of 1886, Vancouver itself – a few stock exchange pillars, factory chimneys, the remnants of the Bank of Montreal), just the guide; and Roderick, while returning Tansy's glance of mocking wide-eyed pleasure at this mysterious statement, knew he'd done his best to avoid him.

It was not precisely because he, Roderick, was mean, Roderick felt, nor was it precisely because there happened to be few things more natively loathsome to him than the whole business of bargaining and tipping, no, he'd avoided the guide out of a kind of ridiculous fear. For he'd so signally failed to make himself understood on this trip, often, as just now at the Restaurant Vesuvius, in the most elementary commerce, that the failure was beginning to strike at his amour propre. And so, rather than spoil matters at the outset by making a fool of himself, he liked rather to wander, to drift alone with Tansy, letting this sense of the strange and utter meaninglessness, to him, of his surroundings, be absorbed in that of their happiness just of being together, which certainly was real, in *her* happiness at being in Europe – just as he would have liked to let it be absorbed wandering with her now around Pompeii. Moreover at such times he had some opportunity for imagining that he (as he damned well should be, as he really wanted to be) was the cicerone: Tansy was too intelligent to be deceived, but she was also too kind to appear undeceived; but in any case the ruse would actually work, and romance be begotten or preserved in the shape of a sort of mutual astral body of inattention outside which Tansy's own intelligence and delighted personal response no doubt operated independently, yet out of which, as if it were a godlike cloud, Roderick could imagine his most banal utterance sounding useful and informative, such as just now, he had planned to say something like, 'Temple of Vespasian,' or 'Doric and Corinthian,' or even 'Bulwer Lytton.'

But the guide had been waiting for them, sitting between two ruinations, and in the twinkling of an eye they were in his clutches. And as a matter of fact he half remembered Tansy saying that you couldn't escape those clutches, you were legally bound to take a guide. He'd left the bargaining this time entirely up to Tansy, even though carried on in English. But Tansy was fortunately too caught up in her delight at the immediate situation to perceive Roderick's shame which had not, however, inspired in him any antipathy to the guide himself, who vaguely reminded Roderick of his eldest brother. He was a swarthy, swift-moving, eagle-nosed fellow, of medium height, with a flashing eye, threadbare clothes, and a military walk.

'Pompeii was a school of immorality. No hypocrite life like ours,' he was announcing thoughtfully as he marched along a little ahead of them. 'Blue mountains, blue sky, blue sea, and a white marble city.'

The Fairhavens smiled. The mountains and sky were indeed blue, now the thunderstorm had rolled away, and could one have seen it from this point, no doubt the Bay of Naples would have appeared blue too.. But there was something extraordinarily eerie about the way the guide had said this to them, Roderick thought, as they followed him through the truncated and darkened stumps of the inundated and exhumed city, adding, proudly smiling to Tansy, 'Si, I am Pompeiian!' as though to him this old Cuernavaca-cum-Acapulco of the Romans, and manufacturer of fish sauce and millstones, were not a heap of ruins but were still here, gleaming, alive, peopled and thriving, and with the sea, now withdrawn miles away, at their very doorstep; 'After Pompeii was destroyed,' he went on rapidly, but still thoughtfully, glancing up a moment at Vesuvius, 'Christians make-a the strong propaganda. They say their God have destroyed Pompeii for its wickedness. Now Pompeiians they say: Pompeii is immoral town? If that were-a so, Vesuvius must-a come every day to punish us.'

Roderick smiled, liking the guide, and he also looked again at Vesuvius which, now clear, with its conventional plume of smoke, seemed too far away and insignificant to have done much damage anyhow. Still, out of fairness to the volcano it seemed proper to note that its physical insignificance must be largely due to the damage it had done, Roderick went on to say to Tansy.

Alas, poor old Vesuvius had really waged a war of attrition on itself in the last century. No longer did the fire-spouting mountain wax and grow taller on the sacrifice of those beneath him, all the territory it had demolished of late years had been at its own expense, every explosion and inundation it had sent forth had decreased its own stature until now, having literally blasted its own cone off, it appeared little more than a distant hill. Vesuvius was Paricutìn in reverse. Though it might still, even now at this moment, be working up more fury, perhaps the god that wished to be believed in should be wary too often of speaking through fire, of giving too many direct signs of his presence.

Actually, he was frightened of Vesuvius, in so far as he could bring himself to think of it at all. All of which caused him to remember that Tansy and he had climbed it only the day before yesterday in the company – 'visiting their old stamping ground,' Tansy said – of some Greeks. And he certainly would not have cared to belittle it then, Roderick thought, crossing himself as they passed the Temple of Venus and went on into the Forum. The cinders got into their shoes, the guides, with their staffs, shrouded in fog and resembling black magicians, had urged them on with loud cries toward the top, where Tansy lamented it was not now possible to descend, like Lamartine, into the crater because a recent earthquake had caused great clefts in the path down into the noisome and shattered abyss. Roderick had, by placing it in the earth, lit a cigarette to bring him luck.

It was difficult to keep up with the guide who now seemed to wear a somewhat different appearance, perhaps because his complete air of belonging, even of ownership, had begun to invest him with a curious and different dignity: he had, or had now, the aspect to Roderick of a stout, prosperous and jovial businessman, quite carefully dressed, in conservative business clothes: dark gray striped coat, light gray flannel trousers, dark gray tie, white shirt. His coat, from whose pocket papers protruded, was too tight over his stomach, the sleeves drew up on his shirt, while the trousers were frayed: this had given the effect of shabbiness. But at the same time he had this hearty soldierly quality about him, and this swift military walk of Roderick's brother, a walk which carried him, and Tansy with him, often quite far ahead of Roderick's measured pace. They crossed the Forum obliquely and disappeared ahead of him amid some huge blackened pillars.

'You see, Temple of Augustus,' he was saying when Roderick overtook them. 'You see? Acorn and Laurel: force and power. The Romans say, "Each moment of love lost is a moment of happiness spoiled ..." The Romans say, "Life is a very long-a dream with open eyes," ' he greeted Roderick, ' "when eyes closed all-a finished, all is-a dust ..." Lovers just like-a beasts ... They spend life in honey, sweet life.' 'He means bees,' Tansy explained to Roderick, turning to him conspiratorially. 'Beasts, bees ... Acorn, laurel, butchers, fish beefmarket. Ventilation from sea, breeze come inside, to smell out.'

'Ah yes,' said Roderick ... 'Der Triumphbogen der Nero.'

'What, darling?'

'The Arco di Nerone. Only I thought it sounded better in German.'

'Si. Arco di Nerone ... The Romans say: "Life is a series of formalities, too seriously taken," ' the guide assured them, turning around. He possessed an admirable name: Signor Salacci.

And there was no doubt about it, Roderick thought again, this town, that both was and was not here, was obviously very real and complete to the excellent Signor Salacci: he saw it all. And moreover he was utterly adjusted to it. In a far realer sense than an actor lives in his scene Signor Salacci *lived* here, in Pompeii. Meantime these arches and temples and markets created and uncreated themselves before Roderick's eyes so that he almost began to see them with the guide's eyes. What was strange was this tragic – tragic because almost successful – effort at performance. It looked sometimes as though the Romans here had made all their dreams come true in terms of convenience, wicked and good alike. Vesuvius had long since destroyed Pompeii's old inhabitants, but there seemed an immortality about the conveniences, which was a disturbing thought.

'Pompeii may have been beautifully proportioned, but it was not, so far as I know, a town singular in its era for any remarkable nobility of conception,' he said. 'On the other hand –'

'If you compare it with Bumble, Saskatchewan –'

'But what seems most remarkable to me is that no one has attempted to draw a moral from this relative survival of Pompeii, when so much breath has been wasted on the divine judgment of its destruction. Of the two the survival seems the more sinister ... Compared with St Malo or parts of Rotterdam it's a triumph. In fact alongside of what's left of Naples it seems to me to have a positive civic grace.'

The junipers that died of fear ... Ruins, ruins, ruins –

– The first night they arrived in Naples they had taken a cab and driven for an hour behind the sidestepping horse along the promenade. What was left of this great city of stupendous history where Virgil had written the Aeneid and which was once the extreme western point of the Greek world? No doubt much had survived. Yet to him it had appeared, where it was not simply a heap of gray rubble, like a second-rate seaside resort, with ugly soulless buildings and mediocre swimming, on the northwest coast of England. Surely, he'd thought, as he held Tansy's hands in the clopping and sideslipping cab, he could invest it with more excitement than that for her.

That night they wandered through the incredibly steep dark back streets of the Neapolitan slums, past the shrines, the niches, the children setting up Catherine wheels, up the long smelly wonderful stairways between houses, past the bedsteads set right on the street, the sailors lurchingly carrying the girls' bags – the Rembrandt Supper at Emmaus around every corner. From a high top window of a narrow tall building a basket was lowered, little by little, and at the bottom filled with wine, and bread and fruit, and, jerkily, withdrawn. And that was what travel was supposed to be, thought Roderick, like that basket that is lowered down into the past, and is brought back again, safely through one's window, filled with the spiritual nourishment of one's voyaging. And that, he profoundly hoped, would be what it was for Tansy ... Here were the poor, here were the ruins, but the great difference between these man-made ruins and the ruins of Pompeii was that the ruins for the most part had not been found worth preserving or had been carried away ... Life itself was something like the desolation that comes to one eternally wading through the poem of *The Waste Land* without understanding it. Awestruck by his callousness, his ignorance, his lack of time, his fear that there will be no time to build anything beautiful, fear of eviction, of ejection, man no longer belongs to or understands the world he has created. Man had become a raven staring at a ruined heronry. Well, let him deduce his own ravenhood from it if he could.

They came to the Casa dei Vettii, or the Domus Vettorium, the most famous house in Pompeii, which partly accounted for their guide's haste; Pompeii closed at five and they had a late start.

Signor Salacci produced a key, unlocked a door, and they entered: 'You want lady-wife to see pictures? Only marrieds can see,' he explained. 'Each house a little town: garden; theater: vomitory, to vomit, and a love room inside.'

'And to the right of the entrance is a Priapus,' observed Roderick, reading from the guidebook, 'only shown by request. However, Tansy,' he continued, 'here "one has the best possible picture of a Pompeiian noble's house since the beautiful paintings and marble decorations have been left as they were in the peristyle which has been furnished with plants. One portion of the house has been provided with a roof and windows so as to protect the surprisingly well-preserved and most wonderfully executed murals depicting mythological scenes. There is a kitchen containing cooking utensils, and adjoining a locked private cabinet (obscene paintings) which belonged to the master of the house and here too is a statue of Priapus intended as part of the fountain . . ." I hope,' Roderick added, 'this is not what your mother showed you on the stereopticon.'

'Basin for goldfish,' the guide was saying. 'Peacocks and dogs. Put phosphorus on stone. White columns and a blue sky. Difficult to believe . . . original . . .' Signor Salacci sighed.

'You mean – ?'

'Water jets and flying birds and phosphorus in the pavement,' sang Signor Salacci, 'and the walls lacquered red and then waxed, with Afrika leopard, and an erotic frieze –'

'They had torches burning so that the inside of this room was in red light to make everyone excited,' Tansy was explaining to Roderick, who'd been standing at a little distance. 'But in contrast to this the garden was all in white marble, with cool fountains playing and open to the moonlight.'

'Usually gave these orgy feasts to the full moon,' the guide mused nostalgically.

'And during these orgy feasts?'

'Slaves had to pray for them –' they had arrived at a shrine to the household gods, the Lares and Penates (how would their old kettle be, their stove, Tansy's copper pans?) – 'for bachelors had,' he said devoutly, 'too much to do bachelor.'

The guide was now opening the padlock on an oblong wooden cover, that he folded back to reveal, momentarily, an oblong framed picture, about eighteen inches long, and a foot wide, evidently of some kind of unusual Cyrano de Bergerac, painted (and from all appearances quite recently subtly improved upon in Marseilles) in black, ocher and red, of a Cyrano engaged in weighing, it seemed at first sight, upon a sort of Safeway scale, his nose, which emitted curious carmine sparkles: 'Where there is money, there is art, there is taste, there is intelligence, there is perdition, there is fight – that is Pompeii!' glowed Signor Salacci, turning the key in the padlock again upon this jealously preserved and athletic relic.

'I always heard there was a reproduction of the Screw of Archimedes in Pompeii,' Roderick observed. 'But I thought he worked it with his feet.'

'But I don't understand about the windows, Rod,' Tansy was giggling, perhaps to conceal her embarrassment, or her embarrassment at evincing before the guide that she was one in whom a natural innocence and decency were combined with a restrained yet wholeheartedly Rabelaisian appreciation.

'Well, it's just as he said, Tansy dear. There aren't any bloody windows, or rather there weren't. Just as the walls weren't marble, but covered with stucco imitation of marble facing. They're simply paintings of windows to give the impression you're looking through a real window.' Roderick filled his pipe. 'Of course according to Swedenborg the real sunrise is an imitation too ... The technique seems vaguely literary in origin.'

'You've got to admit it has certain advantages of privacy –'

'Och aye . . . In short, with certain obvious reservations it's much the same bastard-mansard ye olde Wigwamme Inne Cockington Moosejaw and Damnation-in-the-Wold —'

'What did you say, Rod ? '

'I said, do you remember the man who wanted to pebble-dash Gerald's house ? Or perhaps I was thinking of those sheets of fabric on Percy's garage that are painted to look like red brick.'

'First wine, everyone will be drunk, and afterwards brothel,' announced Signor Salacci, locking the Casa dei Vettii behind them and with the air of an indulgent host in the middle of a debauch proposing further delights.

They left the house and drifted off at a great pace through the sunshine down the Vico dei Vettii, and after casting a glance down the Strada dee Vesuvio in the direction of the mountain, turned into Strada Stabiana.

'It was a silly place to put a volcano,' said Roderick as now, passing the Casa di Cavio Rufo on their right, they arrived at a crossroads made by the intersection of the Strada degli Augustali with the Strada Stabiana.

They turned right again into a narrow, rough, and extremely crooked and winding street that had the appearance of going on forever.

'Vico dei Lupanare. Wine woman and song street,' crowed the guide triumphantly. 'First wine, and afterwards brothel,' he repeated. 'Bread and woman, the first element in life, symbolic . . . All symbolic . . . wait! One entrance — bachelors downstairs; marrieds, priests and the shamefuls upstairs.'

There are, unless you happened to be Toulouse-Lautrec, few things in life less profitable than going to a brothel, unless, Roderick reflected, it was going to a ruined brothel. This was a whole street of ruined brothels. The houses had been built of stone but it was necessary to use considerable imagination to people them, least of all with delights. To him they resembled at first rather a series of disjasked ovens, or, if one could imagine pigpens made of brick, pigpens, but with shelves and niches, so that they seemed to have been made to accommodate the consummations of some race of voluptuous dwarfs.

'Roderick, do look, honey, here at the mills where the flour was ground! – and the ovens, see, there's even a petrified loaf of bread!'

'Si, first bread, then wine, then woman on this-a street,' Signor Salacci was nodding importantly. 'First elements of life, all symbolic!'

Roderick was aware now of a certain blasé obtuseness. Still, a whole street of dead brothels, that had so miraculously survived – relatively – the wrath of God – that was perhaps something to stimulate the lower reaches of the mind after all! Or if not, the ruined pharmacist's, which the guide was pointing out so conveniently placed on the corner, might have indeed. It was abundantly clear too, that once again, so far as Signor Salacci was concerned, these places not merely existed, but were, for him, doing a lively, if ghostly, trade. Particularly their guide seemed pleased by the Cyranesque-priapic trade emblem that, set from time to time amidst the cobbles, indicated waggishly the direction in which even now the phantom bachelors of Pompeii were perhaps proceeding to their grisly quarters downstairs where, once ensconced, past them an eternal ascending procession of marrieds, priests and shamefuls floated on their way to be vampired and counter-whored upstairs. Signor Salacci's romantic attachment touched and delighted Roderick. He was making the afternoon a success. It was not even impossible – Roderick saw him once brushing away what might have been a tear – some great grief, some romance, survived, for him, here.

Nonetheless Roderick found himself suddenly hating this street with an inexplicable virulence. How he loathed Pompeii! His mouth positively watered with his hatred. Roderick was almost prancing. It seemed to him now that it was as though, by some perverse grace, out of the total inundation of some Pacific Northwestern city, had been preserved a bit of the station hotel, a section of the gasworks, the skeletal remains of four or five palatial cinemas, as many bars and several public urinals, a fragment of marketplace together with the building that once housed the Star Laundries, what was left of several fine industrialists' homes (obscene paintings), a football stadium, the Church of the Four Square Gospel, a broken statue of Bobbie Burns, and finally the remains of the brothels in Chinatown which, though the mayor and police force had labored to have them removed right up to the time of the catastrophe, had nonetheless survived five thousand nine hundred and ninety-nine generations whereupon it was concluded, probably rightly, that the city was one of the seven wonders of the world, as it now stood, but wrongly that anything worthwhile had been there in the first place, with the exceptions of the mountains. The guide had just said too that even the noise of traffic had been so deafening in Pompeii that during certain hours they'd had to put a stop to it altogether, as one could well imagine on the stone paved streets – God how one must have longed to get away! And then he remembered that Pompeii was not a city at all, it was only a small town, by the, by the –

– Roderick had found his book among a collection of old *American Mercurys* that must have been there since he'd built the house, and started back; but when he came out on his porch he stopped: the beauty of the scene was phenomenal, terrifying, ominous and yet oddly reassuring at once. The moon had come out and now it shone high in a sky of fleece, in which were patches of sky the color of dark blue serge, twinkling with brilliant stars. The tide was at high slack, the water so calm and still the whole heavens were reflected as in a dark mirror. Then he realized that it was not the moonlight or even the inlet that gave the scene its new, unique beauty, but precisely the oil refinery itself, or more precisely still, the industrial counterpoint, the flickering red pyre of the burning oil waste. Now over the water (so still he could hear the Wildernesses talking softly together two hundred yards away) came the slow warning bell of a freight train chiming on the rail over Port Boden as for a continual vespers, now closer, now receding, now Byzantine in its timbre, as it vibrated in the water, now dolorous like Oaxa-queñian bells, now a blue sound, now as it approached, fuller, more globular, then fading, but always as if some country sound heard long ago that might have inspired a Wordsworth or Cole-ridge to describe church bells borne over the fields to some wan-dering lovers at evening. But whereas the moonlight washed the

color out of everything, replacing it by luminousness, providing
illumination without color, the flaming burning vermilion oil
waste below the moon to the right halfway up the opposite bank
made the most extraordinary lurid color, enormously real, as it
were, bad: as the bell continued to chime intermittently along
the rail, the continual vespers not receding, or drowned by an
occasional mournful whistle and distant clunking of wheels on
iron, Roderick thought how different Eridanus would look from
the refinery side. What would they see? Nothing at all, perhaps
only the oil lamp in his father-in-law's house and the illumined
open windows of the Wildernesses', nothing else, probably not
even the Wildernesses' pier which looked so magnificent in the
moonlight, striking down into its reflection with its geometric-
ally beautiful cross-braces, just the shadowy bulk of his father-
in-law's shed, perhaps, and then the dark bulk of the forest,
and the mountains rising above; they wouldn't see even the
shapes of the shacks, or perhaps that there was a bay at all; the
whole perhaps inseparable from its own shadow.

The Wildernesses' cat debouched itself from his father-in-
law's house and followed him, bounding up the steps and along
the trail, leading him back to the Wildernesses, stopping for
him to catch up, then leaping on again. Once he stopped to pet
the creature which suddenly seemed to him like some curious
aspect or affection of eternity and for some reason, standing
there in the forest, it had struck him as strange that cats must
have looked and behaved exactly the same in, say, not merely
Volney's but Dr Johnson's day. Meanwhile with his flashlight
he sought one of the passages from Volney's *Ruin of Empires*
that he'd recalled and wanted to read : 'Where are the ramparts
of Nineveh, those walls of Babylon, those palaces of Persepolis,
those temples of Balbec and Jerusalem –' It was absolutely
the most obvious kind of dithyrambic tripe, but considering
when it was written might be, so he felt at that moment anyhow, interesting in his discourse with Wilderness, to compare
with Toynbee. '– the temples are fallen, the palaces overthrown,
the ports filled up, the cities destroyed, and the earth, stripped
of its inhabitants, has become a place of sepulchres. Great God !
Whence proceed such fatal revolutions? What causes have so

changed the fortunes of those countries? Wherefore are so many cities destroyed ... where are those brilliant creations of industry ...?'

Going through the forest that night with the bounding and whirling cat all at once it had seemed to him, as if he stood outside time altogether, that in some way these cities of Volney's had not been exactly destroyed, that the ancient populations *had* been reproduced and perpetuated, or rather that the whole damned thing was happening now, at this moment, continually repeating itself, that continually those empires and cities were being created and destroyed and created again as it were before his eyes: then again he began to think that, far more mysterious than any of the questions Volney posed, was the fact that people still found it necessary to ask them, or answer them with unsatisfactory explanations. Had Toynbee really said anything new? Had Volney in his day? With his flashlight, while the cat impatiently sharpened its claws on a tree, he had recourse to the forgotten Volney once more. 'Individuals will feel that private happiness is allied to the public good.' Well, that seemed a point worth discussing at any rate: but what was the public good? What was private happiness?

'In Germany, England, red light,' Signor Salacci was saying. 'Roman better idea. Cock outside.'

Well, St Malo was wiped out, Naples defaced, but a cock in the street outside an antique Pompeiian brothel still survived. Well, why not?

'Aesculapius snakes outside, a doctor ...' the guide went on. 'The chemist and public bathwash ... Soldiers, students, cheapest prices. Just before the war, in Mussolini time, they had just like this. Regular price is fifteen lire. For students and soldiers half price seven-fifty – but cheap is always dangerous ... Chemist and public bathwash,' he pointed down the Vico dei Lupanare. 'In southern Italy is plenty clap. Seventy per cent of people have-a the clap but now is American penicillin – whissht, in a few days! – so nobody know percentage.'

Roderick purred ... Man, excellent in wit, had discovered how to cure clap in twenty-four hours. Without resource he meets nothing that must come! So with his resource therefore he saw, in this marvelous discovery, the possibility of catching a different kind of clap every day for the next seventy-two days, perhaps on the seventy-third an absolutely unique kind.

'Wine street, woman street, and public bathwash,' the guide was intoning in somber, almost biblical tones ... 'In Pompeii you pay advance. Many men come. Étrangers. Strangers, and sailors, you understand. No speak-a the Latin. But Romans make it easy. In every room is painted different position and man pick-a what he want. Ah, wine woman and song street! Wait,' he added, raising an admonitory finger as Roderick seemed about to say something, 'All street symbolic. All anchored east and west, north and south. Except crooked street, wine street and woman street ... A man drunk can-a say, "I don't know where I am. I don't-a know where I was." So streets are straight except for curved, so he can't say I don't know where I was. Si,' he said, as now they walked on down the circumambient Vico dei Lupanare toward the Strada dell'Abbondanza. 'So streets are straight except for curved so he can't-a say I don't know where I was.' He shook his head.

– Roderick's last memory of Eridanus was of a colossal fire: the *Salinas* meekly unloading crude oil at the refinery, innocent rakish smokestacks aft, and then bang, and up went the wharf, sirens wailing as though it were suddenly the lunch hour; then the tanker backing out silently into the inlet, or rather pulling, breaking her mooring lines, and the flames on the tanker apparently subdued as a mushroom of smoke went up on its extending columnar stalk a thousand feet into the air from the refinery: bang, bang, as the oil drums exploded: the noise of crackling even at a distance of two miles and the huge hoses visible: bang and the freight train that rushed soundlessly through the refinery: bang, bang, watching the fire from the Wildernesses' pier, for it looked like a major and terrifying disaster to the whole waterfront, his knees trembling so hard that he couldn't hold the binoculars still: bang, and the *Salinas* now motionless right opposite, and the fire getting worse, the noise of crackling, roaring, and the two-toned moaning rockets of sound of sirens, whirring diminuendo, and then, after half an hour or so, the arrival of the magnificent turreted fireboat, neighing like

a horse, from the town, like a urinating dinosaur, a monitor, a
medieval but supermodern fantasy, a creation of Leonardo da
Vinci – and the disaster averted – unless the oil on the ebbing
tide should catch fire: and the trellis work of the oil company
pier clearly silhouetted against the smoke and steam: the planes
flying overhead trying to photograph it for the newspapers:
and the *Salinas* that seemed to have no one aboard slowly,
slowly and silently steaming guiltily down and away to Port
Boden: and then the excitement over, and then all afternoon
the maniacal aspect of the sky, the sun like a fiery hub to a
gigantic black-disked wheel tired by a rainbow, and the stink
of fried oil drifting over the water, and in the evening the
curious sightseers rowing over to the hissing wharf: and then
to see, the next morning, though the wharf seemed half destroyed, by God, the *Salinas*, with a guilty expression, sneaking
slowly and silently back to the refinery from Port Boden: the
cottage on the opposite green bank slowly sliding aft of the
bridge, aft of the mainmast, aft of the funnel, as with her fire-
scarred paintwork to starboard she now silently soundlessly
and slowly and wearing that guilty expression approached the
refinery again, on which wreckage a single hose was still playing like a distant flickering white line, the *Salinas* now wearing
an expression like a drunk with a hangover approaching at
early morning the pub from which she has been thrown out the
previous night, the necessary flag pretended to fly on the stunted
foremast like a ragged tie tied with trembling hand, and the
American flag at the stern as if her shirt tail were hanging out
drooping aft in the windless gloomy air of seven bells in the
morning, obviously half wanting to give the refinery a wide
berth, but just as obviously having to pass it (and as obviously
wanting to stop in), invested as it was for her with her abhor-
rence and like some subdued roguish Don Quixote – because
of excesses there, which she did not know or could not remember but in any case would probably be blamed for, tip-toeing
past the refinery, but next moment – and by God she had guts,
she had character to brave the irate and weary oiltender this
morning – as large as life, as if propped on elbow against the
ravaged and wrecked bar of the refinery, in exactly the same

place as the day before ... 'As I was saying, fellow, when we
were so rudely interrupted ...' And that evening, hours and
hours later, with a shameless but unmistakably rakish raffish
list to starboard toward the wharf, in exactly the same place, as
if talking her head off. And then – so much for symbols and
presciences of disaster! – the next morning dawning blue and
clean and fresh, with white horses running past the refinery
wharf, that now looked completely undamaged, and the *Salinas*
gone, to be plunging innocently somewhere in the blue Pacific
her hangover washed away and the fire gone, and the smell
and noise and sirens gone, and the fresh green of the forest,
the blowing blue and white smoke of sawmills against the
green hills, and the maniacal sky gone and the mountains high
and the sea blue and cold and clean and an innocent sun over
all ...

'Where there is-a too much religion, is perdition – white, red
light and a cock outside,' the guide mused, discovering another
horizontal emblem in the pavement outside the ex-respectable
lupanar. 'Formalities!' He regarded this dislocated and unusual signpost – perhaps the great-grandfather of all signposts
– a moment. 'Friend ask –' he began. 'But how to find this-a
house? Friend say: go to fountain thirty paces on left pavement is cock pointing. Friend go ...' He gestured significantly,
as if having gone. 'Why for this? He goes in. Very nice, very
clean, separate rooms for love and fine garden where walk
around first to get excited ...' Signor Salacci was tired and sat
down for a moment on a ruined wall. The abomination of
desolation sitting in the unholy place. 'Very dirty streets,' he
added as now they started to move on once more. 'Contrasts,'
he said musingly, 'in everything. Roman Empire start-a in
Pompeii to-a going down ... old marbles a-broken,' he said
sadly. He pointed to a lone bust, sad in the brilliant sunshine. 'A
facsimile of Apollo – exactly the same size but –' he hissed
and made a long expression – 'with a lady-face, because the
Greeks make everything so sweet and gentle, but the Romans
make everything like this:' – he drew down a growth of savage
hair from his chin – 'with beards.'

'Roman exaggerations is,' he continued after a while, 'each

exaggeration in life is defeat, and therefore downfalls ... You see,' he said, pointing out an example of this phenomenon, 'Lime is-a stronger than stone, stones worn out, lime still good. Attention, gentlemen, the curve!' He guided their steps around a pre-Roman Doric column. 'In Italian we laugh and we say, "Attention, gentlemen, the curve." A pun,' he explained. 'Curva also mean lost woman ...' They approached a heap of rubble. 'Americans drop bombs here ... Americans will drop bomb anywhere,' he lamented delightedly. 'Students walking in garden.' The Fairhavens looked around but they didn't see them. 'Greek theater, soldier barrack, night theater, pine trees,' he hummed. 'Where is too much religion is perdition,' he added; 'white, red light, and a cock outside. Formalities! See, modern plumbing.' And Roderick reflected, looking at the twisted pieces of big lead pipes, that once upon a time it was true, the Romans *did* have modern plumbing.

Until a man has built (or helped to build – for he had helped the Wildernesses build their house) a house with his own hands, Roderick thought, he may feel a sense of inferiority before such things as Greek columns. But if he happens to have helped build so much as a summer shack upon the beach he will not feel inferiority, even if he does not understand in the aggregate the entire meaning of a Doric temple. The baseless shaft, the capital, and the lower fascia, that would connect the columns, at least become clear. The shaft was analogous to the cedar piles that they had sunk into the hardpan. Capitals they had achieved without meaning to, solely because it would turn out that a pile had unintentionally been sunk too deep for the stringer and the post to be square, so between the stringer and the post they would insert a block. The wooden stringer, say a two- or three-inch plank, corresponded to the lower fascia, though if one had been completely successful the stringer would rest directly upon the post: thus, the capital, as something deliberate, perhaps had no function, and was the result of an original disharmony, when people built with wood; someone had decided, perhaps on some occasion when a mistake on one side had been balanced by a similar mistake on the other, that it was an aesthetic improvement. These curious thoughts occurred to Roderick as, bent over his camera, he was trying to get Tansy and the guide, who were having a conversation over by the Temple of Apollo, into focus, for the light from the slowly westering sun was good now and the ruins were full of interesting, if pretty obvious, shadows. Ridiculous and far-fetched though it might sound, what he had been thinking gave Roderick, finally, a certain kinship with the builders of Pompeii ... But these Pompeiians – what had they built for? What was this instinct that made men herd together like partridges, like sardines in tomato paste, this cowardly dependence on the presence of others?

Suddenly he thought he knew what was wrong. This – in Pompeii, in Naples – this had happened to him, to Roderick McGregor Fairhaven, the visitor from Ultima Thule. What it amounted to was a feeling that there was not going to be time. Did you want to harrow yourself looking at what had been only temporarily spared, at what was finally doomed? And Roderick could not help but wonder whether man too was not beginning to stand, in some profound inexplicable sense, fundamentally in some such imperfect or dislocated relation to his environment as he. Man once stood at the center of the universe, as Elizabethan poets stood at the center of the world. – But the difference between the man-made ruins and the ruins of Pompeii was that the man-made ones had not for the most part been found worth preserving, or had been carried away. Had some precious part of man been carried away with the ruins? Partly it was as if man built with ruin in view ... See Naples and die!

'Thank you, Tansy dear,' Roderick said, clicking the shutter. 'Now may I take one of you alone, Signor?'

'Si,' the guide said, evidently finishing something he'd been saying to Tansy. 'Si, I am Pompeiian.'

And suddenly laughing as if to please them, the guide, that perfectly adjusted man, made a Roman salute, and Roderick snapped him standing there – right arm upraised, so that it drew his coat very tight under his arms, and the papers stood out of his pocket – between the pillars of the demolished Temple of Apollo.

'We thank you very much indeed for everything, Signor,'

Roderick said, winding the film forward and replacing the camera in his pocket.

They were about to leave Pompeii by the Porta Marina and Signor Salacci said to them: 'The gate is built like a funnel, for a ventilation, to suck up fresh air from the sea, blowing up to the mountain and ventilate town – street banked very straight to the right. So when it rains, water runs to right, you walk dry on left.

'Slaves and animals on one side,' he reminded them as they shook hands at the portal. 'People on the other.'

They all stood looking back over the ancient town toward Vesuvius and Roderick asked:

'And when do you think there's going to be another eruption, Signor?'

'Ah . . .' Signor Salacci wagged his head somberly. And then as he regarded the mountain a look of enormous pride came over his face. 'But yesterday,' he said, 'yesterday she give-a the beeg-a shake!'

GIN AND GOLDENROD

It was a warm, still, sunless day in mid-August. The sky did not appear so much cloudy as merely a uniform pearly gray, like the inside of a seashell, Primrose said. The sea, where they saw it through the motionless drooping trees, was gray too, the bay looking like a polished metal mirror in which the reflections of the lead-gray mountains were clear and motionless. In the forest it was very quiet, as though all the birds and small creatures had abandoned it, and the two figures of the man and his wife walking along the narrow footpath, and their little cat bounding along beside them, seemed the only things alive, so that when a vermilion and black and white garter snake wriggled off into the dry leaves and twigs it sounded loud as a deer crashing through the bracken.

Primrose was looking everywhere for the pair of goldfinches, whose nest, with its exquisite pale blue-white eggs, they had found in a trammon tree only six feet from the ground in May, and which they had watched all summer with delight, but their birds were nowhere to be seen.

'The dear goldfinches have gone to Alcapancingo,' she said.

'Not so early ... They're just gone because they don't like it here any more, with all these new houses going up and their old haunts destroyed.'

'Don't be gloomy, Sig darling. It'll be all right.'

Primrose and Sigbjørn Wilderness were now approaching the few houses on the fringe of the forest. The cat, black and white, with platinum whiskers, sat sniffing at a clump of spring beauty. He would go no further. Then he vanished. Sigbjørn and Primrose came out of the woods into a place where the ground was being cleared, then as by common consent turned off before they reached the store that had come in sight – which was being partly dismantled in order to create a larger one – taking another side path to the left. This transverse path had also once led through the woods, but the ground on one side had been cleared for building. The bushes had been allowed to remain, and it was still a pleasant leafy way of thimbleberries and salmonberries, that in winter, in frost, in moonlight, made a trillion moons.

It brought them out abruptly on a dusty main highway, upon either side of which, as far as the eye could reach, lay sections of brown drainpipe and where a signpost said: *To Dark Rosslyn.*

Sigbjørn's emotions now were entirely those of the cat's — or what the cat's would have been had he had the poor sense to accompany them this far: terror, fear, distrust, anger, anguish, and a hatred so pure in its intensity it was almost beautiful to experience. It was mid-afternoon, and Sunday, and now the cars honked and whizzed by in an all but continuous uproar, each sending up its private cyclone of dust from the road, against which the two had constantly to pause and turn their backs. The bus for Dark Rosslyn came past, snarling like a wild beast crashed by, leaving a backwash of air in which the trees thrashed for some moments. For there were trees again now, on either side of the road, for a short distance, then where there had been the woodland, through which they would have continued their path, there was a huge area of rubble, from which stumps of trees, blackened, hollow, some in cactus shapes, protruded as if blasted by lightning. Near at hand, on the highway, with no thought of privacy, some new houses had already been built, but owing to the law, no trees were left near them. Nevertheless, the destruction of the forest had opened up a magnificent view of the mountains and the inlet, that had been invisible from the road before, and you would have thought that all this evidence of growth and rebuilding would have been productive of anything but despair. On either side of the road a shallow ditch fell away to what, in other seasons, was a small brook, now dry and choked with weeds. Primrose, searching for wildflowers wherever a trace of moisture remained in these ditches, was wandering back and forth across the road, or even pausing vaguely in the middle to search the banks on either side. At these times Sigbjørn would shout at her or even seize her by the waist or shoulder and push her into the side.

'Look out!' 'My God, there's a car –' 'Primrose! There's a –' 'I know it. Look, darling –' and she was off again, swift and graceful in her scarlet corduroy slacks.

Sigbjørn's anxiety shifted now, as for the moment she walked in single file ahead of him – though every time a car went by he almost jumped into the ditch himself – to their goal in Dark Rosslyn. He doubted his ability to find it in the maze of roads that wandered around the hillside at the edge of the town, wondered if he would recognize the house again, through the heavy dolorous recollections of the previous Sunday, and feeling in his right side still the pain of the fall in the black woods, he began to sweat. Now he wished to take off his shirt, knowing that if he said so Primrose would say brightly, 'Well, why don't you?' and somehow unable to do so on this main highway.

They passed the office of the Rosslyn Park Real Estate and Development Company: *Rosslyn Park, Enquire Here, Scenic View-Lots. Approved for National Housing Loans. Cash or Terms:* past the hideous slash of felled trees, bare, broken, ugly land crossed by dusty roads and dotted with new ugly houses where only a few years ago rested the beautiful forest they had loved.

Look Out for Men! said a sign: *Soft Shoulders: Keep away: Private:* and now the road was half torn up and the ditches where the brook had been and the wildflowers of spring once grew were being filled in with a pipe line, bringing water and all the commercial comforts and plumbing of civilization to their once wild and lonely haven. Here, in a particularly vicious slash, where some rank thistles and huge dandelions grew, they saw their goldfinches feeding among the thistles, and paused. Among them was a new bird, like a tiny yellow and black striped sparrow, and Primrose ran across the road again, followed by Sigbjørn, looking both ways at once.

'Look! It's a pine martin.'

'A martin's a kind of rat.'

'Yes, that's right; but there's a bird called a purple martin.'

'You mean a pine siskin.'

'Of course. But what's it doing here on the coast? They only live in the high altitudes. Oh, isn't it sweet.'

The pine siskin darted away and they walked on past, now, thank God, the end of ugsome Rosslyn Park and the little new 'coffee bar' – Sigbjørn glanced at it with pure hatred, it was Sunday, but anyhow you could only buy Coca-Cola and Seven-Up – the big new schoolhouse, a great concrete block of mnemonic anguish, and reached a short stretch still comparatively unspoiled. What did he mean by this – 'comparatively unspoiled'? Were one's emotions of horror even quite the truth? Canada was indeed a pretty large country to despoil. But her legends, nearly all her most valuable and heroic history was the history of spoliation, in one form or another. But man was not a bird, or a wild animal, however much he might live in the wilderness. The conquering of wilderness, whether in fact or in his mind, was part of his own process of self-determination. The plight was an old-fashioned one, that had become true again: progress was the enemy, it was not making man more happy or secure. Ruination and vulgarization had become a habit. Nor – though they had found a sort of peace, a sort of heaven, and were now losing it again – had they, very consciously, been looking for peace. Nevertheless he could not help thinking of the green loveliness of their lost woodland, etc. etc., and all these conflicting clichés buzzed in his head as he followed Primrose, who had found a deep spot where a pool of water from the brook still lingered and here, shaded from the dust and heat of summer, a mass of wild blue forget-me-nots shone fresh and bright among damp emerald moss and near it some American brooklime.

But Sigbjørn could not climb down and pick them for her, he could not, even, remember the name, though he himself had first found and identified this latter flower in June. She didn't want them now, Primrose said, they would be all wilted before they even reached Dark Rosslyn; perhaps he could pick her some on the way back. And now she had seen some goldenrod, growing among a great bank of pearly everlasting; the first goldenrod of the year. They would pick that on their way back too.

'I'm even more doubtful now,' he said.

'Of what?'

'That I can find the house.'

'But I phoned the taxi driver this morning. You told me to. I said we'd be along this afternoon. He knows where it is, doesn't he?'

'I don't think I can face him ... *With his knowing grin,*' he added.

'There's the taxi driver's house just ahead, honey. Come on, it'll soon be over now.'

'Besides, I wanted to save money,' Sigbjørn said.

'*Save!*'

'Don't be angry. I'm sure I can find it,' Sigbjørn said, standing at the crossroads. 'It's just up there and off to the left, I think.'

'Well ... how far is it?' Primrose said dubiously.

'Not too far. Well — perhaps it's a fair distance but if we don't find it we can always come back and get the taxi.'

Primrose hesitated, then took his arm and they went off up the side road. The road was unpaved and dusty but at least they were rid of the momentous traffic and the taxi driver, and Sigbjørn felt rather less sick and almost hopeful. But the intrusion of the taxi driver at all disturbed and confused him. Why had he told Primrose to phone the taxi driver? He thought he remembered him in relation to last Sunday but the connection between him and the object of their visit was vague. Nonetheless he had been sufficiently conscious of such a connection to think it worth getting Primrose to phone. And then, there was always the question that he'd thought he would never have been able to make it walking at all.

The road went downhill briefly toward the sea, turned sharply right, then left again and now ahead of them was a long steep hill. He gazed at it in dismay, for it didn't look familiar at all. Had he really come this way? Or should he have made that other turn off to the left, as Primrose suggested was more likely. He hesitated, listening to the distant sound of traffic: the klaxons sounded like blended mouthorgans.

'No, I'm sure it's this way. Come on,' Sigbjørn said, and they started up the hill doggedly. Now, the traffic behind, a suburban dementia launched itself at them: flat ugly houses, the cleared land, stricken and bare, left without a tree to give shade or privacy or beauty; or strewn with half burned stumps and rubbish. Wy Wurk, Wy Wurry, Amble Inn (again), Dew Drop Inn, Dunwoiken, Kozy Kot, crowned by the masterpiece: Aunty So-Shall. But behind each one of these bourgeois horrors was still the dark forest, waiting, one hoped, for revenge.

They trudged slowly up the hill and now Sigbjørn really began to sweat, for it was hot here, with a sultry damp heat that made the air feel thick and hard to breathe, and his side was hurting again. He looked anxiously back at Primrose who had removed her scarlet corduroy jacket and was panting and scowling behind him, for though she loved to walk she hated climbing hills, and at this moment she meant him to know it. Sigbjørn went ahead, but he could already see that it was as she said: the road wound directly away from Dark Rosslyn and back toward home. But there, too, just at the turn, was a rustic wood arch at the left which said *Whytecliffe Resort, Riding Academy, Horses by the Day or Hour. Refreshments.*

Sigbjørn waited unhappily until Primrose caught up with him.

'Well,' she said. 'Did you go to Whytecliffe?'

'I don't think so. No.'

'Surely you'd remember that thing.' She pointed to the arch.

'I don't know . . . but we might as well go and see.'

'You go then. I'll sit here and catch my breath.'

Tall cedars, Douglas firs, grew beyond the arch as he went up the bridle path, and it was a little cooler, a breath from the sea below freshened the air, and now he could see the bay beneath him, and for some reason this made him feel better. There, below him and to the right were the stables; people were getting on and off horses, calling to each other, and a young couple mounted and paced up the hill toward him: 'What do I do?' 'You just pull on the right rein and it'll do it for you.' And that was true too, once on it, the horse would do everything for you, even to throwing you off. It was hard to be angry with a place where you could hire horses, or see a riding academy as a symptom of modernity. He and Primrose always talked of riding together, though they never had. And how much better the money might have been spent here, with her – well, it was no use looking, he knew it wasn't here he'd been the previous Sunday, and he turned back.

'Isn't this where Greenslade lives now – at Whytecliffe somewhere,' she said when he returned to the arch.

'I think so . . . Yes.'

'We might go and find him then. He'll know where it is.'

'No!' Sigbjørn said. 'No. I'll find it, for Christ's sake . . . or we'll get the taxi driver. Come on.'

'But Greenslade was with you. He'll know –'

'No.' Sigbjørn started distractedly down the hill. 'You said no yourself. You said you'd rather be in hell than meet Greenslade again.'

'He's a horrible man.'

'Yapping about the benefits of civilization. How easy it is for people to talk about the benefits of civilization, who've never known the far greater benefits of not having anything to do with it at all!'

Halfway down the hill Primrose suddenly took his arm.

'Look, Sigbjørn, there – those birds with the white stripes on their tails.'

'Vesper sparrows?'

'No. They don't have so much white. Oh, what are they?'

'Pipits. Some kind of pipits. American pipits,' Sigbjørn said, as the birds lighted on a nearby alder tree. 'Yeah. See how they're bobbing their tails?'

'How clever you are –' Primrose held his arm tightly to her side. 'And brave too. I think you're swell. I know this is perfectly bloody for you.'

'Thank you. I think you're very fine too. But all this isn't easy to do. And I don't see why I'm doing it.'

'But you said you wanted to make a new start, you said it was to be –'

'Yes it was. *It is.*'

Watz-it-2-U. Opposite this house, a little further on, a narrow rutted road turned off to the right and Sigbjørn halted again; it didn't look familiar yet he had the feeling the place was off in that direction. At the juncture of the road a stone house was in process of being built. The foundations were in, the walls were part way up, the window frames had taken their square or oblong gaping shapes and inside this half-built house three people were standing: a man, his wife, and a little boy about seven or eight. They were walking around it, they leaned on the windowsills, they pointed, now, toward where the roof would be, their every expression and gesture one of such hope and excitement and joy that Sigbjørn turned away: even were the fate of this house to be called Amble Inn, it was not right to look at them thus, he felt, gruesome though their odious nest might be.

He walked on quickly, but as the road made a sharp turn he halted suddenly before three houses in front of which there seemed to be a policeman, or a man in shirt sleeves and a navy blue cap like a policeman's. He turned and almost ran back to where Primrose was lingering, around the bend, gazing at some more goldenrod.

'I think it's over this way, but there's a policeman there –'

'A policeman? Where?'

Primrose walked on around the bend then turned, beckoning. The policeman was a taxi driver. But he was not 'their' taxi driver. He was a strange one, probably from the city, but if not a policeman, why a taxi driver *here* at this place, and why these other people standing nakedly and unguiltily about, but as it were too consciously *unl*ooking – but no, the taxi driver was merely shepherding two elderly women who were looking rather too curiously at Sigbjørn, or so it seemed, and he hurried on again past the three houses and began to climb yet another hill that ran out of sight. But at the top of this hill the road stretched out, turning toward the highway with, oh God, yet another long, long, steep hill ahead.

'I won't do it. I won't,' Primrose said. She stamped her foot. 'If we'd got the taxi driver we'd have been there and had it all over by now. I won't –'

'Please. Oh please, Primrose. Don't be angry. As a matter of fact I'm sure it's just down there,' Sigbjørn yelled in a soft whisper. 'Look, maybe it's that –'

'I won't –'

'Christ you said you didn't want to see Greenslade. And Christ I'm doing my best. And Christ I think this is the house.'

It might be. He hurried on and stopped at a corner where three more houses made a blind T. Here it was – or was it? There was this house on the near corner, a high-roofed, wooden house, in need of paint, with a bare, littered yard in which a little black kitten and a puppy were playing together and a small girl playing with a saw stared at them.

'Well, is this it?' Primrose caught up with him, tight-lipped and pale.

'Oh hush! You insisted on coming with me, now you might be –'

'*What?*'

'Oh for God's sake, Primrose.'

'I never did any such thing. You know you begged me to come, Sigbjørn –'

Sigbjørn, exasperated beyond endurance and smarting under his own unfair and untruthful charge at Primrose, gave one despairing glance around and rushed to the door where he knocked loudly.

'Why not try the back door?' Primrose suggested after a while.

The back door was open and they could see through into a dirty, dark kitchen with dirty dishes and bits of stale bread and food on the floor and sink. A radio played loudly. Sigbjørn knocked again. There was a deceptive air of slatternly inno-cence in a teapot sitting on the cookstove and though the place had something familiar about it he still couldn't be sure. And if Al – Al? didn't answer the door who on earth was he to ask for? He took the letter out of his pocket and tried again to make out the signature: 'Dear Sigbjørn – you asked how you could send that $26.00 Your wife exerted so much pressure for me to be on my way the other morning that I forgot to leave you my address. Which is Yours truly F. Landry (Landing? Fanbug?) P.O. Box 32 Dark Rosslyn.' This same pressure he must have felt exerted upon himself, for it seemed he moved from the door, and was contemplating going around to the front again.

Primrose suddenly took his arm, then she kissed his cheek.

'There now, Sig darling, it'll soon be over now my brave one.'

He took a deep breath and knocked again, loudly; the radio was turned off somewhere in the front of the house and footsteps sounded. Sigbjørn turned around.

'You promised,' he whispered, 'you promised to be nice – and to have a drink with him, if he offers us one.'

And now someone, a man, the man Al, appeared, a short muscular fellow with untidy hair, dressed in unpressed trousers, suspenders over a soiled shirt, while his shoes were curled up at the toes and broken at one sole. Sigbjørn felt Primrose stiffen behind him, taking in every detail of his loose fat mouth, bad teeth and squinting eyes.

'Hello,' Sigbjørn said.

'Hello. Come in.' He opened the door and they filed into the squalid kitchen where Primrose sat down quietly on a chair and Sigbjørn stood beside the sink. 'Haven't got a thing in the place,' the man was saying, 'but Al can get you a bottle.'

Sigbjørn, who had thought this man was Al, was confused, and now the beacon, the pharos, of the possible drink at the bootleggers' that had shone before him all the way was gone. He remembered the rather hopeless, nearly empty bottle at home and glanced at Primrose, but she was gazing out the door, her clear, cold profile and glassy polite smile gave him no hope on this plane.

'I came to pay you the debt I owe you from last Sunday,' Sigbjørn said. 'I got your letter.'

'Yeah? I've quit. Well, I've quit for a while anyways. After last Sunday. But there was no hurry about that. You could have sent me a check or something.'

'Do I really owe you twenty-six dollars?'

'That's right. There was eight bottles of gin drunk up here last Sunday. First time I ever served drinks in my house. I tried to get you to go, you know, but then the Indians came.'

'Indians?'

'Yeah.'

'But I paid for the first two bottles. I had the money, remember?' Sigbjørn said. 'And Greenslade paid for his didn't he? Or didn't he?'

'He paid. But he went, after the first bottle was gone. He didn't drink so much. He took his bottle and left. But you wouldn't go. You wanted to take them two bottles home to drink with your wife, remember? But then them Indians came and you started buying them drinks and that's bad stuff. You know. Indians. It ain't safe. I was on hot bricks.'

'I'm sorry if I caused you any trouble,' Sigbjørn said.

'Oh, that's all right, bud. But I never saw a man drink so much and stay on his feet. Them Indians passed out – one was laying on the floor over there, remember? And he was getting tough – you know how they do when they're drinking. They feel insulted.'

'They do,' Sigbjørn said. 'And by God –'

'Giving drinks to Indians, that's bad. I tried to get you out, then to get you to lay down a little and you says: I'm going to lay down and sleep for exactly twenty minutes and then I'm going to get up and have another drink. And by God you done just that. Never saw anything like it, Missus.' He turned to Primrose. 'That's just what he done. Exactly twenty minutes.'

'Yes,' she said.

'Well now, I hate to see a man get taken advantage of. Them Indians ought to of paid for some of it. You know when you get it from me on a Sunday, like, when the liquor stores is closed, I gotta charge a bit more and all. Tell you what, though, suppose we settle for twenty, how's that?'

'Thank you . . . How did I spend thirty-nine dollars?'

'Well, brother, you drank it. Never saw a man drink so damn much and stand on his feet. I got a taxi and took you home, remember? That is, I let you off there by the store and you said you'd make it the rest of the way all right. And I put a bottle in your pocket, you wanted to take to your wife, did you get home with that?'

'I got lost in the forest.'

'It's the first time you've ever done it,' Primrose said.

'Well I'm damned.' The man grinned. 'You sure had a time for yourself, bud. But you got home O.K.?'

'Yes, I got home O.K. You saw me the next morning. I mean the morning after the next morning.' Sigbjørn stared at the floor: but not that night. Where, actually, had he spent that night? Had he slept on the ground? drunk the bottle? where had he fallen? And the new sports jacket, precious because Primrose had given it to him for his birthday, worn only the second time that night –

'I've quit,' the man was saying to Primrose now. 'The person next door is very religious . . . one of them Indians fell down outside and he was quite obscene in his language . . .'

And why not, Sigbjørn thought, Christ why not! and he remembered the time when the deer used to come down through the woods and swim across the bay and there hadn't been any bootlegger in Dark Rosslyn to sell you firewater on Sunday, or, come to that, any reason for drinking it. How easy to make a judgment here. The deduction made, another lie would speed to its total doom, were it wholly untrue: the evil is in its half-life, where it coalesces with all the other half-truths and quarter-truths to confuse us, the esemplastic medium of oversimplifications in which we live. The bootlegger, in times of prohibition, in great cities, has one function. The bootlegger, in times of partial prohibition, has another. The bootlegger, on Sundays, where there is Sunday prohibition, is a secular savior. The bootlegger, in rural places, is as fundamental as the prostitute in the city –

'I've been batching it for three weeks – the wife's in Saskatoon. That's why the place is in such a mess,' the man was saying apologetically to Primrose, and then to Sigbjørn: 'Well, we'll settle for twenty dollars, is that O.K.? And I'll tell you what, there's one of them Indians I know pretty well and maybe I can get a bottle out of him to help pay his share. If I can I'll bring it along, how's that?'

'O.K.' Sigbjørn said, handing over the twenty dollars.

Primrose went to the door. 'It looks like rain,' she said, 'perhaps we'd better get started.'

'Well, good-by.'

'So long, bud. See you in jail.'

'Ha ha.'

'Ha ha.'

Sigbjørn and Primrose Wilderness walked silently side by side

213

down the road toward the long hill until they felt themselves out of sight of the houses. Then Primrose suddenly threw her arms around Sigbjørn.

'Darling Sig. Please forgive me for being so foul. I really was perfectly foul and God I'm sorry ! Say you forgive me.'

'Of course. I was disgusting too.'

'You weren't. You were brave. I know how awful that was for you and I – I thought you were gallant !'

'There are the pipits again – there.'

'So they are.'

Watz-it-2-U ... Walking hand in hand they came to the bottom of the long hill and there was a new footpath branching off through the woods toward the highway, a short-cut which would eliminate the hill. 'But Primrose, honey, maybe it's private property. What if it ends up in somebody's garden ?'

'It doesn't say so. Oh come on, Sigbjørn, let's try it anyhow.'

Primrose started down the path which, at first fairly wide, became more and more narrow and overgrown though now, just ahead, they could hear the snorting obscene traffic of the highway. Then suddenly the path debouched into a garden and there in front of them was a woman, hoeing. Sigbjørn and Primrose started to apologize together but the woman straightened up and smiled.

'Oh, that's all right. Somebody comes in here every once in a while from that path. You can get through to the road. Just go round the garage there and down our drive.'

They thanked her and Sigbjørn led the way, Primrose following behind.

Once more they were on the highway, pushed into the side of the ditch by the passing cars. Primrose was gathering pearly everlasting and tall dusty purple asters, she gathered them, for Sigbjørn could scarcely bend for the pain in his side, so he carried them for her and walked behind. Kozy Kot. Amble Inn.

The rain began to fall, soft and gentle and cool, a benison. They came to the little boarded shelter of the bus stop and halted for a moment as they saw the bus approaching.

'Shall we take the bus ?'

'Oh no. Let's walk.'

'But you'll get wet. Won't it spoil your clothes?' Sigbjørn said, for he loved her scarlet corduroy slacks and jacket.

'Not these. I don't think it's going to rain very hard anyhow. And I do want some goldenrod!'

The bus whizzed past and they turned their heads from that disgusting smell and blast which progress has schooled us to believe – as Proust observed – was nostalgic too. A silent ambulance looking, Sigbjørn thought, like a hearse, came up the road from the city and stopped before a house on the corner.

'Look –' Primrose said. 'Do you remember that chap who used to sit on that porch typing every time we came by?'

'Oh yes – on the big heavy office typewriter. I hope he's not –'

They lingered, watching the ambulance driver in conversation with a gray-haired woman on the porch, but it appeared he was only inquiring his way, and they started on, obscurely relieved that it wasn't the man of the typewriter, to whom they'd never spoken a word.

Primrose walked ahead, carrying a single stem of scarlet bunch-berries, that species of tiny dogwood they had discovered one spring, and Sigbjørn behind, carrying the goldenrod. He was watching Primrose in her scarlet slacks and the scarf she was wearing now over her head against the rain, which was of scarlet and cobalt and emerald and black and white and gold in the design of a curious bird with cobalt beak and emerald feet.

'I have a confession to make, Sigbjørn,' she said.

'May I know what?'

'You didn't lose that bottle of gin. You gave it to me when you came back the next morning. But I put it away and then you thought you'd lost it.'

'Then we have it now.'

'Sure. And we can have a cocktail when we get back.'

'Good girl.'

They stepped into their own woods and the cat came leaping to meet them. In the cool silver rainy twilight of the forest a kind of hope began to bloom again.

THE FOREST PATH TO THE SPRING

To Margerie, my wife

At dusk, every evening, I used to go through the forest to the spring for water.

The way that led to the spring from our cabin was a path wandering along the bank of the inlet through snowberry and thimbleberry and shallon bushes, with the sea below you on the right, and the shingled roofs of the houses, all built down on the beach beneath round the little crescent of the bay.

Far aloft gently swayed the mastheads of the trees: pines, maples, cedars, hemlocks, alders. Much of this was second growth but some of the pines were gigantic. The forest had been logged from time to time, though the slash the loggers left was soon obliterated by the young birch and vines growing up quickly.

Beyond, going toward the spring, through the trees, range beyond celestial range, crowded the mountains, snow-peaked for most of the year. At dusk they were violet, and frequently they looked on fire, the white fire of the mist. Sometimes in the early mornings this mist looked like a huge family wash, the property of Titans, hanging out to dry between the folds of their lower hills. At other times all was chaos, and Valkyries of storm-drift drove across them out of the ever reclouding heavens.

Often all you could see in the whole world of the dawn was a huge sun with two pines silhouetted in it, like a great blaze behind a Gothic cathedral. And at night the same pines would write a Chinese poem on the moon. Wolves howled from the mountains. On the path to the spring the mountains appeared and disappeared through the trees.

And at dusk, too, came the seagulls, returning homeward down the inlet from their daily excursion to the city shores — when the wind was wailing through the trees, as if shot out of a catapult.

Ceaselessly they would come flying out of the west with their angelic wings, some making straight down the inlet, others gliding over the trees, others slower, detached, staggering, or at a dreadfully vast height, a straggling marathon of gulls.

On the left, half hidden among the trees in monolithic attitudes of privacy, like monastic cells of anchorites or saints, were the wooden backhouses of the little shacks.

This was what you could see from the path, which was not only the way to the spring but a fraction of the only footpath through the forest between the different houses of Eridanus, and when the tide was high, unless you went by boat, the only way round to your neighbors.

Not that we had any neighbors to speak of. For the greater part of the year we were often almost alone in Eridanus. My wife and myself, a Manx boatbuilder named Quaggan and occasionally some of Quaggan's sons, a Dane, Nicolai Kristbjorg, and a Channel Islander called Mauger, who had a fishing boat, *Sunrise*, were usually the sole inhabitants, and once we were quite alone the whole winter.

Yet for all their air of abandonment most of the little shacks were prettily and neatly painted and some had names too. Next to ours was Dunwoiken, and by the spring, on the right, the steps went down to Hi-Doubt, which, as if indeed in doubt, was not built upon piles sunk in the hardpan of the beach, but on log rollers, so that the whole could be floated away the easier if necessary to another place, and in this country it was not an uncommon sight to see a house, mounted on such rollers, its chimney smoking, drawn by a tug, sailing downstream.

The very last and northernmost shack of all, the one nearest the mountains, was called Four Bells, and was owned by a kindly engine driver, whose real home was in the Prairies.

On the opposite side, the right of the path, across the mile of water, ran the railway track along the other bank of the inlet, in the same way that the path ran along our bank, with more little shacks mysteriously under the embankment.

We always thought we could tell when the engine driver was bringing his train back with the prospect of a sojourn at Four Bells, where perhaps he could just make out over the water from his cab his sailing craft tugging at anchor like a little white goat, by the way he would sound his whistle gloriously in welcome. It was his fireman no doubt did so but Mr Bell whom one felt to be the artist. The sound after hallooing across the inlet to us would echo for fully a minute down the gorges and back and forth across the mountains and always the day after this happened, or that evening, smoke would be seen coming out of the chimney of Four Bells.

And on other days during the storms in the same manner thunderclaps would go crashing and echoing down the inlet and the gorges.

Four Bells was not called Four Bells because its owner was an old seafarer, as I had been, but because his name was Bell, his family was three, so they were indeed Four Bells. Mr Bell was a tall rawboned man with a red weather-beaten face and the quizzical poetical longing and responsible look appropriate to his profession, but no sooner was the smoke going, and himself tacking up and down in his catboat, than he was once more happy as the child who had dreamed of being an engine driver.

Deep-sea freighters came down the inlet silently to the timber port invisible round the point beyond Four Bells or with a great list, tilted like wheelbarrows, sailed outward bound, their engines saying:

> *Frère* Jacques
> *Frère* Jacques
> *Dor*mez-vous?
> *Dor*mez-vous?

Sometimes too, on the seaboard of the night, a ship would stand drawn, like a jeweled dagger, from the dark scabbard of the town.

Since we were in a bay *within* the inlet, the city, like the town – by which latter I mean Eridanus Port at the sawmill – the city was invisible to us, *behind* us on the path, was our feeling; almost opposite us was Port Boden, seen only as power lines ruled across the dawn or gentian and white smoke of shingle mills, and on the opposite bank too, though nearer the city, was the oil refinery. But the point southward blocked for us what would have been, beyond wide tide flats, a distant view of the cantilever bridges, skyscrapers and gantries of the city, with more great mountains that way too, and on this southerly point stood a lighthouse.

It was a whitewashed concrete structure, thin as a match, like a magic lighthouse, without a keeper, but oddly like a human being itself, standing lonely on its cairn with its ruby lamp for a head and its generator strapped to its back like a pack; wild roses in early summer blew on the bank beside it, and when the evening star came out, sure enough, it began its beneficent signaling too.

If you can imagine yourself taking a pleasure steamer down the inlet from the city some afternoon, going toward the northern mountains, first you would have left the city harbor with its great freighters from all over the world with names like *Grimanger* and ΟΙΔΙΠΟΥΣ ΤΥΡΑΝΝΟΣ and its shipyards, and then to starboard would be the railway tracks, running away from the city along the bank, through the oil-refinery station, along the foot of steep cliffs that rose to a high wooden hill, into Port Boden, and then, curving out of sight, beginning their long climb into the mountains; on the port side beneath the white peaks and the huge forestation of the mountain slopes would be tide-flats, a gravel pit, the Indian reserve, a barge company, and then the point where the wild roses were blowing and the mergansers nested, with the lighthouse itself; it was here, once around the point with the lighthouse dropping astern, that you would be cutting across our bay with our little cabins under the trees on the beach where we lived at Eridanus, and that was our path going along the bank; but you would be able to see from your steamer what we could not, right around the next point at Four Bells, into Eridanus Port – or, if this happens to be today, what was Eridanus Port and is now a real estate subsection; perhaps you would still see people waving at you before that though, and the man with the megaphone on your steamer who points out the sights would say contemptuously, 'Squatters; the government's been trying to get them off for years,' and that would be ourselves, my wife and me, waving to you gaily; and then you would have passed our bay and be sailing directly northwards into the snow-covered mountain peaks, past numerous enchanting uninhabited islands of tall pines, down gradually into the narrowing gorge and to the uttermost end of that marvelous region of wilderness known to the Indians as Paradise, and where you may even today, among the advertisements for dyspeptic soft poisons nailed to trees, have, for the equivalent of what used to be an English crown, a cup of chill weak tea with a little bag in it at a place called Ye Olde Totemlande Inne.

This side of Four Bells were two nameless shacks, then Hangover, Wywurk, Doo-Drop-Inn and Trickle-In, but no one lived in these houses save in summer and they were all deserted for the rest of the year.

At first, rowing past it – for the names appeared on the side of the houses facing the water – the majestic name Dunwoiken had struck my imagination and I thought it must have been built by some exiled Scotsman, remembering his former estate, fallen on evil days, yet living amidst scenery that reminded him of the mountains and lochs of home. But that was before I understood its name was cousin-german to Wywurk and that both words were, in a manner of speaking, jokes. Dunwoiken had been built by four firemen – that is to say city firemen, not ship's firemen, as I had been – but immediately they built it they lost interest and never came back to the beach, though they must have rented or sold it, for over the course of years people came and went there.

Having once seen the joke about some of these names – and intended timbre of pronunciation, more sinister than at first met the eye – they began to irritate me, especially Wywurk. But apart from the fact that Lawrence wrote *Kangaroo* in a house called Wyewurk in Australia (and he was more amused than irritated), though I did not know this at the time, the irritation itself really springs I now think from ignorance, or snobbery. And in these days when streets and houses are mere soulless numbers is it not a survival of some instinct of unique identity in regard to one's home, some striving with ironic humor and self-criticism of this very estate of uniformity, for identity itself, in however bad taste. And even were it not, were they any more pretentious or unimaginative than the lordly sources they parodied? Is Inglewood a more imaginative name than Dunwoiken? Is Chequers? Or The White House? Is Maximilian's Miramar to be preferred to Maple View? And is Wuthering Heights not merely weathered out of its cuteness? But irritate me they did then, and most especially Wywurk. The holophrastic brilliance of this particular name, and more obvious sympathetic content, never failed to elicit comment from the richer passersby in motorboats, who, having to shout in order to make themselves heard on board above the engine, could be very well overheard on shore. But in later years, when we lived nearer to it, I soon learned to be grateful for the distraction this name provided.

For the sea-borne comments, carrying to our ears and which were invariably hurtful or cruel and cut us to the heart before the motorboats reached Wywurk, never failed to be appreciative on their passing Wywurk itself. First there was the brilliance of the pun to be discussed as it dawned upon them, then its philosophic content to be disputed among the boat's occupants, as a consequence of which they would disappear round the northward point in that mood of easy tolerance that comes only to the superior reader who has suddenly understood the content of an obscure poem.

Hangover – no doubt simply a statement of fact commemorating some cherished and even forgotten or perhaps permanently catastrophic state of mind, for we never saw anyone enter or leave this house and have not till this day – rarely inspired more than a passing chuckle. While Four Bells, whose name had been chosen with love, rarely excited comment either.

Eventually I realized that the hamlet was really two hamlets, that it was divided almost precisely into the houses with names, and the houses without names, though these two hamlets, like interpenetrating dimensions, were in the same place, and there was yet another town, or sort of town, by the sawmill round the northward point sharing our name Eridanus, as did the inlet itself.

The houses with names – with the exception of Four Bells, for Mr Bell's sojourns were any season – Hangover, Wywurk, Hi-Doubt and so on, belonged to people who just came to Eridanus for the week-end in summer, or for a summer holiday of a week or two. They were electricians, loggers, blacksmiths, mostly town-dwellers earning good salaries but not sufficient to afford summer houses at one of the settlements further up the inlet where land could be bought if, which was a point indeed, they would have cared to buy it; they built their little shacks here because it was government land and the Harbor Board, upon whom I often felt must have sat God Himself, did not object. Most of these summer people had children, most of them liked to fish for sport, and to do what they felt they were supposed to do on a summer holiday. When they came most of them had a wonderful time doing these things and then they went away again – I regret to say much to the relief of ourselves and the sea-birds – in some few cases no doubt to turn into the very sort of people who later would make cruel remarks, as from the superior vantage of their motorboats they observed the lowly homes of the squatters who still actually lived in such places.

The others, who lived for the most part in the houses without names, were all, with one exception, deep-sea fishermen who had been here many many years before the summer people came, and who had their houses here by some kind of 'foreshore rights' allowed to fishermen. The exception was the Manx boat-builder whose boat shed was large as a small church and built of hand-split cedar shakes, and whose floating pier bisected the bay and constituted its own general landing, the only thing perhaps that made the little impromptu port an entity, and he seemed to be the father or grandfather of most of the other fishermen, so that, in the way of Celts, it was a little like a big family the entrance to which, for an outsider, I was to find by no means easy.

Sometimes when it was stormy, in the later days, we used to sit in his shack strewn with a litter-like neatness, with bradawls and hacksaws, frows and nailsets and driftbolts, and drink tea, or when we had any, whisky, and sing the old Manx fishermen's hymn while the tempest howled across the inlet and the water, scarcely less loud, rushed with a mighty enthusiasm down his hemlock flume.

Because we were drinking tea or whisky inside while his sons, the fishermen, were outside – and moreover the strange life we were leading had made my wife and me by this time have an aversion even to fishing – now and then we sang it a bit ironically. Nonetheless in our way we must have meant what we sang. I had a guitar salved, not from my days as a jazz musician, but an older one from my days as a ship's fireman, my wife had a beautiful voice, and both the old man and I had not bad bass voices.

There is no hymn like this great hymn sung to the tune of Peel Castle with its booming minor chords in which sounds all the savagery of the sea yet whose words of supplication make less an appeal to, than a poem of God's mercy:

> Hear us, O Lord, from heaven Thy dwelling place,
> Like them of old in vain we toil all night,
> Unless with us Thou go who art the Light,
> Come then, O Lord, that we may see Thy face.
>
> Thou, Lord, dost rule the raging of the sea
> When loud the storm and furious is the gale,
> Strong is Thine arm, our little barks are frail,
> Send us Thy help, remember Galilee...

When the wild roses began to blow on the point by the light-house in June, and the mergansers swam in and out of the rocks with their little ducklings perched on their backs, these fishermen went away, sometimes singly, sometimes in pairs, sometimes three or four boats joined together, like proud white giraffes their newly painted fishing boats with their tall gear would be seen going round the point.

They went to sea, and some of them never returned, and as they went to sea, so Eridanus was taken over by the summer people.

Then on Labor Day, as if swept away by the great wash of the returning fishermen's craft wheeling across the bay and breaking all along the length of the beach, reaching within the bay at last with the successive thunder of rollers, the summer people would depart, back to the city, and the fishermen, their boats singly or in pairs, would have come home again.

They were only a bare half-dozen fishermen all told who lived in Eridanus so that one stormy equinox, when Kristbjorg, who had been sailing alone up to Alaska, in his sturdy snub-nosed old tub painted green, to differentiate it from the others, had still not returned, he left a gap.

Quaggan, my wife, and myself, were repairing Quaggan's iron stove with a mixture of wood ashes, asbestos and salt, and at the same time singing the fishermen's hymn, when Kristbjorg, a bald strong wide but childish-faced Dane, who lived as he fished absolutely alone too, walked right in. Soon we were all singing something very different – a Danish song of his, his translation of which may be written as follows:

> It blew a storm in the red-light district
> It was blowing so hard that not a sailor
> Was blown off the sea but a pimp was blown
> Off the street. It blew through the windows,
> And it rained through the roof –
> But the gang chipped in and bought a pint.
> And what is better
> When a bunch of soaks are together –
> Even when the roof is leaking?

Kristbjorg always came round to say good-by with solemnity before he sailed for the summer, as if for the last time. But we found that he sometimes liked to delay his return beyond the period necessary so that he would be missed by us, and missed indeed he was.

'We were anxious about you, Nicolai, we thought you were never going to get back in this weather.'

But it would turn out that he had been back and had been lurking in the city for a week.

'... In the city got a little exercise. Been sitting humped up in the old boat so long. I never saw a street flusher. They just letting the old grime go. The streetcars are getting so humpy and dumpy! – I ran into a couple of bottles of rye.... I thought a little walking would speed the old ticker....'

Quaggan loved all kinds of wood and did not care much to fish (save locally, off the end of his pier, just before he went visiting his grandchildren). 'Hemlock is very sweet that way,' he would say tenderly of his doughty flume that had survived a quarter of a century without decay.

There was another lonely man from the Yorkshire moors, who lived quite alone down beyond the lighthouse, and though he seldom came up to our little bay we saw him, from time to time, when we walked down to the point. It was his joy to make sure that the automatic lighthouse was working, he told us, and in fact he would start to talk, as if half to himself, as soon as he saw us approaching.

'The heagles, how they fly in great circles! Nature is one of the most beautiful things I ever saw in my life. Have you seen the heagle yesterday?'

'Yes, we did, Sam –'

'Why the heagle went round to get his bearings, to look over the country. Two miles wide, hin great circles ... Pretty soon you'll see crabs under these stones, and then it will be spring. They're some crabs in spring no bigger than a fly. Now have you ever seen how an elephant was constroocted? And where did those old Romans get them shields but from the rooster's wings?'

'Roosters, Sam?'

'Aye. And take in the desert now – the Sahara – where camels stamp with hooves like great spittoons upside down. One day they build a railroad –' he would lean against his lighthouse, nodding his head, '– but *hin*sects heat up all the wooden ties. Aye. So now they make the ties out of metal shaped like camels' hooves. . . . Nature is one of the most beautiful . . . And soon the birds, and pretty soon the crabs will bring the spring, my dearies, and the deer swimming right across the bay with their hantlers, beautiful, sticking up like branches on a floating tree, swimming, swimming across to this here lighthouse, right here, in spring. . . . Then you'll see dragonflies like flying machines back-pedaling. . . .'

The summer people rarely saw the fearful depredations their houses had to suffer in the winter, nor knew, during those hard months, what it was like to live in them. Perhaps they wondered why their summer homes had not been swept away by the storms they had heard shrieking and whipping against their city windows, the timbers they could imagine striking the piles and foundations of their shacks, the tempest, always the worst since 1866, that they read about in the city paper called the *Sun*, bought at a time of day when the real sun had gone down without, for that matter, sometimes ever having come up : the day after that they might motor out, leaving their cars – for unlike us they had cars – up on the road, and shake their heads to find their houses still there. How well we built, they would say. It was true. But the real reason was that there was that about Eridanus, existing by grace of God and without police or fire or other civic protection, that made its few inhabitants thoughtful. And a spirit would have seen that the fishermen during the winter had protected those summer houses as their own, but by the time summer arrived the fishermen had gone, not asking or expecting thanks. And while the fishermen were away it is also true that the summer people would not readily see damage happen to a fisherman's house, if they had lived long enough on the beach to think about it, that was, or happened to have been fishermen themselves, as was sometimes the case, or were old people.

This was Eridanus, and the wrecked steamer of the defunct Astra line that gave it its name lay round the point beyond the lighthouse, where, its engines failing, it had been driven ashore in a wild faen wind decades ago, carrying a cargo of cherries-in-brine, wine, and old marble from Portugal.

Gulls slept like doves on its samson posts where grasses were blowing abaft the dead galley, and in early spring pecked their old feathers off to make room for their new shiny plumage like fresh white paint. Swallows and goldfinches swept in and out of the dead fiddley. A spare propeller blade upright against the break of the poop had never been removed. Down below lever weight and fulcrum slept in an eternity of stillness. Grass grew too from the downfallen crosstrees, and in the dead winches wildflowers had taken root – wildflowers, spring beauties and death camass with its creamy blooms. And on the stern, seeming to comment on my own source, for I too had been born in that terrible city whose main street is the ocean, could still be almost made out the ghost of the words : *Eridanus*, Liverpool –

We poor folk were also Eridanus, a condemned community, perpetually under the shadow of eviction. And like Eridanus itself, in its eternal flux and flow, was the inlet. For in the heavens at night, as my wife first taught me, dark and wandering beneath blazing Orion, flowed the starry constellation Eridanus, known both as the River of Death and the River of Life, and placed there by Jupiter in remembrance of Phaethon, who once had the splendid illusion that he could guide the fiery steeds of the sun as well as his father Phoebus.

Legend merely states that Jupiter, sensing the danger to the world, shot a thunderbolt which, striking Phaethon, hurled him, his hair on fire, into the River Po, then that, in addition to creating the constellation in Phaethon's honor, in pity he changed Phaethon's sisters into poplar trees that they might always be near and protect their brother. But that he went to all this trouble suggests that he, even as Phoebus, was impressed by the attempt, and must have given the whole matter some thought. Recently our local paper, showing a surprisingly sudden interest in classical mythology, has claimed to see something insulting in the name of our town of a political, even an international nature, or as denoting foreign influences, as a result of which there has been some agitation, on the part of some distant ratepayers, with I know not what motives, to change its name to Shellvue. And undoubtedly the view in that specified direction is very fine, with the red votive candle of the burning oil wastes flickering ceaselessly all night before the gleaming open cathedral of the oil refinery –

II

It was on Labor Day, years ago at the beginning of the war, just after we had been married, and thinking it would be both our honeymoon and our first and last summer holiday together, that my wife and I, strangers from the cities, myself almost from the underworld, came to live in Eridanus. But we did not see it at all then as I have described it now.

The beach was crowded, and when we first came down to it from the road, after having taken the bus from the city, and emerged on it from the cool green benison of the forest, it was as if we had suddenly stumbled upon a hidden, but noisy popular resort. Yet it must have been the garishness and strangeness of daylight and the sun itself which gave it to me, long used to the night and sleeping fitfully during these daylight hours, the quality of a nightmare.

It was a scorching hot afternoon and seven Scots were sitting inside the tiny cabin we'd been told we might rent for a small sum by the week, with the woodstove going full blast, and the windows shut, cackling, and finishing, as their last holiday meal, some sort of steaming mutton broth.

Outside the mountains were covered with heat haze. The tide was out – so far out it did not occur to me it would ever come in – the foreshore, along the whole length of which people were digging for clams, was stony, or covered with huge barnacled rocks, that made me fear for my young wife's feet, for which, since they were so small and delicate, I had a special feeling of protection. Further down by the water's edge the beach was strewn with seaweed and detritus and didn't even look like a possible place to swim.

Nor was anybody in swimming, though children shouted and squealed, paddling in the mud, among the tide-flats, from which arose the most impressive and unusual stink I ever smelt in my life. This archetypical malodor on investigation proved partly to emanate from the inlet itself, which was sleeked as far as the eye could reach with an oil slick I quickly deduced to be the work of an oil tanker lying benignly at the wharf of the refinery I have mentioned opposite the lighthouse, so that now it looked as though one certainly could never swim at all; we might as well have come to the Persian Gulf. And to add to the heat, which further suggested the Persian Gulf, as we crunched thoughtfully over the barnacles and exoskeletons of crabs, or avoiding the deposits of tar or creosote, sank up to our ankles instead in slippery reeking slime, or splashed into pools themselves preened with peacock feathers of oil, came, from high up the beach, a blast of hot breath and ashes from a dozen clambakes, round the fires of which, it seemed to us, hundreds of people were howling and singing in a dozen languages.

As human beings we loved no doubt to see people enjoying themselves, but as a honeymoon couple seeking privacy we felt increasingly we had come to the wrong place, all the more so since it began to remind me of arriving in some fifth-rate seaside resort for a one-night stand.

That is how selfish lovers are, without an idea in their heads for anyone save themselves. As against this the worthy Scot from whom we rented the cabin, though poor himself and clearly struggling with that thrift in his own nature which so long supposed to be traditional had now become a fact, was extremely generous. He saw at once that we had come because it was all we could afford and before he and his fellow Scots had departed the shack was ours for the month at a rental of twelve dollars, he having lowered this from fifteen himself.

'But do ye ken boots, young man,' he asked sharply.

'Boots?'

'Aye, lad, I'm fussy about me boot.'

So the Scotsman's boat was generously thrown in. I had once been a ship's engineer, I explained, not caring to say ship's fireman.

But could you rent Paradise at twelve dollars a month? was our thought, the next morning, as from the porch of the shack, gazing on the scene of absolute emptiness and solitude, we watched the sunrise bringing the distant power lines across the inlet at Port Boden into relief, the sun sliding up behind the mountain pines, like that blaze behind the pinnacles of a Gothic cathedral, hearing too, from somewhere, the thrilling diatonic notes of a foghorn in the mist, as if some great symphony had just begun its opening chords.

From the oil company's wharf just visible down the inlet the oil tanker had vanished, and with it the oil slick; the tide was high and cold and deep and we swam, diving straight off the porch, scattering into dividing echelons a school of minnows. And when we came up, turning round, we saw the pines and alders of our forest high above us. To us lovers the beach emptied of its cheery crowd seemed the opposite of melancholy. We turned again and there were the mountains. After that we swam sometimes three and four times a day.

We rowed the Scotsman's boat down the inlet and picnicked on an island, uninhabited, with a deep cover where we drew up in the boat, among wild asters and goldenrod and pearly everlasting. The further reaches of the inlet, under the soaring snow-capped mountains, were now in September a deserted heaven for ourselves alone. We could row all day and once beyond Eridanus Port scarcely see another boat. One day later we even rowed to the other side of the inlet, across to the railway. This was partly because right under the railway embankment on the opposite side were dimly to be discerned, as I said, some more little shacks, scattered and smoke-blackened, but above which sometimes a strip of the metals themselves at noontide would seem to be rippling in motion with the inlet sparkling just below; still, we used to wonder how ever people could live so close to the noise of trains. Now our curiosity would be satisfied. The row over toward the railway, that had promised to be anything but picturesque, grew more beautiful by the minute as we drew out of our own bay. For these people – a few old pioneers and retired prospectors, maybe a handful of railroadmen and their wives who didn't mind the noise – poor like ourselves but whom we had patronized in our minds for being yet poorer, were richer in that they could see round the point of the inlet and right down it, could see beyond the timber port of Eridanus, the very highest mountains of all, the Rocky Mountains themselves, that were for us hidden by the trees of our forest, though both of us saw range beyond range of the Cascades – the great Cordilleras that ribbed the continent from Alaska to Cape Horn – and of which Mount Hood was no less a part than Popocatepetl. Yes, fine though our view was, they had a finer, for they saw the mountains to the south and west too, the peaks beneath which we lived, yet could not see at all. As we rowed along the shore in the warm late afternoon light these great peaks were reflected in and shadowed the flowing water, and seemed to move along with us, so that my wife spoke of Wordsworth's famous peak, that strode after him; this was something similar, she said, though very different, because there was nothing threatening about this apparent movement; these peaks that followed us were, rather, guardians. Many times were we to see this phenomenon, as of a whole mountainside or ridge of pines detaching themselves and moving as we rowed, but never did it, or they, seem 'after' us: it seemed a reminder of duality, of opposing motions born of the motion of the earth, a symbol even while an illusion, of nature's intolerance of inertia. When we finally rowed back the sunset light was falling on the tiered aluminium retorts of the oil refinery, so that it looked to us, so infatuated were we (though this was before the time I would have thought it looked like an open cathedral at night, for the flickering candle of oil waste wasn't there), like a strange and beautiful musical instrument.

But still we did not see Eridanus as a place to live. The war was on, many of the ships that passed and sent the commotion of their washes over the beach were cargoed with obscenities toward death and once I had found myself saying to my wife:

'It's a hell of a time to live. There can't be any of this non-sense about love in a cottage.'

I was sorry I'd spoken like that for I seemed to see a trembling hope die out of her face, and I took her in my arms. But I had not intended to be cruel; nor was she a sentimentalist, and anyhow we hadn't got a cottage, nor much hope of having one in the foreseeable future. The shadow of the war was over everything. And while people were dying in it, it was hard to be really happy within oneself. It was hard to know what was happy, what was good. Were we happy, good? Or, being happy at such a time, what could one do with one's happiness?

One day when we were out rowing we came across a sunken canoe, a derelict, floating just beneath the surface in deep water so clear we made out its name: *Intermezzo*.

We thought it might have been sunk on purpose, perhaps by two other lovers, and it was this that kept us from salving it. And we reflected, yes, that was perhaps all our lives here would be, an intermezzo. Indeed we had not asked for, or expected, more than a honeymoon. And we wondered where those other lovers were now.

The war? Had the war separated them? And would the war separate us? Guilt and fear came over me and anxiety for my wife, and I began to row back gloomily and in silence, the calm sunlit peace of the inlet turned for me into the banks of some river of the dead, for was not Eridanus also the Styx?

Before I had married, and after I left the sea, I had been a jazz musician, but my health had been ruined by late hours and one-night stands all over the hemisphere. Now I had given up this life for the sake of our marriage and was making a new one – a hard thing for a jazz musician when he loves jazz as much as I.

At the beginning of the war I had volunteered. I had been rejected, but now, with my new life, my health was beginning vastly to improve.

Even now, as I rowed, sluggishly and unhappily though I was pulling, I could feel the improvement. Little by little self-discipline, a sense of humor and our happy life together were wreaking a miracle. Was this effort toward life and health merely to be a probationship for death? Nonetheless it was a matter of simple honor to attempt to fit myself for the slaughter if humanly possible, and it was as much this as for my marriage that I had given up my old life of night clubs, and incidentally nearly my only means of making a reasonable living, though I had saved enough for us to live on for a year and possessed a small income from royalties on records, for a few of which I was part composer.

What if we should continue to live here? The idea did not strike me seriously, or from any considered depths of my mind, merely flickered across my horizon like one of those sourceless evanescent searchlight beams that used occasionally to flash over the mountains from the vague direction of the city, 'where they were probably opening a grocery store,' as my wife laconically used to observe. Cheap it would certainly be. But then honeymoons were surely not events that by their nature were supposed to continue. And far worse than the notion of 'intermezzo' was that, on one plane, it would be like living on the very windrow of the world, as that world had not hesitated to remind us.

And while a summer holiday, even a protracted summer holiday, was one thing, how hard it would be to actually live here, for my wife to cope with the old cookstove, lack of plumbing, oil lamps, no ordinary comforts of any kind in cold weather. Ah yes, it would be too hard for her, even with my help (for though I had a sort of slow-witted strength, I did not have the co-ordinated handiness and practicality usually native to the sailor).

It might be fun for a week, even a month, but to live here meant accepting the terms of the most abject poverty, would be almost tantamount, I thought, to renouncing the world altogether, and when I reflected in what dead earnest we would be playing the game in winter, I simply laughed: of course it was out of the question.

I backed water with my oars, turning the boat round. High up the alders and the pines swayed against the sky. The house stood prettily on its simple lines. But below the house, underneath it, on the beach, were its foundations of piles and wooden stringers and its interlaced tracery of cross-braces, like the frozen still machinery between the two paddleboxes of a paddle-steamer.

Or it was like a cage, as I rowed nearer, where one-by-twos, through which I saw the machinery, were nailed vertically to the stringers of the front porch, acting, one might explain, re-motely like a train's cowcatcher, to prevent timbers at flood tide from drifting beneath the house and undermining the foundations.

Or beneath, it was like a strange huge cage where some am-phibious animal might have lived, there on the beach, when often at low tide, resetting a cross-brace, amidst the seaweed smells, I felt as if I were down in the first slime, but in which work I delighted as I delighted in the simplicity of the stresses of the foundations I was looking at, that unlike most founda-tions were of course above ground, as in the most primitive of all houses.

It was simple and primitive. But what complexity must there have been in the thing itself, to withstand the elemental forces it had to withstand? A ton of driftwood, launched with all the force of an incoming high tide with an equinoctial gale behind it, the house would thus withstand, and turn aside harmlessly.

And suddenly, as I helped my wife out and tied up the boat, I was overwhelmed with a kind of love. Standing there, in de-fiance of eternity, and yet as if in humble answer to it, with their weathered sidings as much a part of the natural surround-ings as a Shinto temple is of the Japanese landscape, why had these shacks come to represent something to me of an indefinable goodness, even a kind of greatness? And some shadow of the truth that was later to come to me, seemed to steal over my soul, the feeling of something that man had lost, of which these shacks and cabins, brave against the elements, but at the mercy of the destroyer, were the helpless yet stalwart symbol, of man's hunger and need for beauty, for the stars and the sunrise.

First we had decided to stay only till the end of September. But the summer seemed just beginning and by the middle of October we were still there, and still swimming every day. By the end of October the glorious Indian summer was still golden and by the middle of November we had decided to stay the winter. Ah, what a life of happiness had now opened before us! The first frosts came, and there was silver driftwood on the beach, and when it grew too cold to swim we took walks through the forest where the ice crystals crackled like rock candy under our feet. And then came the season of fogs, and sometimes the fog froze on the trees and the forest became a crystal forest. And at night, when we opened the window, from the lamps within our shadows were projected out to sea, on the fog, against the night, and sometimes they were huge, menacing. One night, coming across the porch from the woodshed with a lantern in one hand and a load of wood under the other arm, I saw my shadow, gigantic, the logs of wood as big as a coffin, and this shadow seemed for a moment the glowering embodiment of all that threatened us; yes, even a projection of that dark chaotic side of myself, my ferocious destructive ignorance.

And about this time we began to reflect with wonder: this is our first home.

'Moonrise of the dying moon.'

'Sunrise of the dying moon, in a green sky.'

'White frost on the porch and all the roofs ... I wonder if it's killed poor Mr McNab's nasturtiums. It's the first heavy frost of the year. And the first clear sunrise in a month.'

'There's a little flotilla of golden eyes under the window.'

'The tide is high.'

'My poor seagulls, they're hungry. How cold your feet must be down there, in that icy water. The cat ate all your bones – I found them on the floor – the wretch. The bones I saved from the stew last night.'

'There's a raven sitting on the top of the big cedar, and a fine, foul, fearsome creature he is too !'

'Look – now ! The sunrise.'

'Like a bonfire.'

'Like a burning cathedral.'

'I must wash the windows.'

'Part of what makes this sunrise so wonderful isn't just pure nature. It's the smoke from those wretched factories at Port Boden.'

'The sunrise does things to these mists.'

'I must put out some breakfast for the cat. He'll come in very hungry from his dawn prowl.'

'There goes a cormorant.'

'There goes a great loon.'

'The frost sparkles like diamond dust.'

'In a few minutes now it will melt.'

So each morning, before the really cold days when I got up myself, I would be awakened by my wife's comments while lighting the fire and making the coffee, as if now upon a continual sunrise of our life, a continual awakening. And it seemed to me that until I knew her I had lived my whole life in darkness.

III

Now the great tides and currents in their flux and flow fascinated us. It was not merely because of the exigencies of our boat, which was not our property, which we could not anchor, and which it was not always possible to keep on a float, that it was necessary to watch them. In the great high tides of winter, with the Pacific almost level with our floor, the house itself could be in jeopardy, as I have said, from the huge timbers or uprooted trees racing downstream.

And I learned too that a tide which to all appearances is coming in may be doing so only on the surface, that beneath it is already going out.

Quaggan, the Manx boatbuilder whom we had now met, told

us, rocking under our windows in his boat one warmer evening when the settlement was like a minuscule Genoa or Venice in a dream, of the Manx belief that at the new moon the birds on the ninth wave out from the shore are the souls of the dead.

Nothing is more irritating and sorrowful to a man who has followed the sea than the sound of the ocean pounding mercilessly and stupidly on a beach. But here in the inlet there was neither sea nor river, but something compounded of both, in eternal movement, and eternal flux and change, as mysterious and multiform in its motion and being, and in the mind as the mind flowed with it, as was that other Eridanus, the constellation in the heavens, the starry river in the sky, whose source only was visible to us, and visible reflected in the inlet too on still nights with a high brimming tide, before it curved away behind the beautiful oil refinery round the Scepter of Brandenburg and into the Southern Hemisphere. Or, at such a time of stillness, at the brief period of high tide before the ebb, it was like what I have learned the Chinese call the Tao, that, they say, came into existence before Heaven and Earth, something so still, so changeless, and yet reaching everywhere, and in no danger of being exhausted: like 'that which is so still and yet passes on in constant flow, and in passing on, becomes remote, and having become remote, returns.'

Never was the unfortunate aspect of the beach on that first day exactly to repeat itself. If oil sometimes appeared on the waters it was soon gone, and the oil itself was oddly pretty, but in fact the discharge of oil by tankers into the harbor reaches was about that time put a stop to by law. But when the law was broken and the oil slicks appeared it was miraculous with what swiftness the flowing inlet cleansed itself. It was the cleanest, the coldest, freshest, most invigoratingly beautiful water I have ever swum in, and when they spoke of damming the inlet, when a British brewery interest later talked of turning the whole place into a stagnant fresh water basin, perverting even those pure sources and cutting it off from the cleansing sea altogether, it was as if for a moment the sources of my own life trembled and agonized and dried up within me. Tides as low as those on that first day, also, were of course exceptional. And at low tide the mud flats themselves were interesting, seething with every imaginable kind of strange life. Tiny slender pale turquoise starfish, fat violet ones, and vermilion sunstars with twenty pointed arms like children's paintings of the sun; barnacles kicking food into their mouths, polyps and sea-anemones, sea-cucumbers two feet long like orange dragons with spikes and horns and antennae, lone strange wasps hunting among the cockles, devilfish whose amours sound like crackling machine-gun fire, and kelp, with long brown satin streamers, 'when they put their heads up and shake them, that means the tide is slackening,' Quaggan told us. Round the point north-wards beyond the seaport were indeed miles of muddy flats at the lowest tides with old pilings like drunken giants bracing each other up, as if staggering homeward evermore from some titanic tavern in the mountains.

At night, sometimes all seemed still, at rest on the beach and the flats, wrapped in a quietude of reflection. Even the barnacles slept, we felt. But we found we had never made a greater mis-take. It is only at night that this great world of the windrow and tide-flats really wakes up. We discovered that there were little shellfish called Chinese Hats that only walked at night, so that now when night fell, we had a standing joke, and would turn to one another laughing to say in sepulchral tones:

'It is night, and the Chinese Hats are on the move!'

And equally the rocks on the beach that at first had seemed only to threaten my wife's tiny feet became a factor of delight. The difficulty of walking over them at half tide down to swim was simply overcome by wearing old tennis shoes. And in the morning when one got up to make the coffee, with the sun blaz-ing through the windows so that it was like standing in the middle of a diamond – or looking out through the windows into the inlet where in the distance the struggling sunlight turned a patch of black water into boiling diamonds – I began to see these intermediate rocks as with Quaggan's eyes, the eyes of a Celt, as presences themselves, standing round like Renan's immutable witnesses that have no death, each bearing the name of a divinity.

And of course we got much of our wood from the beach, both

for making repairs round about the place and for firewood. It was on the beach we found one day the ladder that was later to be so useful to us and that we had seen floating half awash. And it was also on the beach that I found the old cannister that we cleaned and that in the end I used to take each evening to the spring for water.

The Scot had left us two small rain barrels for rain water, but long before I found the cannister drinking water had begun to constitute one of our most serious problems. On the highway beyond the forest was a general store and garage with a water tap next to the petrol pump and it was in every way possible, though tiresome, to take a bucket and obtain water from this source and bring it down through the forest, and most of the summer people would do just this. But we discovered that where possible the real beach dwellers avoided doing so, though this was largely a point of honor, for the storekeeper, a good man, did not mind, and the beach people provided him a major source of revenue. But he paid taxes and we did not, and also the rate-payers in the district were in the habit of using the slightest excuse to make a public issue of the existence of the 'wretched squatters' at all upon the beach, whose houses, 'like malignant sea-growths should be put to the torch' — as one city newspaper malignantly phrased it. What use saying to such as they: 'Love had he found in huts where poor men lie.' For these reasons the permanent residents, or even the summer people who had been there for some time, preferred to obtain their water from a natural spring or source. Some had sunk wells, others, like Quaggan, had flumes which conducted water down from the mountain streams flowing through the forest, but we did not find that out until afterwards, for at this time we had scarcely met those who were to become our neighbors and friends, and a good quarter of a mile separated us from each of our two nearest ones, from Quaggan to the north, and Mauger to the south. The Scotsman had left us a small barrel filled with fresh water and told us that he always replenished this by rowing to a spring about half a mile away, round the point with the lighthouse, and beyond the wharf of the barge company. So every few days I would load the barrel and a bucket into the boat and my wife and I rowed there with them. This stream ran all the year round but was so shallow you couldn't scoop your bucket into it. You had to fill it where a waterfall, about a foot high, poured through rocks, where you could put your bucket under.

The beach here, in a no man's land between the barge company and the Indian reserve, was very flat and low, not sandy, but covered with a deep slimy ooze and growths of seaweed: when the tide was low the boat was grounded about a hundred feet from the waterfall on the shore, and you had to wrestle the barrel back from the creek over the ooze and through shallow water, sinking in the muck. On the other hand at high tide the sea came right up over the waterfall covering it completely, though afterwards it was pure again. So that you had to time it exactly at half tide when you could come in fairly close with your boat or it was an all but impossible task. Even at best it is difficult for me now to see how we got so much fun out of that particular chore. But perhaps it just seems like fun now because of the memory of our despair on the day when we found we couldn't go there any more; for the moment it seemed that on this account we would really have to leave Eridanus altogether.

It was by now late in November, and less than a month to the winter solstice, and we were still lingering on; the sparkling morning frosts, the blue and gold noons and evening fogs of October, had turned suddenly into dark or stormy sunrises, with sullen clouds driving through the mountains before the north wind. One morning, in order to take advantage of the half tide, I, having taken over from my wife, rose well before sunrise to make the coffee. Jupiter had been burning fiercely and when I rose, though it was eight-fifteen, the waning moon was still bright. By the time I'd brought my wife her coffee there was a dawn like china, or porcelain. Earlier there had been a black mackerel sky with corrugated rose. Always my wife loved me to describe these things to her, even if inaccurately, as was more often the case, as she would describe them to me when she got up first in warmer days.

But apparently I was wrong about the sunrise, as I had been wrong about the tide's incoming, because later, toward ten

o'clock, we were still drinking coffee and still waiting for the
sun to come up and the tide to come in. It had become a calm,
rather mild day with the water like a dark mirror and the sky
like a wet dish clout. A heron standing motionless on a stone
by the point looked unnaturally tall, and for a moment we remembered we had seen men working out there with lanterns the
other night : perhaps the heron was some kind of new buoy. But
then this tall buoy moved slightly, mantling itself in condor
wings, then stood motionless as before.

All this time, though, the sun actually had been rising, had,
for other people beyond the hill across the water, already risen.
I say the hill, for no longer as in September did the sun rise in
the east, over the sea, over Port Boden, with the power lines
ruled across it, or in the northeast where the mountains were,
but ever more toward the south, behind this wooded hill above
the railroad tracks.

But now suddenly an extraordinary thing happened. Far
south of the power lines, directly above the invisible railway,
above where the blackened shacks under the embankment were,
the sun struggled up, the only live thing in a gray waste, or
rather it had abruptly appeared, the sun, as a tiny circle with
five trees in it, grouped round its lower rim like church spires
in a teacup. There was, if you shut your eyes and opened them
wide again hard, no glare, only this platinum circle of sun with
the trees in it, and no other trees to be seen for fog, and then
clouds minutely drawn over the top, the sun taking in more
trees along the hilltop as it slanted up. Then for a moment the
sun became suffused, then it looked like a skull, the back of a
skull. We shut our eyes and opened them again and there was
the sun, a tiny little sun, framed in one of the window panes,
like a miniature, unreal, with these trees in it, though no
other trees were to be seen.

We took the boat and rowed to the creek and found a new
notice:

PRIVATE PROPERTY KEEP OFF

But we decided to fill the barrel anyhow this last time. Someone came running down the slope gesticulating angrily and in

my haste to get the boat away, which was hard aground with the increased weight of the barrel, one of its hoops became loosened, and by the time we'd got home not only was the barrel nearly empty but we had nearly sunk the Scotsman's boat too. My wife was crying and it was now raining and I was angry; it was wartime and we could scarcely buy another barrel, and in the quarrel – one of our very first – which ensued, we had almost decided to leave for good when I caught sight of the cannister on the beach left by the receding tide. As I examined it the sun came half out, casting a pale silver light while the rain was still falling in the inlet and my wife was so entranced by the beauty of this that she forgot all the harsh things that had been said and began to explain about the raindrops to me, exactly as if I were a child, while I listened, moved, and innocently as if I had never seen such a thing before, and indeed it seemed I never had.

'You see, my true love, each is interlocked with other circles falling about it,' she said. 'Some are larger circles, expanding widely and engulfing others, some are weaker smaller circles that only seem to last a short while. . . . The rain itself is water from the sea, raised to heaven by the sun, transformed into clouds and falling again into the sea.'

Did I know this? I suppose so, something like it. But that the sea itself in turn was born of rain I hadn't known. Yet what she said was uttered with such inexpressible wonder I repeat that, watching, and listening to her, it was like the first time I'd witnessed the common occurrence of rain falling into the sea.

So terrible and foreign to the earth has this world become that a child may be born into its Liverpools and never find a single person any longer who will think it worth pointing out to him the simple beauty of a thing like that. Who can be surprised that the very elements, harnessed only for the earth's ruination and man's greed, should turn against man himself?

Meantime the sun was trying to burst forth again and we knew that its showing itself as a skull had been a pose. As if it were the beam from that lighthouse at Cape Kao that they say can be seen seventy-six miles away, so we saw spring. And that I think was when we really decided to stay.

As for the cannister it was of a kind that I had seen on shipboard used in the bosun's or engineer's mess as a filter in those days when I had been a fireman and I surmised that it had been thrown overboard from an English ship. Whether it was my imagination or not, it smelled of lime juice. Such filters are intended for water but it used to be common practice to put lime juice in them. Now the lime juice that is standard for the crew on English ships is so strong undiluted that they used to use it for scrubbing the mess tables white – a few drops in a bucket of water would do the trick – but on metal it can have a corrosive as well as a cleansing effect and it struck me that some green mess boy had possibly put too much lime juice in this filter by mistake, or with insufficient dilution, the bosun had come off duty thirsty, drawn himself a draught of nice quenching rust, torn the filter off the wall, threatened to crown the unfortunate mess boy with it, and then thrown it overboard. Such was the little sea story I made up for my wife about it as I set about converting it into a good clean water container for ourselves.

Now we had a cannister but still no honorable place to get water. The same day we met Kristbjorg on the path.

'– and there's your wand,' he said.

'What?'

'Water, Missus.'

It was the spring. Wand, or a word like it, though not pronounced the way it looks, was apparently either the Danish or Norwegian for water, or if not the word Kristbjorg sometimes used. It had been there all the time, not a hundred yards from the house, though we hadn't seen it. No doubt because it had been an extremely dry and protracted Indian summer, it had not started running till late, by which time we had got used to its not being there, so we hadn't seen it. But for a moment it had been as if Kristbjorg had waved a magic wand and suddenly, there was the water. And the kind soul went and brought a bit of iron piping to make it easier to fill our cannister from it.

IV

Nor shall I ever forget the first time I went down that path to the spring for water. The evening was highly peculiar. In the northeast a full moon like a burning thistle had risen over the mountains. Mars hovered over the moon, the sole star. On the other side of the water a bank of fog stretched along the coastline the length of the inlet, luminous in the east opposite the house, but becoming black toward the south and west to the far right beyond the trees on the headland – that was, from our porch, from the path, the headland with the lighthouse was behind me, but it was such a strange evening I kept turning round – through which the fog showed like spirals and puffs of smoke, as though the woods were on fire. The sky was blue in the west, shading down to a pastel-like chalky sunset against which the trees were etched. A spindly water tower stood out above the fog over there. It had been dark inside the house but now I was outside on the path it was light. This was six o'clock and in spite of the blue sky to the west a patch of moonlight was reflected in the water by a diving float. The tide was high below the trees. In one instant, however, when I reached the spring, the moon went behind a cloud and it was dark: the reflection disappeared. And when I got back there was a blue fog.

'Welcome home,' my wife smiled, greeting me.

'Ah yes, my darling, it really *is* home now. I love those curtains you made.'

'It's good to sit by the window and look when it's beautiful outside, but when it's a gloomy twilight I like to pull the curtains, and feel from the dark night withdrawn, and full of lamplight inside.'

'None of this nonsense about love in a cottage?'

I was lighting the oil lamps as I said this, smiling as I reflected how this unprophetic and loveless remark had become a loving catchphrase, and enchanted now by the golden color of the flame of the lighted oil lamps against their pretty blue holders backed with fluted tin brackets like haloes, or a monstrance.

'But now it's night, and the Chinese Hats are on the move!'

We laughed, as I turned down the flame of a wick that was smoking the chimney.

And outside the tide was sweeping in still further from the Pacific until we could hear it washing and purling under the house itself. And later we lay in bed listening to a freighter's engines as they shook the house:

> *Frère* Jacques
> *Frère* Jacques
> *Dormez*-vous?
> *Dormez*-vous?

But the next morning when the gulls sailed outward bound to the city shores the clear cold sun streamed right into the two rooms of our house filling it with brilliant incessant water reflections and incandescence of light as if it knew that soon the world would start rolling through the mountainous seas of winter toward inevitable spring. And that evening after the last gulls had come to rest, when the moonlight came in there was time for it to embroider the waving windows of our house with their curtains on the unresting tide of Eridanus that was both sea and river.

Thereafter at dusk, when the gulls came floating home over the trees, I used to take this cannister to the spring. First I climbed the wooden ladder set into the bank and made into steps that had replaced the Scotsman's old broken steps, that led up from our porch to the path. Then I turned right so that now I was facing north toward the mountains, white plumaged as gulls themselves with a fresh paint of snow; or rose and indigo.

Often I would linger on the way and dream of our life. Was it possible to be so happy? Here we were living on the very windrow of existence, under conditions so poverty stricken and abject in the eyes of the world they were actually condemned in the newspapers, or by the Board of Health, and yet it seemed that we were in heaven, and that the world outside – so portentous in its prescriptions for man of imaginary needs that were in reality his damnation – was hell. And for these illusory needs, in that hell of ugliness outside Eridanus, and for the sake of making it a worse hell, men were killing each other.

But a few evenings later, returning homeward along the path, I found myself possessed by the most violent emotion I had ever experienced in my life. It was so violent it took me some time to recognize what it was, and so all-embracingly powerful it made me stop in my tracks and put my burden down. A moment before I had been thinking how much I loved my wife, how thankful I was for our happiness, then I had passed to thinking about mankind, and now this once innocent emotion had become, for this is indeed what it was, hatred. It was not just ordinary hatred either, it was a virulent and murderous thing that throbbed through all my veins like a passion and even seemed to make my hair stand on end and my mouth water, and it took in everyone in its sweep, everyone except my wife. And now, again and again I would stop on the path as I came back with water, putting down my burden as I became possessed by this feeling. It was a hatred so all-consuming and so absolutely implacable that I was astounded at myself. What was all this hatred? Were these really my feelings? The world, surely, one could hate the world for its ugliness, but this was like hatred of mankind. One day, after I had been turned down again for the army, it occurred to me that in some mysterious way I had access to the fearful wrath that was sweeping the world, or that I stood at the mercy of the wild forces of nature that I had read man had been sent into the world to redeem, or something that was like the dreadful Wendigo, the avenging man-hating spirit of the wilderness, the fire-tortured forest, that the Indians feared and believed in still.

And in my agonized confusion of mind, my hatred and suffering *were* the forest fire itself, the destroyer, which is here, there, all about; it breathes, it moves, and sometimes suddenly turns back on its tracks and even commits suicide, behaving as though it had an idiot mind of its own; so my hatred became a thing in itself, the pattern of destruction. But the movement of the forest fire is almost like a perversion of the movement of the inlet: flames run into a stand of dry inflammable cedar, yellow flames slice them down, and watching, one thinks these flames will roll over the crest of the hill like a tidal wave. Instead, perhaps an hour later, the wind has changed, or the fire has grown too big for itself, and is now sucking in a draft that opposes its advance. So the fire doesn't sweep up the hill, but instead settles back to eat the morsels of the trees it felled during its first rush. So it seemed was the hatred behaving, turning inward and back upon myself, to devour my very self in its flames.

What was wrong with me? For nearly all was unselfishness in our little settlement. Like benevolent mountain lions, I had discovered, our neighbors would wait all day, only to perform an unselfish act, to help us in some way, or bring a gift. A smile, a wave of the hand, a cheery greeting was a matter of great importance here too. Perhaps they thought us a bit shiftless but they never let us know it. I remembered how Mauger, the Channel Islander, would reconnoiter in his boat, looking at our house, trying to pick the best time to bring us some crabs, or salmon, without inconvenience to us, for which he would accept no payment. To the contrary, he would pay us for the privilege of giving us the crabs by enriching us with stories and songs.

Once he told us of a salmon he saw drown an eagle. The eagle had flown away with a salmon in its claws that he had not wanted to share with a flock of crows, and rather than give up any part of its booty it had allowed itself finally to be dragged under the waves.

He told us that in the northern regions where he fished there were two kinds of ice, blue and white: live and dead. The white was dead so could not climb. But the blue ice would come and calmly ravish an island of all her beauty of trees and moss, bleed her lichen to the rock, and leave her bare as the Scotsman's door he had come to help us mend.

Or he would tell us of Arctic visions, of winds so strong they blew in the outgoing tide in which were found strange fish with green bones –

When he came back in September he loved to sing:

> Oh you've got a long way to go
> You've got a long way to go
> Whether you travel by day or night

And you haven't a port or a starboard light
If it's west or eastward ho –
The judge will tell you so –

Or he would sing, in his curious jerky voice with its accents
of the old English music hall, and which was more like talking:

Farewell, farewell, my sailor boy
This parting gives me pain ...

And we too had grown unselfish, or at least different, away
from the tenets of the selfish world. Eternally we watched Quaggan's float to see that it was safe and if it broke away without
his knowledge, or when he was in the city, we brought it back,
no matter how bad the weather, honestly hoping he would not
know it was us, yet proud that it had been ourselves, for had it
not been, it would have been someone else.

No one ever locked their doors, nobody ever discussed anyone
else meanly. Canonical virtues must not be assumed for the
inhabitants of Eridanus however. Though one point should be
made in regard to the womenfolk of the fishermen. With the
exception of those who were married, there never were any
women. The unmarried fishermen often lent their shacks to
their friends in the summer, but they were sacrosanct when they
returned. What they did in the city was their own business, yet
they never brought whores, for example, to their shacks. The
attitude of the solitary fisherman toward his shack, and his boat,
was not dissimilar. In effect his love for the one was like his love
for the other. Perhaps his shack was less a part of him than his
boat and his love for his shack was more disinterested; I think
one reason for this is that their little cabins were shrines of their
own integrity and independence, something that this type of
human being, who seems almost to have disappeared, realizes
can only be preserved without the evil of gossip. And actually
each man's life was in essence a mystery (even if it looked like
an open book) to his neighbor. The inhabitants varied in political
and religious beliefs and unbeliefs and were certainly not sentimental. There was at one time, in later years, a family with
three children living in Eridanus by necessity and not by choice
and they were indeed convinced that it was 'beneath them', and

that the true values were to be found in 'keeping up with the Joneses.' They let themselves sink into degradation, as seeming to be the conventional counterpart of poverty, without ever having looked at a sunrise. I recall that their dishevelment and general incapacity caused some rather sharp comment among the fishermen and everyone was relieved when they left, to move into a slum in the city, where they certainly did not have to carry their water from a spring and where their only sight of a sunrise was behind warehouses. And even ourselves were not entirely absolved from identifying such a life with 'failure,' something we certainly should have outgrown. And I remember very well how we used to drift along in our little boat in the sun, or sit by the fire in the gentle lamplight if it was night and cold weather, and murmur together our day-dreams of 'success', travel, a fine house, and so on.

And everything in Eridanus, as the saying is, seemed made out of everything else, without the necessity of making anyone else suffer for its possession: the roofs were of hand-split cedar shakes, the piles of pine, the boats of cedar and vine-leaved maple. Cypress and fir went up our chimneys and the smoke went back to heaven.

There was no room for hatred, and resuming my load of the cannister, I resolved to banish it – after all it was not human beings I hated but the ugliness they made in the image of their own ignorant contempt for the earth – and I went back to my wife.

But I forgot all my hatred and torment the moment I saw my wife. How much I owed to her! I had been a creature of the night, who yet had never seen the beauty of the night.

My wife taught me to know the stars in their courses and seasons, and to know their names, and how she always laughed like a peal of merry little bells telling me again about the first time she made me really look at them. It was early in our stay at Eridanus while I, used to being up all night and sleeping during the day, could not accustom myself to the change of rhythm, and the silence, and darkness all around us. Because I found it hard to sleep, in the small dark hours of one moonless night she took me walking deep into the forest; she told me to put out my electric torch and then, in a moment, she said, look up at the sky. The stars were blazing and shooting through the black trees and I had said, 'My God, I never saw anything like that in my life!' But I never could see the patterns she pointed out and she always had to teach me afresh each time, until one late autumn night there was a brilliant full moon. That night there was frosted driftwood and a slow silver line of surf on the beach. Above the night itself flashed with swords and diamonds. Standing on the porch she pointed out Orion – 'See, the three stars of his belt, Mintaka, Alnilam, Alnitak, there's Betelgeuse above in his right shoulder, and Rigel below in his left knee –' and when I saw it at last she said, 'It's easier tonight because the moonlight drowns all but the brightest stars.'

I reflected how little I had known of the depths and tides of a woman until now, her tenderness, her compassion, her capacity for delight, her wistfulness, her joy and strength, and her beauty, that happened through my wild luck to be the beauty of my wife.

She had lived in the country as a child and now returning after her years in the cities it was as if she had never left it. Walking through the forest to meet her returning from the store I would sometimes come upon her standing as still and alert as the wild creature she had seen and was watching, a doe with her fawn, a mink, or a tiny kinglet on a bough over her head. Or I would find her on her knees, smelling the earth, she loved it so much. Often I had the feeling that she had some mysterious correspondence with all nature around her unknown to me, and I thought that perhaps she was herself the eidolon of everything we loved in Eridanus, of all its shifting moods and tides and darks and suns and stars. Nor could the forest itself have longed for spring more than she. She longed for it like a Christian for heaven, and through her I myself became susceptible to these moods and changes and currents of nature, as to its ceaseless rotting into humus of its fallen leaves and buds – nothing in nature suggested you died yourself more than that, I began to think – and burgeoning toward life.

My wife was also an accomplished cook, and though the woodburning cookstove we had reminded us of Charlie Chaplin's in *The Gold Rush*, she somehow turned our limited and humble fare into works of art.

Sometimes, when we were most troubled in heart because of the war, or fear we would be separated, or run out of money, she would lie in bed laughing in the dark and telling me stories to make me laugh too, and then we would even make up dirty limericks together.

We found we could rarely do any outside work together, like splitting wood, or making repairs, or especially when we built the pier, without singing; the jobs begat the songs, so that it was as if we had discovered the primitive beginnings of music again for ourselves; we began to make up our own songs, and I began to write them down.

But it was the accompaniment of her speech, of her *consciousness* of everything that impressed me then, half absurd, wholly perceptive, it intensified our whole life.

'See the frost on the fallen leaves, it's like a sumptuous brocade.' 'The chickadees are chiming like a windbell.' 'Look at that bit of moss, it's a miniature tropical forest of palm trees.' 'How do I know the cascara from the alder trees? Because the alders have eyes.' 'Eyes?' 'Just like the eyes on potatoes. It's where the young shoots and branches drop off.' 'We shall have snow tonight, I can smell it on the wind.' Such was our small talk, our common gossip of the forest.

My old life of the night, how far away that seemed now, my life in which my only stars were neon lights! I must have stumbled into a thousand alcoholic dawns, but drunk in the rumble seat I passed them by. How different were the few drinks we drank now, with Quaggan or Kristbjorg, when we could afford it or when there was any. Never had I really looked at a sunrise till now.

Once or twice on Sundays some of the boys who'd played with me came out to see us, when they happened to be filling a week's engagement in the city at the Palomar Dance Hall, or on the stage at the Orpheum cinema. Many combinations had been broken up during the war and my old band was not the same now, but whatever the world may think jazz musicians not merely possess unusual integrity but are among the most under-

standing and spiritual men and they did not tempt me back to
my old life, knowing that would kill me. It was not that I imagined that I was transcending jazz : I could never do that or wish
to, and they wouldn't have let me get away with that illusion
either. But there are some who can stand the racket and some
who cannot. No one can be fool enough to think that Venuti or
Satchmo or the Duke or Louis Armstrong have 'ruined their
lives' by living what I have pretentiously called 'a life of the
night.' For one thing it is their lives and it has for me the aspects
of a very real glory, of the realest kind of true acceptance of a
real vocation. On one plane I can see them laughing their heads
off at this kind of language. But they would know that what I
say is true.

I belonged, somehow, way in the past, to the days of prohibition – as a matter of fact I have still not quite lost my taste
for bootleg booze – and Beiderbecke, who was my hero, and
Eddie Lang who taught me to play. Jazz had advanced since
those days and Mr Robert Hackett is capable of flights that
would have been difficult even for Bix. But I was attached
romantically to those days as I was to the obsolete days of stokeholds. I had never been able to play sweet music, and I had
rarely been able to play very sober either, and I was in danger of
worse when I quit, and all this my colleagues, filled with grave
polite wonder at this extraordinary life I was leading, and on
whose hangover-concealing faces the pieces of plaster betrayed
the heroism and decency of their visit at all, thoroughly appreciated. They had brought me an old gramophone which could
be wound by hand, since of course we had no electricity, and a
collection of our old recordings, and I understood too, through
the familiar jargon into which we all would familiarly fall,
that their serious impression was that I would have to do something creative with my life if I did not want somehow to go to
pieces, for all my happiness.

One bitter gray day with the north wind shrilling through
bare iron trees and the path through the forest almost unnegotiable with ice and frozen snowdrifts, there was a sudden commotion outside. It was some of the boys from my old band and
they had brought me a small, second-hand cottage piano. Can

you conceive of the self-sacrifice, the planning, the sheer *effort* inherent in this act? They had taken up a collection, had somehow found the instrument, and since it was only on Sunday they could visit me, and being Sunday they could not hire anyone to help them, they had hired a truck and driven out, and finally brought this piano to me through the frozen forest, over that all but impassable path.

After this my friends sent me from time to time many hot arrangements to work on for them. And they also made it possible for me to supplement my income in a manner that gave me great pleasure and is besides, so far as I know, unique. That is, I was able to provide on many occasions the titles for certain hot numbers, when it came to recording them, that had grown out of improvisation. In the old days such titles would seem to grow out of the number itself, and in this category are the titles for such numbers as For No Reason at All in C, and the piano solos In a Mist, In the Dark, of Beiderbecke. Walking the Dog is the title of an unknown masterpiece of Eddie Lang's, Black Maria is another. Little Buttercup – the tune so far as I know having nothing to do with the air in H.M.S. *Pinafore* – and Apple Blossom are two of Venuti's in a poetical vein, and Negroes have always been particularly good at titling such numbers. But latterly despite some brilliant tiltings in bebop, and some superlative efforts such as Heavy Traffic on Canal Street (a swing version of Paganini's Carnival in Venice) and the Bach Bay Blues by the New Friends of Rhythm, even the genius of our brother race has begun to fail in this respect. One day my friends got stuck for a title in San Francisco and half joking, half serious, asked my advice on a Christmas card for a number they were recording with a small combination shortly after the New Year. We wired them: Suggest Swinging the Maelstrom though cannot be as good as Mahogany Hall Stomp God bless you happy new year love.

Thereafter I received many inquiries of this nature and most of my suggestions being used, half joking but wholly considerate, I would receive a sum of money out of all proportion to what I would ordinarily have earned from any royalties on the sale of the record in question. Some titles which I supplied and you may recognize are, besides Swinging the Maelstrom – Chinook, Wild Cherry, Wild Water, Little Path to the Spring, and Playing the Pleiades – and I did a variation on Bix that I worked out on the piano, calling it Love in a Mist.

Little Path to the Spring! In this extraordinary manner I had earned enough, the way we were living, to keep us for the next two or three years, and to provide some reassurance for my wife were I eventually to be called up. And all these things I used to think of on the path itself while I was getting water, like some poverty-stricken priest pacing in the aisles of a great cathedral at dusk, who counting his beads and reciting his paternoster is yet continually possessed by the uprush of his extraneous thoughts. Ah, little path to the spring! It struck me that I must be at bottom a very humble man to take such creative pleasure from such an innocent source, and that I must be careful not to let my pride in this humbleness spoil everything.

That first winter in Eridanus was a difficult one for us, in many ways; used as we were to city life our primitive existence here on the beach – simple enough in summer and warm weather – propounded problems every day for which we had no answer, and yet always we solved them somehow, and it forced upon us feats of strength or endurance which we often performed without knowing how or why; and yet looking back on it now I remember much profound happiness.

V

In our part of the world the days are very short in winter, and often so dark and gray it is impossible to believe the sun will ever shine again; weeks of icy drenching rain, interspersed by the savage storms that sweep down the inlet from the mountains when the sea roared around and under us and battered our shack until it seemed sometimes January would never end, though once in a long while would come a day of blinding sunlight and clarity, so cold the inlet fumed and the mist rose from the water like steam from a boiling caldron, and at night my wife said of the stars, 'Like splinters of ice in a sky of jet.'

The wintry landscape could be beautiful on these rare short

days of sunlight and frostflowers, with crystal casing on the slender branches of birches and vine-leaved maples, diamond drops on the tassels of the spruces, and the bright frosted foliage of the evergreens. The frost melted on our porch in stripes, leaving a pattern against the wet black wood like a richly beaded cape flung out, on which our little cat tripped about with cold dainty paws and then sat hunched outside on the windowsill with his tail curled round his feet.

One dark windy day deep in January, when there seemed no life or color left in a sodden world and the inlet looked like the Styx itself, black water, black mountains, low black clouds shuddering and snarling overhead, we walked down to the lighthouse.

'– And soon the crabs will bring the spring –' Sam called to us. 'But crabs ... I had a friend, a diver – thief he was in private life, never come home without somethink, even if it was only a nail. Aye. Basement like a junkyard ... Well, this time he goes down, down, down, you know, deep. Then he gets scairt. – Why? Migrations of billions of crabs, climbing all around him, migrating in the spring, aclambering around him, aswallering and stretching their muscles.'

'I'

'Aye. Perhaps they see somethink *else* down there – who knows? Because he was so crazy scairt he wouldn't speak to no one for two weeks. But after that, he sings like nightingales, and he'd talk the head off any wooden duck.... And soon the crabs, my dearies, and soon the birds will bring the spring....'

It was about this time we began to read more. I went to the city library and took out a 'country card' which entitled me to take away a shopping bag full of books at once. The city, that already, in a few hours, had begun to render our existence an almost impossible fable, so that I seemed to know with sad foresight how even its richest comforts that one day we might in cowardice yearn for, and finally have, would almost suffocate all memory of the reality and wealth of such a life as ours, the city, with its steam heat, its prison bars of Venetian blinds, its frozen static views of roofs and a few small dingy gardens with clipped shrubs that looked, in the winter dusk, like chicken croquettes covered with powdered sugar. And ah, after being away from my wife for all these hours, to return from the city to discover the house still in place and the inlet sleeked and still, the alders and the cedars high, the pier there – for we had built a little pier – the sky wide and the stars blazing! Or, making my way down the sodden slippery path with the trees tossing and groaning about me in the tempest and the darkness, to make again the port, the haven of lamplight and warmth.

But then at night sometimes the elemental despair would begin again and we would lose all hope for terror at the noise, the rending branches, the tumult of the sea, the sound of ruination under the house, so that we clung to one another like two little arboreal animals in some midnight jungle – and we were two such animals in such a jungle – until we could laugh again at the very commotion, the very extremity of duty to a house filled with an anxiety of love like that of officers for a sailing ship in a gale. Though it was in the early mornings of high tide when getting breakfast that this wild elemental menace often proved the most unnerving, with the gray sea and white caps almost level with the windows, and the rain dashing against them, the sea crashing and hissing inshore under the house, causing horrible commotions of logs, jarring thunders dithering the whole little shack so that the lamp brackets rattled with the windows, past which a drifting timber sailed threatening the pier, and beyond the smoke of the factories in Port Boden was just a rainy gray, while leaves were falling into the sea; then our boat hurling itself about down below would seem in jeopardy, at the same time there would be the sound of breaking branches in the forest, the great maple tree would seethe and roar, while the tossing floats squealed piteously, and the loops of Mauger's fishing nets hung on the porch would flap like mad ghosts; and then be motionless; and all the anxiety that had been stretched to its utmost tension repeating, would the poor boat be hurt, the pier against which a thud was like a blow at the heart, relaxed too: though only an instant, the next moment it had all started again, so that what with the wind, the thunderous boomings, the delight in the swiftness outside, the anxiety within and without, the pride that one had survived, the sense of life, the fear of death, the appetite for breakfast as the bacon and coffee smells went singing down the gale every time one opened the door – I was seized sometimes with an exuberance so great that I wanted to dive swiftly into that brimming sea to acquire a greater appetite still, either that or because the sea seemed safer than the house.

But then we went out to a morning of wild ducks doing sixty downwind and golden-crowned kinglets feeding in swift jingling multitudinous flight through the leafless bushes, and another day of winter companionship would draw down to an evening of wind, clouds, and seagulls blowing four ways at once, and a black sky above the trembling desolate alders, the heart clothed already in their delicate green jewelry I had never really seen, and the gulls whitely soaring against that darkness, where suddenly now appeared the moon behind clouds, as the wind dropped, transillumining its own soaring moonshot depths in the water, the moon reflected in the half-moonlit clouds in the water down there, and behind, in the same translunar depths, the reflection of the struts and cross-braces of our simple-minded pier, safe for another day, disposed subaqueously in some ancient complex harmony of architectural beauty, an inverse moonlight geometry, beyond our conscious knowledge.

With February the days were noticeably longer and brighter and warmer, the sunrise and sunset were sometimes bright and beautiful again, there would be a sudden warm bright noon, or even a whole day that melted the ice in the brooks and set them running, or a day of sunlight where one could look through the trees at heaven, where luminous Aconcaguas sailed God's blue afternoon.

In the evening when I went for water, which I always liked to time to coincide with the seagulls' evening return over the trees and down the inlet, the twilight was growing longer, and chickadees and kinglets and varied thrushes flitted in the bushes. How I loved their little lives, now I knew their names and something of their habits, for my wife and I had fed them all winter and some were even quite tame, regarding me fearlessly near at hand. Just past Dunwoiken the path took a sharp dip down toward the beach, at a steep gradient, then it turned to the left, up a small slope, and there was the spring that came down from the mountains, where I filled my cannister. Ah, the pathos and beauty and mystery of little springs and places where there is fresh water near the ocean.

We called it the spring though in one way it was not. It was a lively little brook but it was called the spring because it was only a little further up that it emerged from underground. It was a source of water, a source of supply; that is why it was called the spring; it is a nuisance, but not insignificant, that I have to use the same word for this as for the season.

One evening on the way back from the spring for some reason I suddenly thought of a break by Bix in Frankie Trumbauer's record of Singing the Blues that had always seemed to me to express a moment of the most pure spontaneous happiness. I could never hear this break without feeling happy myself and wanting to do something good. Could one translate this kind of happiness into one's life? Since this was only a moment of happiness I seemed involved with irreconcilable impulses. One could not make a moment permanent and perhaps the attempt to try was some form of evil. But was there not some means of suggesting at least the existence of such happiness, that was like what is really meant by freedom, which was like the spring, which was like our love, which was like the desire to be truly good.

One cold rainy day I met Quaggan, a wiry homunculus, in a Cowichan sweater knitted by Indians in a series of friezes; he was in the path, cutting cascara bark.

'Proteus path,' he said musingly.

'Proteus?'

'Aye. The man who cut this trail. Blacksmith, lives in the city now. We used to call it the Bell-Proteus path, for 'twas Bell helped him,' said the old man, scuttling off into the dusk with his bright purgative load.

When I returned home I looked up Proteus in the dictionary which had been left behind by the Scotsman (who with uncanny insight had not returned it for twenty years to the Moose Jaw

Public Library) together with some essays on Renan and a Bible, the loan of one Gideon, which was in the woodshed, and discovered – though I can't say I didn't more or less know it before – that he was a prophetic sea-god in the service of Poseidon. When seized, he would assume different shapes.

But how strange this was, I thought. Here Proteus was a man, who had given his name to this path. But he was also a god. How mysterious! And Eridanus too, that was a ship and the name of our hamlet and seaport, and inlet, and also a constellation. Were we living a life that was half real, half fable? Bell's name had no meaning I knew of. Neither had Quaggan's. Kristbjorg might have Christ-like virtues but he was anything but Christ-like. And yet I could not help remembering Hank Gleason, the bull fiddle's, pronouncement on Eridanus that Sunday. 'Out of this world, brother,' he had said. It gave me an uneasy feeling for a moment, like seeing one of those grotesque films in which they use animated cartoons with real figures, a mixture of two forms; it was also the feeling, though I couldn't put my finger on it, such as I had about Wywurk or Hi-Doubt. And yet did the confusion come from pinning the labels of one dimension on another? Or were they inextricable? As when, just about this time, the oil refinery decided to put a great sign over the wharfs, as an advertisement: SHELL. But for weeks they never got around to the s, so that it was left HELL. And yet, my own imagination could not have dreamt anything fairer than the heaven from which we perceived this. (In fact I was even fond of the evil oil refinery itself that at night now, as the war demanded more and more lubrication, was often a blaze of lights like a battleship in harbor on the Admiral's birthday.) But these problems I could never solve: if I could even state them in my 'music' – for I had taken to bouts of composition on the cottage piano – I would be doing well.

And then, before I had time to think, I would seem to be getting water again, walking as if eternally through a series of dissolving dusks down the path. And at last the night would come like a great Catherine wheel.

It was a very still evening, and I had gone later than usual.

There were quiet lamps already gleaming in Quaggan's shack, in Kristbjorg's, and on the point in Four Bells, though I knew none of their owners were at home for I had just seen all three of them through the trees going to the store. I think it was the stillness, the quietude, with the tide in, and the fact of the lamps burning in the empty houses by the sea that must have reminded me of it. Where had I read of the Isle of Delight – in Renan of course – where the birds sing matins and lauds at the canonical hours? The Isle of Delight, where the lamps light of themselves for the offices of religion, and never burn out for they shine with a spiritual light, and where an absolute stillness reigns, and everyone knows precisely the hour of his death, and one feels neither cold nor heat nor sadness nor sickness of body or soul. And I thought to myself, these lights are like those lights. That stillness is like this stillness. This itself is like the Isle of Delight. And then I thought to myself, stopping in the path: what if we should lose it? And with this thought of all-consuming anxiety I would always pause with a sigh. And then came the season spring and I forgot this anxiety too.

VI

Ah, not till that year had I observed a spring!

We went out on the porch and looked at the spring stars: Arcturus, Hercules the giant, the Lion and the Sea Serpent, the Cup, the Crown, and Vega in the Lyre.

One morning we saw our two great loons in their black and white high plumage, diving and calling softly to each other with low clear whistles, and that day the first bright leaves of the green dragons came thrusting through the earth on the path near the spring.

We were speaking together of these things that evening when suddenly we stopped talking at an apparition of terrifying beauty: in the darkness, in the northeast sky, within a circular frame, appeared the crosstrees of a windjammer on fire: the blazing crosstrees of a windjammer in port, no sails, just the masts, the blazing yards: a whole blazing Birkenhead Brocklebank dockside of fiery Herzogin Ceciles: or as if some ancient

waterfront scene of conflagration in neighboring old wind-
jammered Port Boden had been transported out of the past, in
miniature, into the sky: now, to the right within the miniature
frame, turned blackened crumbling yards: and now one lone
silvery mast, ash-gray, with its naked canted yards, a multiple
tilted cross, chording it perpendicularly, sinking below the circular frame, ascending, of blazing gold; we laughed out of sheer
joy, for it was just the full moon rising clear of the pines behind
the mountains, and often it must do this, but who looked at it?
Who could see it? Could anyone else see it? I had never seen
it. Why had God given this to us?

— And often I was to ask this: My God, why have You given
this to us? But when the moon waned, rising further and further south, the sun would rise further and further north. And
the truth of this simple fact, learned also from my wife, for the
first time the following morning, confronted in the sky, not by a
blazing windjammer, but by a spectacle such as might have
been beheld by a shipwrecked seaman on a spar, seeing, at sunrise, the becalmed ship of the Ancient Mariner. Through the
window the sea was so calm in the mist it rose up steep as a
wall. Mr Bell's float seemed above us, halfway up the window,
with far below that — a little later — divided not by sea or reflected mountains but by what seemed space itself, the orange
sun rising still, barred with angry clouds. But the windjammer
stood broadside in the sun; three masts, sad in the doldrums,
tilted yards. And then the next moment had turned so that
there was just this one gigantically tall mast, cross-boomed, coming towards us, changing into the tallest pine on the hill, as the
rising sun left it behind. And I thought of my grandfather, becalmed in the Indian Ocean, the crew dying of cholera, my
grandfather giving orders finally, at the beginning of wireless, to the oncoming gunboat, to be blown up himself with the
ship.

That night there were two evening herons in the moon at
high tide, the herons projected large and primeval before it, the
one flapping high, blocking a moment the moon itself, the other,
engines switched off, gliding low an inch above the moonstruck
swelling water to land noiselessly on the float; a *squark* when

they met, the one waiting for the other, and then flying off together: the bat turned into a firefly before the moon, and the cat's magical rites: and the tide full and high beneath the window: the swim at high tide, and love at high tide, with the windows liquescent on the floor: and waking again the next moment to the full tide again in the dawn, and the lights of the oil tanker still on alongside the oil-refinery port: and waking to the sudden O'Neillian blast of a ship's siren taking your soul to Palembang in spite of yourself, and again, the swim, the swim at dawn! And the shell-pink chiffon, my wife probably said, of factory smoke far in the northeast at Port Boden, and the four aluminum gas tanks, that later would come out in all their ugliness, like four golden pillars (because each was left half in shadow) to a Greek temple, and behind the old chemical factory like a ghost of a Grecian ruin and behind the four golden pillars a silent climbing train like a chain of golden squares: and the wash of a passing motorboat under the window like carved turquoise in onrushing movement toward you: and then the oil tanker lying under the pillars and retorts at the refinery like Troy, the pillars reflected in the water: the wonderful cold clean fresh salt smell of the dawn air, and then the pure gold blare of light from behind the mountain pines, and the two morning herons, then the two blazing eyes of the sun over the Cascade foothills, and the five gaunt growing pines caught tall in the circular frame, and then with such a blast of light it seemed to cut a piece out of the hill, the herons flying, the oil-tanker sailing with the morning tide —

Oh, what light and love can do to four gas tanks at sunrise over the water!

And how different the forest path was now, in spring, from the other seasons we had known it: summer, autumn and winter. The very quality of the light was different, the pale green, green and gold dappled light that comes when the leaves are very small, for later, in summer with the leaves full out, the green is darker and the path darker and deeply shady. But now there was this delicate light and greenness everywhere, the beauty of light on the feminine leaves of vine-leaved maples and the young leaves of the alders shining in sunlight like stars of dogwood blossoms, green overhead and underfoot where plants were rushing up and there were the little beginnings of wildflowers that would be, my wife said, spring beauties, starflowers, wild bleeding hearts, saxifrage and bronze bells. Or on some cool still mornings came the mysterious fogs : 'Anything can happen in a fog,' she said, 'and just around the next corner something wonderful will happen !'

And now it was spring and we had not lost our way of living; in fact, with the money I'd earned we had bought a little house further up the beach between Kristbjorg's and Four Bells under a wild cherry tree for a hundred dollars. No one had lived in this house for years and it was badly in need of repairs and of cleaning so that we did not move into it until May and we worked very hard to make it clean and sound and beautiful.

In early spring we had not yet moved into our second house and this is the time I am really thinking of when I say that each evening at dusk I used to go down the path for water. Carrying my cannister I would pass along the back of Dunwoiken, descend the sharp gradient toward the beach, then turn left again, up a little slope, to the spring. Then I set the cannister under the iron piping Kristbjorg had put there and waited for it to fill. While it filled I watched the gulls coming up the inlet or gazed up the trunks of the trees to the highest pinnacles of the smallest branches trembling like a moonsail, and breathed the scents of evening : the rich damp earth, myrtle and the first wild crabapple and wild cherry blossoms, all the wild scents of spring, mingled with the smell of the sea and from the beach the salt smells, and the rasping iodine smell of seaweed.

But one evening I forgot to do this and found myself to my surprise not looking at anything nor smelling anything. And now, all of a sudden, very different seemed the journey back. Though the cannister only held four gallons, and since I had become stronger, the task ought to have seemed much lighter than before, yet on this evening it began to weigh a ton and it was just slip and slide, one foot after another. I found myself stopping for breath every moment. The worst part was the dip down which on the way to the spring I had run so gaily, but

which had become a veritable hill of difficulty on the return journey, so that I had to drag rather than carry my cannister up
it. And now I stopped and cursed my lot. What had happened
now? Now that the spring we had so longed for had come, now
that our life on the beach seemed doubly secure with our new
house – what was I bothering about now? It seemed to me as
though all our prayers having been answered and myself for
once having nothing in the world to worry about, for the
moment, I had to find something to irk me in this chore. It was
as though man would not be contented with anything God gave
him and I could only think that when God evicted him from
Paradise it served him right.

And now no matter how happy I had been all day the awe-
inspiring thoughts were as if waiting for me here at the spring.
Somehow I always made it back, but somehow too, for the first
time, I came to dread this simple little chore. It wasn't as if this
were a mere malaise of self-centeredness. Each of us thought
more of the other than of himself. Nor was it a matter of mutual
self-absorption. Sincerely we considered our neighbors. Quaggan had indeed grown so fond of us he made a red mark on his
calendar every time we went to see him.... One day I saw an
old frayed but strong rope on this path, cast away on a tree
stump, and I thought: yes, that is the awful end of such thoughts.
Had I actually been tempted to kill myself? Aghast at the
thought I took the rope back and reaved it up for use.

But at the same time that I dreaded it I was also aware that
I looked forward to it, looked forward to the walk to the spring,
which was like going toward the future, toward our new little
house. It was a sweet time of the day when the sun sank and the
only part of the day in which I was really apart from my wife,
unless I counted my 'work.' I did not look forward to it because
I would be separated from her but precisely because I was then
able to enjoy the pleasure of returning to her, as if after a long
journey. The journey might be, or had become, a sort of anguish, but we always met again with cries of joy and relief
after this interminable separation of not more than twenty minutes.

But again, I thought, was the chore even anguish? In the

surroundings there was everywhere an intimation of Paradise, in the little job, so far from mechanical, a sense of simple human accomplishment. I thought of the old ladder we had salved from the beach. This too was an accomplishment. At first we had pushed it away, but it had drifted back again and this seemed like a sign to use it. And I reflected : yes, and like this vermiculated old ladder, stinking with teredos and sea-worms, washed down from the sawmill, this sodden snag, half awash when I first saw it, is the past, up and down which one's mind every night meaninglessly climbs !

But I had salved this ladder last autumn, in the days when I used to lie awake brooding in the night, which now I never did. And the ladder no longer stank, or smelled of teredos. Much of it was good, and hacking out the rotten wood, I had put its frame to use, and indeed converted it into these very steps I was even now climbing down to greet my wife on the porch, with joy after my gloomy thoughts, carrying my burden, the same steps up which I had set forth twenty minutes ago on my path to the spring.

Yet a ladder was a ladder, however transmuted, and the past remained. It was in this way I came to the conclusion that it was not the chore itself, because it was heavy, but something to do with my thoughts, something that was always elicited on my return journey, especially when I came to the hill, that I really dreaded. Though I did not understand this until after I had met the mountain lion, and shortly after I had met the mountain lion something else happened that put it right out of my mind for many years, until, in fact, the other day.

The cougar was waiting for me part way up a maple tree in which it was uncomfortably balanced, to one side of the hill section of the path, and what is strange is that I should have met it on the return journey without having noticed it, just as I hadn't noticed the rope, if it was there, on my way to the spring.

A logger had once told me that if you set fire to your mittens and throw them at a mountain lion that would take effect, and I know that bears are often very susceptible to human laughter. But this folklore – and there is a great deal about mountain lions in these parts – did not help. All I immediately knew was that I had no sort of weapon, and that it was impractical as well as useless to make any movement of running away. So I stood traditionally and absolutely still. Then we simply waited, both of us, to see what the other would do, gazing straight into each other's eyes at short range; in fact it was only his gleaming topaz eyes and the tip of his tail twitching almost imperceptibly that showed me he was alive at all.

Finally I heard myself saying something like this to the mountain lion, something extraordinary and absurd, commanding yet calm, my voice as unreal to myself as if I'd just picked myself up from a lonely road after falling off a motorcycle and in shock were adjuring the wilderness itself to aid, a fact one half recalls under chloroform afterwards. 'Brother, it's true. I like you in a way, but just the same, between you and me, get going!' Something like that. The lion, crouched on a branch really too small for him, caught off guard or off balance, and having perhaps already missed his spring, jumped down clumsily, and then, overwhelmed, catlike, with the indignity of this ungraceful launching, and sobered and humiliated by my calm voice – as I liked to think afterwards – slunk away guiltily into the bushes, disappeared so silently and swiftly that an instant later it was impossible to believe he'd ever been there at all.

At the time I completely forgot the rest of my return journey, though ludicrously it turned out I had not failed to bring the cannister with me, nor do I have any recollection at all of coming down the steps. I had to warn my wife not to go out, then row round to warn the neighbors and see that the alarm was given to the forest warden; I rowed, close inshore, straining my eyes through the gloom to warn anyone else I might see on the forest path. But night was coming on and I saw no one.

I didn't even see the lion again, which, when he ran off, according to later reports, did not stop until ten miles away when he jumped right through the glass window of a trapper, who offered him his elbow to eat while with the other hand, I truly regret to say, the man reached for a carving knife to cut the beast's throat, after which the trapper was obliged to row for several hours, as penance, to get aid in his underdrawers; when we heard this we mourned the animal a bit, in our way.

But that night as we lay in bed, and the moon shone through the window, with my arms around my wife and our cat purring between us, I saw that the only reason I had not been afraid of the mountain lion – otherwise I must have been a fool and I do not for this reason escape the charge – was that I was more afraid of something else. It was true, though this was less due to courage than a naïve ignorance, that I was not very afraid of mountain lions even when there was a report of them. But then I did not really believe in them. I must have been afraid – I mean I must have been afraid in some way of the lion – but at the hill on the spring path have been already gripped by the anticipation of a so much greater fear that the concrete fact even of a lion had been unable to displace it. What was it I feared? Lying in bed with my arms around my wife, listening to the roar of the surf we couldn't see, for it was a fierce low tide – I felt so happy that all of a sudden I could not for the life of me give it a name. It seemed something past, and that was what it was, though not in the sense in which I was thinking. Even when one is happiest it is possible to entertain, with one section of one's mind, the most ghoulish reflections, and so I did now, before I went to sleep, but now as at a distance, as if in retrospect. It was as though I had entered the soul of a past self, not that of the self that merely brooded by night, but an earlier self to whom sleep meant delirium, my thoughts chasing each other down a gulf. Half conscious I told myself that it was as though I had actually been on the lookout for something on the path that had seemed ready, on every side, to spring out of our paradise at us, that was nothing so much as the embodiment in some frightful animal form of those nameless somnambulisms, guilts, ghouls of past delirium, wounds to other souls and lives, ghosts of actions approximating to murder, even if not my own actions in this life, betrayals of self and I know not what, ready to leap out and destroy me, to destroy us, and our happiness, so that when, as if in answer to all this, I saw a mere lion, how could I be afraid? And yet mysteriously the lion was all that too.

But the next night, and upon nights after, something even more curious happened, as I say, that caused me to forget this till now.

The next evening when I went for water all I can remember is that on my way there, or on setting out, I was certainly prepared for another encounter with the mountain lion, of whose sad demise we had not yet heard, and prepared to be conventionally afraid of him, I suppose, though I went unarmed (it was because I didn't have a gun) and my wife, who had no fear of anything on earth save spiders, was curiously unapprehensive about it and had implicit faith in me. Actually, at the bottom of her mind, so great was her love of wild animals and her understanding of them, a love and understanding I came to share, I felt sometimes she may have wished I had charmed the animal home for a companion instead of scaring him away.

Something about the aspect of the mountains that evening distracted me from the lion. Though it was a warm evening, it was windy, and the mountains were wild with chaos, like an arctic island seen through snow. And indeed it had snowed far down on the mountains in the last three nights, though I was not reminded by this snow that it was this changeable weather that had driven the cougar down to the warmer regions in search of food. The wind roared and howled through the rolling treetops like an express train. It was a chinook — the kind of faen wind that years before at night had driven the S.S. *Eridanus* — Liverpool — ashore with her cargo of old marble, wine, and cherries-in-brine from Portugal. The further mountains grew nearer and nearer until they looked like the precipitous rocky cliff-face of an island gashed with guano. The nearer hills were very light but their inner folds grew ever darker and darker. In the chaos high up there appeared a church of blue sky by mistake, as if put in by Ruysdael. A gull whose wings seemed almost a maniacal white suddenly was drawn up, driven straight up perpendicularly into the tempest. One of Quaggan's sons passed me running on the path :

'It's blowing real hard. I'm just dashing madly to see how things were.'

I remember this Celtic way of expressing it delighted me :

267

maybe his boat, or more likely Kristbjorg's, who was in the city, was dragging its anchor, and I said to give me a shout if he wanted any help. I remember filling the cannister with the cold mountain water pouring down. Gulls were blowing backwards above the trees and one came to rest on the roof of Hi-Doubt. How touching the gull, dovelike there, with his white blowing feathers! But the next thing I remembered was that I was singing and had passed the hill without remembering a single step I had taken or with any recollection of its difficulty; and the next thing I was down the steps, cannister and all, with no clear vision once more of how this had been managed, and my wife was greeting me as usual, as if I'd come back from a long journey. To the mountain lion I had given no thought at all. It was like a dream, with the difference that it was reality.

The next time I set off with the cannister I recall almost a precisely similar thing happened, though this was just a quiet spring evening, the mountains remote and still, muffled at their base by a great scarf of mist that rose without division from the calm reflecting sea. The journey to the spring seemed much the same, though even this seemed more dreamy, mysterious, and accomplished in a shorter time. But once more, on the way back, I was only conscious of the hill when I realized that I had traversed it without effort.

At the same time I became conscious of my gloomy thoughts again, but in a quite different way: how can I say it? It is as if I saw those thoughts at a distance, as if below me. In one sense I did not see them but heard them, they flowed, they were like a river, an inlet, they comprised a whole project impossible to recapture or pin down. Nonetheless those thoughts, and they were abysmal, not happy as I would have wished, made me happy in that, though they were in motion they were in order too: an inlet does not overflow its banks, however high the tide, nor does it dry up, the tide goes out, but it comes in again, in fact as Quaggan had observed, it can do both at once; I was aware that some horrendous extremity of self-observation was going to be necessary to fulfill my project. Perhaps I have not mentioned my project, or rather what I conceived my project to be.

VII

Though this may at first seem inconsistent with my dismissal of this project as 'my music,' 'my bouts of composition,' or 'my work,' I had been haunted for months by the idea of writing a symphony in which I would incorporate among other things, for the first time in serious music (or so I thought), the true feelings and rhythm of jazz. I did not share, among other perplexities of my vocation, the vocation that I had not yet discovered, the common romantic conception of the superiority of music over words. Sometimes I even thought poetry could go further, or at least as far, in its own medium; whereas music, destined to develop in terms of ever more complex invention (I knew this because I had mastered, almost accidentally, the whole-tone scale), seemed to me then to have its unconscious end in silence, whereas the Word is the beginning of creation itself. Despite this I always felt, as a practicing jazz musician, that the human voice managed to spoil a given instrumental record. To contradict this again, my wife and I loved to sing, and sometimes I felt our life together to be a kind of singing.

How well I recall struggling through all these, and many more, contradictions and perplexities. I finally even prayed, and the other day, looking through some scraps of early work saved from our fire, I encountered, half burnt, the edges scorched and crumbling, the following, written as it were over a score: *Dear Lord God, I earnestly pray you to help me order this work, ugly chaotic and sinful though it may be, in a manner that is acceptable in Thy sight; thus, so it seems to my imperfect and disordered brain, at the same time fulfilling the highest canons of art, yet breaking new ground and, where necessary, old rules. It must be tumultuous, stormy, full of thunder, the exhilarating Word of God must sound through it, pronouncing hope for man, yet it also must be balanced, grave, full of tenderness and compassion, and humor. I, being full of sin, cannot escape false concepts, but let me be truly Thy servant in making this a great and beautiful thing, and if my motives are obscure, and the notes scattered and often meaningless, please help me to order it, or I am lost. . . .*

But despite my prayers my symphony refused to order itself or resolve itself in musical terms. Yet I saw what I had to do clearly. I heard these thoughts ordering themselves as if pushed off from me: they were agonizing, but they were clear, and they were my own, and when I returned home I tried again to put them down. But here I was beset by further difficulties, for when I tried to write the music, I had to put it down first in words. Now this was peculiar because I knew nothing about writing, or words, at that time. I had read very little and my whole life had been music. My father – who would have been the first to laugh at this way of putting it – had played French horn in the first performance in 1913 of Stravinsky's Sacre du Printemps. My father was with Soutine too, and knew and respected Cocteau, though he was a very proper kind of Englishman in some respects. Stravinsky he worshipped, but he died at about the age I am now, before the Symphony of Psalms at all events, so I had many lessons in composition and was even brought up, though I had no formal musical education, on Stravinsky's children's pieces. I grew to share my father's wild enthusiasm for the Sacre but to this day I believe it to be in one important respect rhythmically deficient – in a way I won't go into – and that Stravinsky knew nothing at all about jazz, which also goes for most other modern composers. I reflected briefly that though my unconscious, and even conscious, approach to serious music had been almost entirely through jazz, nonetheless my rhythmical touchstone had proved an uncanny method of separating the first-rate from the not quite first-rate, or of differentiating the apparently similar or related in merit and ambition: on this view, of modern composers, both Schönberg and Berg are equally first-rate: but as between Poulenc and Milhaud, say, Poulenc is somewhere, but Milhaud, to my ear, nowhere at all. What I am really getting at is probably that in some composers I seem to hear the very underlying beat and rhythm of the universe itself, but to say the least I am, it is admitted, naïve in expressing myself. However, I felt that no matter how grotesque the manner in which my inspiration proposed to work through me, I had something original to express. Here was the beginning of an honesty, a sort of truthfulness to truth, where there had been nothing before but truthfulness to dishonesty and self-evasion and to thoughts and phrases and even melodies that were not my own. Yet it is queer that I had to try and put all this into *words*, to see it, to try and see the thoughts even as I heard the music. But there is a sense in which everybody on this earth is a writer, the sense in which Ortega – the Spanish philosopher whom I have recently read thanks to one of the summer people, a schoolmaster, and now one of my best friends, and who lent me his books – means it. Ortega has it that a man's life is like a fiction that he makes up as he goes along. He becomes an engineer and converts it into reality – becomes an engineer for the sake of doing that.

I am bound to say that even in the worst of my struggles I did not feel like Jean Christophe; my soul did not boil 'like wine in a vat,' nor did my 'brain hum feverishly,' at least not very loudly: though my wife could always judge the degree of my inspiration by the increasing tempo of my sniffs, which, if I was really working, would follow a period of deep sighs and abstracted silence. Nor did I feel 'This force is myself. When it ceases to be I shall kill myself.' As a matter of fact I never doubted that it was the force itself that was killing me, even though it possessed none of the above dramatic characteristics, and I was in every way delighted that it should, for my whole intention seemed to be to die through it, without dying of course, that I might become reborn.

The next time I went for water, despite the fact that I had forearmed myself consciously against any illusion , almost exactly the same thing happened; this time indeed the feeling came more strongly than ever, so that it seemed in fact, to me, as if the path were shrinking at both ends. Not only was I unconscious of the hill, and the weight of the cannister, but I had the decided impression that the path *back* from the spring was growing shorter than the path *to* it, though the way there had seemed shorter too than on the previous day. When I returned home it was as if I had flown into my wife's arms, and I tried to tell her about it. But no matter how hard I tried I could not express what the feeling was like – beyond saying that it was almost as if a 'great burden had been lifted off my soul.' Some

such cliché as that. It was as if something that used to take a long
and painful time now took so little time I couldn't remember it
at all; but simultaneously I had a consciousness of a far greater
duration of time having passed during which something of vast
importance to me had taken place, without my knowledge and
outside time altogether.

No wonder mystics have a hard task describing their illu-
minations, even though this was not exactly that; yet the experience seemed to be associated with light, even a blinding
light, as when years afterwards recalling it I dreamed that my
being had been transformed into the inlet itself, not at dusk, by
the moon, but at sunrise, as we had so often also seen it, suddenly transilluminated by the sun's light, so that I seemed to
contain the reflected sun deeply within my very soul, yet a sun
which as I awoke was in turn transformed, Swedenborgwise,
with its light and warmth into something perfectly simple, like
a desire to be a better man, to be capable of more gentleness,
understanding, love –

There has always been something preternatural about paths,
and especially in forests – I know now for I have read more –
for not only folklore but poetry abounds with symbolic stories
about them: paths that divide and become two paths, paths that
lead to a golden kingdom, paths that lead to death, or life, paths
where one meets wolves, and who knows? even mountain lions,
paths where one loses one's way, paths that not merely divide
but become the twenty-one paths that lead back to Eden.

But I did not then need the books to be deeply conscious of
this mysterious feeling about paths. I had never heard of a path
that shrank before, but we had heard of people who disappeared
altogether, people who are seen walking along one moment,
and then the next have vanished: and so, overlooking the fact
that the experience might have some deeper significance, and
solely with the purpose of deliciously making our flesh creep,
we made up a story along those lines that night in bed. What if
the path became shorter and shorter until I should disappear
altogether one evening, when coming back with the water? Or
perhaps this story was a means of propitiating fate for the
miraculous fact that we had not been separated by not assuming

it to be a smug certitude, a form of inoculation, since we still might be separated by the war (I had been rejected a second time by then, probably for being half-witted), against such a separation, and at the same time a kind of parable of the 'happy ending' of our lives come what might – for no matter what we might make up about the character on the path, I myself was certainly going to come back from the spring and that journey to end in, for us, a glorious lover's meeting.

But in fact the path did seem in effect to get shorter and shorter, if the impression was never again to be accompanied by quite the same sense of incommunicable experience. No matter how consciously I determined to remember on the outward journey, it always turned out that I had climbed the hill coming back without giving it a thought. And so realistic had our little story become that not many evenings after when I came back with water at dusk my wife came running to meet me, crying :

'Oh my God ! I'm so glad to see you !'

'My darling. Well, here I am.'

So genuine was the relief on my wife's face, and so genuine was my own feeling at meeting her again, that I was sorry we'd ever made up such a story. But it was a wonderful and profound moment. And just for an instant I felt that had she not come down the path to meet me, I might indeed have disappeared, to spend the rest of my extraterritorial existence searching for her in some limbo.

Up above the topmasts of the trees swayed against the April sky. Suddenly the gulls appeared, as if shot out of a catapult, hurtling downwind above the trees. And over my wife's shoulder, coming across the inlet toward the lighthouse, I saw a deer swimming.

This reminded me that despite the wind it was warm enough for me to start swimming again – I had virtually given up in December – so I went straight in, and it was as though I had been baptized afresh.

It was soon after this that we moved into our little house under the wild cherry tree that we'd bought from the blacksmith.

This house burned down three years later and all the music

I had written burned with it, but we built another house ourselves, with the help of Quaggan, Kristbjorg and Mauger, out
of driftwood and wood from the sawmill in Eridanus Port,
which was now being torn down to make way for a real estate
subdivision.

We built it on the same spot as the old house, using the
burned posts for part of our foundations that now, being charred,
were not susceptible to rot. And the music got itself rewritten
too somehow, in a way that was more satisfactory, for I had only
to come back to the path to remember parts of it. It was as if
the music had even been written during some of those moments.
The rest, as any creative artist will understand, was only
work.

But I never could recapture my symphony after losing it by
fire. And so, still struggling with words as well as music, I
wrote an opera. Haunted by a line I had read somewhere: 'And
from the whole world, as it revolved through space, came a
sound of singing,' and by the passionate desire to express my
own happiness with my wife in Eridanus, I composed this opera,
built, like our new house, on the charred foundations and fragments of the old work and our old life. The theme was suggested probably by my thoughts of cleansing and purgation and
renewal and the symbols of the cannister, the ladder and so on,
and certainly by the inlet itself, and the spring. It was partly in
the whole-tone scale, like *Wozzeck*, partly jazz, partly folksongs
or songs my wife sang, even old hymns, such as Hear Us O Lord
from Heaven Thy Dwelling Place. I even used canons like
Frère Jacques to express the ships' engines or the rhythms of
eternity; Kristbjorg, Quaggan, my wife and myself, the other
inhabitants of Eridanus, my jazz friends, were all characters,
or exuberant instruments on the stage or in the pit. The fire
was a dramatic incident and our own life, with its withdrawals
and returns, what I had learned of nature, and the tides and
the sunrises I tried to express. And I tried to write of human
happiness in terms of enthusiasm and high seriousness usually
reserved for catastrophe and tragedy. The opera was called *The
Forest Path to the Spring*.

VIII

Our first little house we had rented from the good Scotsman passed into other hands on his death, though sometimes we used to go down the path by the spring and look at it, and it was only the other day that we did this again. Many years have passed.

Mauger was dead: Bell had gone, and old Sam by the lighthouse; but Kristbjorg and Quaggan, now seventy-five and a great-grandfather, were still very much alive, and living in the same place. As usual people were threatening to throw us off the beach but somehow we were still there. Mauger's shack toward the lighthouse with its newly shingled roof stood desolate, but we did not feel sad to look at it. His life had been too well accomplished and he died saying, 'I never felt better in my life.'

We happened to be completely broke when he died but someone had sent some laurels in the shape of an anchor to his funeral where, in the funeral parlor, a woman sang Nearer My God to Thee through a grille and the minister read the Twenty-third Psalm in an improved version. Our suggestion that this be followed by Hear Us O Lord from Heaven Thy Dwelling Place having been abandoned, since no one save ourselves and Quaggan could sing it, our suggestion was likewise neglected. That almost anything be substituted for Nearer My God to Thee, a hymn he hated since his father had been a stoker on the *Titanic*.

There were huge pretentious faked marble Corinthian pillars in the undertaker's parlor on either side of the minister as he read and I kept seeing these change before my eyes into the stanchly beautiful lousy old wooden piles covered with blue mussels on which Mauger's house (and I doubt not more likely, in heaven, should it stand, St Peter's too) stood. Another fisherman, his brother, was taking the house with its green reticulated nets hanging out to dry. And I thought how selflessly, taking time from their own work, and accepting no money for it, Quaggan and Kristbjorg and Mauger had helped us build our new house, helped us, though all old men, with the cruel work of putting in our foundations, in fact supplied half the foundations themselves. Mauger must have been grateful there were so many who loved him and I was surprised how many at his funeral were summer people we didn't know. Kristbjorg, one of his best friends, had his own ideas about death and had not come at all. Still, he seemed to be there too. When we stopped on the way out to look at Mauger in his coffin he seemed to be smiling, with a twinkling look beneath his heavy mustaches, even mysteriously to be singing to us under his breath:

> Still you've got a long way to go
> You've got a long way to go
> Whether you travel by day or night ...
> The judge will tell you so ...

Our hamlet on the beach had scarcely changed. On the front of our first house where we had been so happy was a large wooden plaque bearing a name that perhaps had no merit even according to the special categories of waggery through which one was obliged to perceive it: Wuzz-it-2-U? But otherwise it had been improved. The porch had been widened, it had a wireless aerial – maybe someone even listened to our opera upon it, but we hoped not. For the local authorities on hearing rumors of an opera by a local composer had seen an excellent instrument with which to belabor our position on the beach again, so that for a while such embarrassing headlines as OPERATIC SQUATTERS ENDANGER DIGNITY OF CITY – WE NEED SEWERS NOT SYMPHONIES – RICH COMPOSER PREFERS RATSNEST OF PERVERSION were not uncommon, until another fourteen-year-old taxpayer's son committed a sex crime, and the next mayor committed a murder; so that fortunately we did not have long to wait. The house now had a roof ladder, though my old ladder still did duty as steps. There was a new roof-jack and a new chimney. Feeling like thieves we peeked in the window. But where else could all nature look in too, and the house still have privacy? For it did. It was not merely that the sunlight came in, but the very movement and rhythm of the sea, in which the reflections of trees and mountains and sun were counter-reflected and multi-reflected in shimmering movement within. As if part of nature, the very living and moving and breathing reflection of nature itself had been captured. Yet it was built in such a cunningly hidden manner that no one could see into it from a neighboring house. One had to peek in like a thief to do that. A tree we had planted in the back was now the height of the shack, a dogwood clustered like white stars, another wild cherry that had failed to blossom for us was a snow of blooms, while our own primroses we had left for the Scotsman were in flower : fireweed too had sown itself from the seeds of that beautiful willow herb, our unbidden guest, blown downwind from our second house. Once during a winter, when we were in Europe, a child had been born there in a snowstorm. There was a new stove, but the old table and two chairs where we ate in front of the window were still there. There was the bunk where we had spent our honeymoon – and what a long honeymoon it had turned out to be – and desired each other and anguished at the fear of losing each other and our hearts had been troubled, and we had seen the stars and the moon rise, and listened to the roar of the surf on the wild stormy nights of our first winter, and the grandmother of the cat that accompanied us now had slept with us and pulled our hair in the morning to wake us up – Valetta, long since gathered to the rest of her strange moonkind. Yet who would think, to look at the place idly, with its ramshackle air, its sense of impermanence, of improvisation, that such a beauty of existence, such happiness could be possible there, such dramas have taken place ? Look at that old hut, the passerby shouts in his motor launch above the engine, laughing contemptuously : oh well, we'll be pulling down all those eyesores now. Start here, and keep going ! Autocamps for the better class, hotels, cut down all those trees, open it up for the public, put it on the map. Nothing but receivers of stolen goods and a few old pirates live in the ratsnests anyway. Squatters ! The government's been trying to get them off for years !

It was there that our own life had come into being and for all its strangeness and conflict, a pang of sadness struck us now. Longing and hope fulfilled, loss and rediscovery, failure and accomplishment, sorrow and joy seemed annealed into one profound emotion. From the porch where we stood we could see dimly – for there was suddenly a spring fog billowing in across the water – right across the arc of the bay to where our next house had burned down and there was no tragedy about that either. Our new house stood clearly visible in its place, though as we watched it began to be swallowed up by the fog.

As the mist rolled up towards us, beginning to envelop us, the sun still trying to maintain itself like a platinum disc, it was as if the essence of a kind of music that had forever receded there, that seemed evoked from the comments of my wife as she looked through this window, out on to this porch in the first days when we'd just meant to spend a week, or in the autumn when we still stayed on, while she was making the coffee, talking to herself partly for my benefit, describing the day to me, as if I had been like a blind man recovering his sight to whom she had to teach again the beauties and oddities of the world, as if it became unlocked, began to play, to our inner ear, not music but having the effect of music, not sentimental at all, but fresh and innocent, and only moving because it was so happy, or because happiness is moving; or it was like a whispering of the ghosts of ourselves. 'Sunrise of the dying moon, in a green sky ... White frost on the porch and all the roofs, the first heavy frost of the year ... There's a little flotilla of golden eyes under the window, and the racoons have been here during the night, I can see their tracks ... The tide is high. My poor seagulls, they're hungry. How cold your feet must be down there, in that icy water ... Look – now! like a bonfire! Like a burning cathedral. I must wash the windows. There's a wash from a fishing boat like a strand of silver Christmas tinsel. The sunrise does things to these mists. ... I must put out some breakfast for the cat. He'll come in very hungry from his dawn prowl. There goes a cormorant. There goes a great loon. The frost sparkles like diamond dust. I used to think it was fairy diamonds as a child. In a few minutes it will melt and the porch will be wet and black, with a sprinkling of harlequin leaves. The mountains look very hazy and far away this morning, that's a sign it will be a good day. ...'

Strange magnificent honeymoon that had become one's whole life.

We climbed the steps – they were the same steps made from my ladder and they still held – and began to walk into the mist and down the path to the spring. The fog was thick in the forest, like smoke pouring toward us as from a funnel beneath the bushes, in which it was curious to hear the intermittent insulated twitterings of birds gradually hushing. Talking of those first days, my wife remembered how once for nearly a month there had been a fog so thick we couldn't see across the inlet, and what boats went by unseen, only known by a mournful continued hooting of foghorns and lonely bells. Sometimes Kristbjorg's boat had appeared dimly as it did now and the point ahead would fade in and out and sometimes we could scarcely see beyond the porch, so that it had been like living at the edge of eternity. And we remembered too the days when it had been dark and freezing with a film of ice on the blackened porch and the steps, and the lamp going until ten o'clock in the morning. And the ships that would steer by dead reckoning listening for the echo of their hooters from the bank, though we could hear their engines, as we heard a ship's engine now, going very softly:

> Frère Jacques
> Frère Jacques
> Dormez-vous?
> Dormez-vous?

And the snowstorms in which there was no echo. And the sense of the snow driving on the night in the world outside too, and such a storm as would yield no echo. And ourselves seemed the only lamp of love within it.

Or there would seem something about these little shacks, as there did now, as mysterious and hidden as the never-found nest of the marbled murrelet, that also haunted these shores.

The path had scarcely changed; nor, here, had the forest. Civilization, creator of deathscapes, like a dull-witted fire of ugliness and ferocious stupidity – so unimaginative it had even almost managed to spoil the architectural beauty of our oil refinery – had spread all down the opposite bank, blown over the water and crept up upon us from the south along it, murdering the trees and taking down the shacks as it went, but it had become baffled by the Indian reserve, and a law that had not been repealed that forbade building too near a lighthouse, so to the south we were miraculously saved by civilization itself (of which a lighthouse is perhaps always the highest symbol) as if it too had become conscious of the futility of pretending that it was advancing by creating the moribund. And it was the same way to the north, where battles between real estate sharks over the living and dead body of Eridanus Port had resulted in the return, little by little, of the jungle itself, and vines and thimble-berry already covered the ill-surveyed lots of the subsection among the few trees that had been left. But some people lived happily there after all, who could afford it. And even beautifully. For man – whose depredations, where they did not threaten the entire country with drought and desolation, sometimes by accident provided a better view – had not succeeded yet in hacking down the mountains and the stars.

The bells of a train, slowly moving northward along the coast tracks, began to sound through the fog across the water. I could remember a time when these bells had seemed to me exactly like the thudding of school bells, summoning one to some unwelcome task. Then they had seemed like somber church bells, tolling for a funeral. But now, at this moment, they struck clear as gay chimes, Christmas bells, birthday bells, harbor bells, pealing through the unraveling mist as for a city liberated, or some great spiritual victory of mankind. And they seemed to mingle with the song of the ship now distant, round the point – but so great a conductor of sound is water that its engines thudded as if at a fathom's distance:

> Dormez-vous?
> Dormez-vous?
> Sonnez les matines!
> Sonnez les matines!

And ourselves? How had we changed? We were many years older. We had traveled, been to the Orient, and Europe, grown rich and poor again, and always returned here. But were we older? My wife seemed young and beautiful and wild as ever, far more so. She still had the figure of a young girl and she had the wonder of a young girl. Her wide frank long-lashed eyes still changed color from green to yellow like a tiger cub's. Her brow could become chaotic with frowns and it is true that despair had once carved lines of suffering on her face, though I thought these signs vanished or came at will with her moods; they vanished when she was alive and interested, and she was uniquely alive, vivid and exciting.

'He no longer loves the person whom he loved ten years ago,' said gloomy old Pascal. I quite believe it. 'She is no longer the same, nor is he. He was young, and she also: she is quite different. He would perhaps love her yet, if she were what she was then.' So gloomy profound old Pascal, the unselfish helper of my youth in other ways, had once seemed to threaten our future age. And yet not so. Surely I loved her now much more. I had more years to love with. Why should I expect her to be the same? Though she was the same in a way, just as this spring was the same, and not the same, as the springs of years ago. And I wondered if what really we should see in age is merely the principle of the seasons themselves wearing out, only to renew themselves through another kind of death. And indeed the seasons themselves in their duration and character had changed, or seemed to have changed, much more than she. Our winters came more forthrightly down from the arctic now, in the East they were getting our old Western winters, and this winter had been the longest and gloomiest we had ever known, and one had almost seemed to feel the onset of another ice age, another search for Eden. So much more welcome and sweeter the spring, now it had come. I myself however had aged in appearance. I had even quite a few white hairs, on one side, and our latest joke was that I was 'graying at the temple.' On the other hand I did not feel older, and bodily I was twice as strong, and I was in every way full of health. The port of fifty now seemed to me quite blithe, and as for old Pascal, he had died younger than I was now. The poor old chap would not have said such things if he'd only lived a bit longer, I thought.

'I wonder where Kristbjorg is, these days.'

'There he is.'

And here he had just appeared, stepping out of the mist. He had been fishing up the Fraser River, because he was 'in death' as he said, his more than explicit phrase for 'in debt.' But the cold for the first time had caused him to move into the city for a while last winter, though he had left his boat for Quaggan and ourselves to look after. He was getting on for seventy, and was much thinner, but hale and hearty, and many lines seemed to have been smoothed from his face. He no longer sang the song about the storm in the red-light district but he still wore the same lumberjacket and good Irish tweed trousers he had worn in his fifties when not ten years older than I was now and I had thought him an old man, though now I thought him nearer my own age.

'Why there you are, Nicolai, we missed you.'

'Ah well, this weather's changing, Missus. . . . Been in town . . . The streetcars are getting so humpy and dumpy, I never saw a street flusher. They just letting the old grime go. . . . I ran into a couple of bottles of rye. . . .'

He passed into the mist and we continued along our path, the Bell-Proteus path, that on the reverse journey had once long since seemed to get so much longer, and then so much shorter. The fog was lifting and I thought:

How wrongly we interpreted that whole strange experience. Or rather how was it that it had never occurred to us, seriously, to interpret it at all, let alone to see it as a warning, a form of message, even as a message that shadowed forth a kind of strange command, a command that, it seemed to me, I had obeyed! And yet, all my heeding of any warning it contained would not have averted the suffering immediately ahead. Only dimly, even now, did I understand it. Sometimes I felt that the path had only seemed to grow shorter because the burden, the cannister, had grown lighter as I grew physically stronger. Then again I could become convinced that the significance of the experience lay not in the path at all, but in the possibility that in converting the very cannister I carried, the ladder down which I climbed every time I went to the spring – in converting both these derelicts to use I had prefigured something I should have done with my soul. Then of course, and pre-eminently, there was the lion. But I lacked spiritual equipment to follow such thoughts through. This much I understood, and had understood that as a man I had become tyrannized by the past, and that it was my duty to transcend it in the present. Yet my new vocation was involved with using that past – for this was the underlying meaning of my symphony, even my opera, the second opera I was now writing, the second symphony I would one day write – with turning it into use for others. And to do this, even before writing a note, it was necessary to face that past as far as possible without fear. Ah yes, and it was that, that I had begun to do here. And if I had not done so, how could we have been happy, as we now were happy?

How could I have helped you, I seemed to be saying to my wife, in the deepest sense even have loved you? However would we have found strength to endure the more furious past that was then ahead of us, to endure the fire, the destruction of our hopes, our house, to be rich and poor, known and unknown again, to endure the fear, the onset and the defeat of disease – even of madness, for to be deprived of one's house may, in a sense, be said to be like being deprived of one's rational faculty. How else have survived the shrieks of a dying piano, even, as a matter of fact, have come, somehow, to see something actually funny about all that? And how, above all, have found strength to rebuild on the same spot, right in the teeth of the terror of fire that had grown up between us and that had also been defeated? And I remembered the time when, homeless, having lost everything we had in the world, we had been drawn, not many weeks after the fire, to the still malodorous ruin of that house, before dawn, and watching the sun rise, had seemed to draw strength out of the sunrise itself for the decision once more to stay, to rebuild that haunted ruin we loved so much that we created our most jubilant memory that very day, when careless of its charred and tragic smell we wonderfully picnicked within it, diving off the blackened posts into the natural swimming pool of our old living room and frightened away I have no doubt the devil himself, who, the enemy of all humor in the face of disaster, as of all human delight, and often disguised as a social worker for the common good – for that we had saved the forest was not so important as that we had seemed to threaten some valuable potential real estate – wants nothing so much as that man shall believe himself unfriended by any higher power than he.

And yet, on the other side, else life would be composed of mere heroics that were all vain gestures to oneself, it had been necessary to go beyond remorse, beyond even contrition. I have often wondered whether it is not man's ordeal to make his contrition active. Sometimes I had the feeling I was attacking the past rationally as with a clawbar and hammer, while trying to make it into something else for a supernatural end. In a manner I changed it by changing myself and having changed it found it necessary to pass beyond the pride I felt in my accomplishment, and to accept myself as a fool again. I'm sure that even old Hank Gleason, though he would put this into better English, or different English, would see my point. Nothing is more humbling than the wreckage of a burned house, the fragments of consumed work. But it is necessary not to take pride in such masterly pieces of damnation either, especially when they have become so nearly universal. If we had progressed, I thought, it was as if to a region where such words as spring, water, houses, trees, vines, laurels, mountains, wolves, bay, roses, beach, islands, forest, tides and deer and snow and fire, had realized their true being, or had their source: and as these words on a page once stood merely to what they symbolized, so did the reality we knew now stand to something else beyond that that symbolized or reflected: it was as if we were clothed in the kind of reality which before we saw only at a distance, or to translate it into terms of my own vocation, it was as if we lived in a medium to which that in which our old lives moved, happy though they were, was like simply the bald verbal inspiration to the music we had achieved. I speak in terms of our lives only: my own compositions have always fallen far short of the great, indeed they will never perhaps be anything more than second-rate, but at least as it seemed to me there was room for them in the world, and I – and we – had happiness in their execution.

We were still on earth, still in the same place, but if someone had charged us with the notion that we had gone to heaven and that this was the after life we would not have said him nay for long. Moreover if we had been charged with formerly having been in hell for a while we would probably have had to say yes too, though adding that on the whole we liked that fine, as long as we were together, and were sometimes even homesick for it, though this life had many advantages over the other.

Still, indeed, we had the hellish fear of losing our third little house but now the joy and happiness of what we had known would go with us wherever we went or God sent us and would not die. I cannot really well express what I mean but merely set this down in the Montaigne-like belief – or as someone said, speaking about Montaigne – that the experience of one happy man might be useful.

The fog began to lift and we saw the train, it was drawn by a diesel engine of sinister appearance (the first one I ever saw in my life but I recognized it from the photogravure pictures in the *Sun*) departing quite silently now into the future to become obsolete and romantic in turn. Men could not do altogether without the nostalgic mountain-borne wailing of the old steam engines it seemed, so it had been equipped with a device, a touching compromise, that mooed like a cow intermittently as it slid along into the mountain pines.

But even in that moo, of nautical timbre, as it slid into the great Cordilleras, among these northern cousins of Popocatepetl, so that those working on the lines must think that a freighter approached, it was possible to detect I thought, that note of artistry which denoted Mr Bell, a signal to his old home, and the good people, English immigrants, an electrician and his family, who now inhabited it.

The wash from the invisible freighter, the wash still invisible itself from where we were on the path, could be heard breaking all along the curve of the beach as it approached us, and simultaneously it began, slowly at first, and gently, to rain, and as the wash of undulating silver rippling into sight transversely spent itself against the rocks we stopped to watch the rain like a bead curtain falling behind a gap in the trees, into the inlet below.

Each drop falling into the sea is like a life, I thought, each producing a circle in the ocean, or the medium of life itself, and widening into infinity, though it seems to melt into the sea, and become invisible, or disappear entirely, and be lost. Each is interlocked with other circles falling about it, some are larger circles expanding widely and engulfing others, some are weaker, smaller circles that only seem to last a short while. And smiling as I remembered my lesson I thought of that first time when we had seen the rain falling into a calm sea like a dark mirror, and we had found the cannister and decided to stay.

But last night I had seen something new; my wife had called me out of bed to the open window to see what she first thought was a school of little fishes breaking the still water just beneath, where the tide was high under the house. Then we saw that the whole dark water was covered with bright expanding phosphorescent circles. Only when my wife felt the warm mild rain on her naked shoulder did she realize it was raining. They were perfect expanding circles of light, first tiny circles bright as a coin, then becoming expanding rings growing fainter and fainter, while as the rain fell into the phosphorescent water each raindrop expanded into a ripple that was translated into light. And the rain itself was water from the sea, as my wife first taught me, raised to heaven by the sun, transformed into clouds, and falling again into the sea. While within the inlet itself the tides and currents in that sea returned, became remote, and becoming remote, like that which is called the Tao, returned again as we ourselves had done.

Now, somewhere in the unseen west where it was setting, the sun broke through the clouds, sending a flare of light across the water turning the rain into a sudden shower of pearls and touching the mountains, where the mist rising now almost perpendicularly from the black abysses fumed heavenward in pure white fire.

Three rainbows went up like rockets across the bay : one for the cat. They faded and there, in the east, a widening rift of clouds had become a patch of clear rain-washed sky. Arcturus. Spica. Procyon overhead, and Regulus in the Lion over the oil refinery. But Orion must have already set behind the sun so that, though we were Eridanus, Eridanus was nowhere to be found. And on the point the lighthouse began its beneficent signaling into the twilight.

And the spring? Here it was. It still ran, down through the jack-in-the-pulpits, down toward Hi-Doubt. It purified itself a bit as it came down from the mountains, but it always carried with it a faint tang of mushrooms, earth, dead leaves, pine needles, mud and snow, on its way down to the inlet and out to the Pacific. In the deeper reaches of the forest, in the somber damp caves, where the dead branches hang bowed down with moss, and death camass and the destroying angel grow, it was haggard and chill and tragic, unsure measurer of its path. Feeling its way underground it must have had its dark moments. But here, in springtime, on its last lap to the sea, it was as at its source a happy joyous little stream.

High above the pine trees swayed against the sky, out of the west came the seagulls with their angelic wings, coming home to rest. And I remembered how every evening I used to go down this path through the forest to get water from the spring at dusk. . . . Looking over my wife's shoulder I could see a deer swimming toward the lighthouse.

Laughing we stooped down to the stream and drank.

FINE WORKS OF FICTION
AVAILABLE IN QUALITY
PAPERBACK EDITIONS FROM
CARROLL & GRAF